A VIEW OF THE WORLD

FICTION

SAMARA

WITHIN THE LABYRINTH

A SINGLE PILGRIM

THE DAY OF THE FOX

THE VOLCANOES ABOVE US

DARKNESS VISIBLE

THE TENTH YEAR OF THE SHIP

A SMALL WAR MADE TO ORDER

FLIGHT FROM A DARK EQUATOR

EVERY MAN'S BROTHER

THE SICILIAN SPECIALIST

CUBAN PASSAGE

A SUITABLE CASE FOR CORRUPTION

NON FICTION

A DRAGON APPARENT

GOLDEN EARTH

THE HONOURED SOCIETY

NAPLES '44

VOICES OF THE OLD SEA

JACKDAW CAKE

A VIEW OF THE WORLD

NORMAN LEWIS

Selected Journalism

ELAND, LONDON
&
HIPPOCRENE BOOKS, INC., NEW YORK

Published by
ELAND
53 Eland Road, London SW11 5JX
&
HIPPOCRENE BOOKS, INC.,
171 Madison Avenue, New York, NY 10016

First issued in this edition 1986
© Norman Lewis 1986

British Library Cataloguing in Publication Data

Lewis, Norman
A view of the world: selected journalism.
I. Title
082   PR6062.E948

ISBN 0–907871–46–1
ISBN 0–907871–41–0 Pbk

Photoset, printed and bound in Great Britain by
Redwood Burn Limited,
Trowbridge, Wiltshire

Cover illustration © Tony Ansell
Cover design © Patrick Frean

Biography

Norman Lewis has written thirteen novels and seven non-fiction
works. Of the latter, his two travel books, *A Dragon Apparent*, and
Golden Earth (travels in Burma) – both best-sellers in their day – describe his journeyings in the Far East at a time when the countries he
visited were passing out of the reach of the ordinary traveller.

His novel, *The Volcanoes Above Us*, based on personal experiences in
Central America in revolt, sold 6 million copies in paperback in
Russia – enormously to his surprise, he says, as the book expressed
no political point of view. *The Honoured Society*, a non-fiction study of
the Sicilian Mafia, was serialised in 6 instalments in the *New Yorker*,
and his best-selling novel *The Sicilian Specialist*, incorporating at that
time undisclosed facts about the Kennedy assassination, was removed from sale in some American cities following a Mafia ban.
Naples '44, a recently published war-diary, which received high critical acclaim, describes his adventures in British Intelligence in the
Italian South.

Norman Lewis regards his life's major achievement as the world
reaction to an article written by him entitled *Genocide in Brazil*,
published in the *Sunday Times* in 1968. This led to a change in the
Brazilian law relating to the treatment of Indians, and to the formation of *Survival International*, the influential body with branches in
many countries, dedicated to the protection of aboriginal people.

Lewis relaxes by his occasional travels to off-beat parts of the
world, which he prefers to be as remote as possible; otherwise he lives
with his family in introspective, almost monastic calm, in the depths
of Essex.

Contents

Author's Note

Most of these pieces were originally written at the instigation of the *New Yorker*, the *Sunday Times*, the *Observer* and the *New Statesman*, to whose editors I make grateful acknowledgement. The first ten pieces were included in *The Changing Sky* (first published in 1959), the next eight are collected within a book for the first time; the final two have never previously been published.

Since the time of writing, changes of political direction have taken place in one or two countries about which I wrote. Occasionally, where it may interest the reader, I have added a date in square brackets; but I have made no attempt to bring the accounts up to date by reference to recent happenings, because what interested me was the background, and the style of life in a country, rather than the colour of threads in the political web.

N.L.

Foreword

Travel came before writing. There was a time when I felt that all I wanted from life was to be allowed to remain a perpetual spectator of changing scenes. I managed my meagre supply of money so as to be able to surrender myself as much as possible to this addiction, and charged with a wonderful ignorance I went abroad by third-class train, country bus, on foot, by canoe, by tramp steamer and by Arab dhow.

My travels started with Spain, where in the early 'thirties a *fonda* would furnish a windowless cell and an austere meal of bread, sausage and wine for the equivalent of a shilling; when Pedro Flores Atocha, last of the flamboyant bandits of Andalusia, was receiving the first of the Spanish film actresses in his mountain hideout, and you sometimes saw a picture of Lenin, or of the bullfighter Belmonte, in the places later occupied by a portrait of General Franco. In this then relatively incorruptible country, where merely by leaving the main road you could plunge immediately into Europe's prehistoric past, I spent – divided over a number of visits – a total of about three years, and I still go there to get away from the insipidity of modern times whenever I can, although the Spain of old has only survived in a few relatively inaccessible parts of the interior.

After Spain it was the African *meridionale* of Italy, the Balkans, the Red Sea and Southern Arabia (in the dhow, 30 tons, undecked, crew of five, without lifeboat: a lifeboat would have been impiously calling into question God's providence), then Mexico, North Africa, three winters in the Far East, Central America, Equatorial Africa, and the less travelled areas of South America: Amazonian Brazil, the Savannahs of Venezuela, Bolivia and Paraguay. At first I believed in pure travel, and that it was necessary never to have a purpose. I arrived, watched a little, and when my amazement began to subside, my impressions to dull, I moved on. When I began to write it was probably, at least in part, in an attempt to imprison some essence of the experiences, the images which were always slipping, fading, dissolving, taking flight. Later I found that the discipline of writing compelled me to see more, to penetrate more deeply to increase my understanding and to discard a little of my ignorance. Still later I began to weave the background and the incidents of travel into my novels, and now, as I observe the change that has taken place over the years, I wonder if I am any longer capable of enjoying travel for its own sake.

Insurgents and bandits, malaria, curtains of various kinds, whether lowered by politicians or by the priest-kings of their day, like the Imam of the Yemen – I am reminded that those parts of the world where I have travelled most happily, those countries which had most preserved their peculiar style and character, always seemed to suffer from these disadvantages, and that on the other hand those that seemed to me hardly worth a visit and certainly not worth writing about were those that had succumbed to a flaccid and joyless prosperity which they were doing their best to export to the rest of the world. Ironically, so much that is of value has been protected by poverty, bad communications, reactionary governments, the natural barriers to progress of mountain, desert and jungle, colonial misrule, the anopheles mosquito.

The pieces in this collection are mostly about places to escape to when one has had a surfeit of the amenities of the modern world. Belize (colonial neglect) is a living museum, a wondrous survival of a Caribbean colony of the last century. Liberia (bad communications plus bad government) offers an extraordinary example of what can be done in the names of Freedom and Democracy when released slaves are turned loose on native Africans, who until the said released slaves appeared on the scene, had had the good fortune to remain free. Guatemala (colonial misrule plus reactionary governments plus endless revolution) is the last home of the uncontaminated Red Man – the Mayan Indian – living, to be sure, in much reduced circumstances, but still defending himself with fair success from all the overtures of the West.

Norman Lewis, 1959

The foregoing was written a quarter of a century ago, and whatever validity my theories about the protective properties of bad government, bad communications etc. may have possessed at that time, it has certainly been lost, and I now repudiate them. The great divide in my writings, the swing round in my viewpoint, followed a visit in 1968 to Brazil on behalf of *The Sunday Times* to investigate the atro-

10

cities committed against the Indians of that country which, had they not been halted, would have long since meant their total extermination. The ensuing article (reproduced in this book) I regard as the most worthwhile of all my endeavours, and I have reason to believe that it at least saved some lives, and probably even benefited the long-term prospects of the Amerindians.

Bad governments preserve nothing, and even good ones have a mediocre record in this direction, and I cannot think of any single place that I have written about that did not appear to have gone down hill – sometimes disastrously so – on a subsequent visit. The war in Vietnam put an end to all the ancient glories of the Indo China I knew. Guatemala, which I used to think of as the most beautiful country in the world, has become after thirty years of puppet military government, imposed from without, the cemetery of its indigenous population. In a single year alone – 1979 – when I wrote of the destruction of the Amazonian forests of Brazil, 3 million hectares were 'cleared' (with all the teeming wildlife they contained) by the now classic method of defoliants followed by napalm. Flying over the jungle for a thousand miles – almost from one end of Brazil to the other – all one saw of it was smoke. The vanished trees will be replaced by cattle ranches, in the certain knowledge that their 'life' will average 10 years, and that the desert will follow.

At the present rate of clearance the Amazonian forest will have ceased to exist somewhere between the years 2000 and 2010, terminal dates also applicable to the great rain-forest of South East Asia, sacrificed in this case not to ranching but to timber extraction interests. It is not possible in the face of such calamities to keep silent, to remain a perpetual spectator.

Norman Lewis, 1985

1

A Quiet Evening in Huehuetenango

In the bleak depths of an interminable English winter, I was suddenly seized with an almost physical craving to write a novel having as its background the tropical jungles and volcanoes of Central America. Having succeeded in persuading my publishers that this would be a good thing from both our points of view, I boarded a plane at London Airport one morose evening in January, and two days later I was in Guatemala City. I chose Guatemala because I had been there before and knew something about it, but also because all that one thinks of as typical of the Central-American scene – primitive Indians, Mayan ruins, the wrecks of grandiose Spanish colonial cities – is found there in the purest concentration.

For three weeks I did my best to absorb some of the atmosphere of life in seedy banana ports of the Caribbean and the Pacific, where bored men in big hats still occasionally pull guns on each other. I went hunting in jungles said to abound with jaguars and tapir without shooting anything more impressive than a species of giant rat. I talked with wily politicians of the country, survivors of half a dozen revolutions, and took tea with exiled fellow-countrymen on isolated coffee plantations, who had lived so long among the Indians that they sometimes stopped in mid-sentence to translate their very proper English sentiments from the Spanish in which they now thought.

My final trip was to the far north of the country, the remote and mountainous area beyond Huehuetenango, which lies just south of the Mexican state of Chiapas and is reached after three hundred miles of infamous roads and stupendous scenery. Here under the Cuchumatanes, the ultimate peaks of Guatemala, even the onslaught of the Spanish Conquistadors faltered and collapsed. And here the mountain tribes were finally left in peace, to live on in the harsh but free existence of

13

the Stone Age, touched only by the outward forms of Christianity, consoled in secret by the ancient gods, and rejecting with all their might all the overtures of Western civilisation.

In the early afternoon of the fourth day, my taxi, driven by a town Indian from Guatemala City called Calmo, reached the top of the 12,000-foot pass overlooking the valley of Huehuetenango. We stopped here to let the engine cool, and noticing that the trees in this wind-swept place were covered with orchids, I astounded Calmo by suggesting we should pick some. 'Flowers?' he said. 'Where? They don't grow at this height!' I stumbled, weak and breathless from the altitude, up the hillside towards an oak, loaded with vermilion-flowered bromeliads. 'Ah,' he said, 'you mean the *parasitos*. Well, certainly, if you like, sir. When you said flowers, I didn't realise... We call these weeds – tree-killers.' Calmo was not only an intrepid driver, but a qualified guide supplied by the State Tourist Office. He spoke a version of English which so effectively stripped the meaning from his remarks that I steered him back to Spanish whenever I could. For the rest, he was gentle, sad-looking and pious, dividing his free time between visits to churches and – although well into middle life – running after girls.

We got into Huehuetenango at four in the afternoon, and it turned out to be an earthquake town, with corrugated-iron roofs on fine churches, squat houses iced over with multi-coloured stuccoes, and a great number of pubs having such names as 'I Await Thee on Thy Return'. We went into one of these, each of us carrying an armful of orchids, Calmo probably hoping that no one he knew would see him bothering himself with such contemptible weeds. The woman who brought the beer had a Mayan face, flat-featured but handsome, and full of inherited tragedy. Calmo told her in his most dignified way, 'This I say with all sincerity. I want to come back to this place and marry you.' The woman said, 'Ah bueno,' shaking off the compliment as if an invisible fly had settled on her cheek. She wore a massive wedding ring, and there were several children about the floor.

After that, Calmo wanted to go into the cathedral to pray for success in that week's lottery. The cathedral had just been freshly decorated for the pre-Lenten festival with huge bouquets of imitation flowers, their stiff petals varnished, and dusted over with powdered glass. Indians were lighting candles among the little separate patches of red and white blossoms they had spread out on the flags to symbolise the living and the dead. Hundreds of candles glimmered in the obscurity of the cleared space where the Indians worship in their own way in the Christian churches, grouped in whispering semicircles round the candles, while their *shamans* passed from group to group, swinging incense-burners and muttering magical formulas. The Indians were dressed in the frozen fashions of the early sixteenth century; the striped breeches of Castilian peasants, the habits of the first few Franciscans who had scaled the heights to reach their villages, the cod-pieces of Alvarado's ferocious soldiery. They had left their babies hidden in the old people's care in the mountain caves, still remembering the days before the conquest, when at this season the rain god had taken the children for his annual sacrifice. These Indians were still surrounded by a world of magic and illusion, living characters in a Grimm's fairy-tale of our day in which the whites they see when they come down to the towns are enchanters and werewolves, who can kill with a glance, but are themselves immortal.

We went out into the sunshine again. A meteorite shower of parakeets fell screeching across the patch of sky stretched over the plaza. Soldiers, shrunken away in their American uniforms, were fishing in space with their rifles over the blood-red balustrade of the town hall, which was also their barracks. The green bell in the cathedral tower clanked five times, and the sleepers on the stone benches stirred a little in the vast shade of their sombreros. Calmo woke up an ice-cream vendor, bought a cornet, then said, 'I cannot eat it. The hot for my teeth is too great.' When speaking English he found special difficulty in distinguishing between opposites such as heat and cold.

We sat down in the car to decide what to do with the evening. The sleepiness of the place was beginning to paralyse us. Nothing stirred but the vultures waving their scarves of shadow over the flower beds. Calmo said, 'Yesterday a market-day, tomorrow a procession; so that today we have no prospect but an early night. There is really nothing to do.' As he spoke, a man came riding into the plaza on a tall, bony horse. The man looked like an Englishman on his way to a fancy-dress ball: he was lean, pink-cheeked, mildly aloof of expression, and his improbable costume of black leather with silver facings had clearly been hired out too often and was on the loose side for its present wearer. He was carrying a bundle of what looked like yard-brooms wrapped up in coloured paper. Calmo explained that these would be rockets for use in the next day's celebrations. The clip-clop of the hooves died away, and the silence came down like a drop-curtain. Huehuetenango was a place of apathetic beauty, built out of the ruin of a devastated Indian city. There was a sadness, a sense of forgotten tragedy in the air; and here it seemed that silence was a part of the natural condition. As Calmo had so often said, 'We Indians are a reserved people. Even in our fiestas. Our joys and our weepings are hidden away inside: for us only, you understand – not for the world.'

There was a notice over the hotel door that said, 'Distinction, Atmosphere and Sympathy'. The atmosphere was all-pervasive. The garden had been turned into a floral jungle encircled by borders of Pepsi-Cola bottles stuck neck-down in the earth. Quite ordinary flowers like stocks and hollyhocks were throttling each other in a savage struggle for living space, and humming-birds like monstrous bees zoomed about the agonised sea of blossom. Goldfish bowls containing roses hideously pickled in preserving fluid, stood on every table-top. The bedroom towels were embroidered with the words, 'Sleep My Beloved'.

Food in this hotel was *American Plan* – words which have now been accepted into the Spanish vocabulary of Central America and no longer refer to the system of charging for accommodation inclusive of meals, but describe a special kind of food itself – the hygienic but emasculated fare supposed to be preferred by American visitors, and now generally adopted on the strength of what are believed to be its medicinal and semi-magical properties. This time *American Plan* meant tinned soup, spaghetti, boiled beef and Californian peaches. The whole loaf of bread and a half-pound of butter of a generation ago had wasted away to two slices of toast and a pat of margarine. The milk was the product of Contented Cows, served in the original tin as a guarantee of the absence of dangerous freshness. We got through the boring ritual of dinner as soon as we could. The other guests – business men drawn from the elite ten per cent of pure white stock – were still inclined to congratulate one another on the downfall of the last government, which had not been approved of in commercial circles. 'A minimum wage. And why not? – I'd be the first. But when all's said and done, friends, what happens when you give an Indian more than 40 cents for a day's work? You know as well as I do. He doesn't show up the next day – that's all. They've got to be educated up to it.'

After dinner I resigned myself to an early evening, and went to bed under a religious picture consisting of an eye projecting rays in all directions, and beneath it the question: 'What is a moment of pleasure weighed in the scales against an eternity of punishment?' I had hardly dozed off when I was awakened by an explosion. I got up and opened the window. The street had filled up with people who were all going in the same direction and chattering excitedly. A siren wailed and a motor-cycle policeman went past deafeningly, snaking in and out of the crowd. There was another explosion, and as this was the homeland of revolutions it was natural to assume that one had started. I dressed and went out into the courtyard, where the hotel boy was throwing a bayonet at an anatomical chart given away with a Mexican journal devoted to home medicine. The boy said that so far as he knew there had been no *pronunciamento*, and the bangs were probably someone celebrating his saint's day. I then remembered the lean horseman.

As the tumult showed no signs of abating I walked down to the plaza, which had filled up with blank-faced Indians moving slowly round in an anti-clockwise direction as if stirred up by some gigantic invisible spoon. There were frequent scuffles and outcries as young men singled out girls from the promenading groups and broke coloured eggs on their heads, rubbing the contents well into the thick black hair. The eggs were being sold by the basketful all over the plaza, and they turned out to have been emptied, refilled with some brittle, wafer-like substance, repaired and then painted. When a girl sometimes returned the compliment, the gallant thus favoured stopped to bow, and said: 'Muchas gracias.'

Calmo, whom I soon ran into, his jacket pockets bulging with eggs, said it looked as if there were going to be a fiesta

17

after all. He couldn't think why. There was really no excuse for it. The fashionable town-Indians, most of them shopkeepers, had turned out in all their finery, headed by the 'Queen of Huehuetenango' herself – a splendidly beflounced creature with ribbon-entwined pigtails down to her thighs, who was said to draw her revenues from a *maison de rendezvous* possessing radioactive baths. There was a sedate sprinkling of whites, hatted and begloved for the occasion.

Merchants had put up their stalls and were offering sugar skulls, holy pictures, plastic space-guns, and a remedy for heart-sickness which is a speciality of Huehuetenango and tastes like inferior port. We found the lean horseman launching his rockets in military fashion from a wooden rack-like contraption. They were aimed so as to hiss as alarmingly low as possible over the heads of the crowds, showering them with sparks, and sometimes they cleared the building opposite and sometimes they did not. Other enthusiasts were discharging *mortaretes*, miniature flying bombs, which leaped two or three hundred feet straight up into the air before exploding with an ear-stunning crack. The motor-cycle policeman on his scarlet Harley-Davidson with wide-open exhaust, and eight front and six rear lights, came weaving and bellowing round the plaza at intervals of about a minute, and a travelling movie-show was using part of the cathedral's baroque façade as the screen for a venerable Mexican film called *Ay mi Jalisco* featuring a great deal of gunplay.

A curious hollow structure looking like a cupola sliced in half had been built on the top of the town hall, and about this time powerful lights came on in its interior and nine sad-faced men in dark suits entered it by an invisible door, carrying what looked like several grand pianos. A moment later these pieces of furniture had been placed end to end to form an enormous marimba, under an illuminated sign that said 'Musica Civica'. A cosmic voice coughed electrically and then announced that in response to the esteemed public's many requests the municipal orchestra would have pleasure in rendering a selection of notable composers' works. Eighteen hammers then came down on the keys with a responding opening flourish, and the giant marimba raced into an athletic version of 'If You Were the Only Girl in the World'.

Calmo and I took refuge from the torrent of sound in a

tavern called The Little Chain of Gold. It was a place of great charm containing a shrine and a newly installed juke-box in addition to the usual accessories, and was decorated with beautiful calendars given away by Guatemalan bus companies, and a couple of propaganda pictures of mutilated corpses put out by the new government after the last revolution. The Little Chain advertised the excellence of its 'hotsdoogs'. Most of its customers were *preparados*, Indians who had done military service and had rejected their tribal costumes in favour of brightly coloured imitations of American army uniforms. Some of them added a slightly sinister touch to their gay ensembles of reds and blues by covering the lower part of their faces with black cloths, a harmless freak of fashion which I was told had originated in a desire to breathe in as little dust as possible when foot-slogging along the country roads.

Calmo said that the main difference between a preparado and a tribal Indian was that the preparado, who had acquired a civilised taste for whisky, couldn't afford to get drunk so often as an uncivilised drinker of aguardiente.

We drank the aguardiente. It smelt of ether and had a fierce laboratory flavour. Every time the door opened the marimba music pressed on our eardrums. Calmo made an attempt to detain one of the serving girls. 'Don't go away, little treasure, and I'll bring you some flowers from the gardens in the plaza, whatever they fine me.' He received so baleful a stare for his pains that he dropped the girl's hand as if she had bitten him. At last the hour of civic music ran out. From where we sat we saw that the Mexican outlaws had ceased to gallop across the cathedral wall. The crowds had thinned into groups of stubborn drunkards. Calmo was becoming uneasy. 'In my opinion it is better to go. These people are very peace-loving, but when they become drunk they sometimes assassinate each other in places like this. Not for malicious reasons, understand me, but as the result of wagers or to demonstrate the accuracy of their aim with the various fire-arms they possess.'

We paid our bill and had just got up when the door was flung open and three of the toughest-looking desperadoes I had ever seen reeled in. These were no shrinking Indians, but hard-muscled *ladinos*, half-breeds who carried in their faces all the Indian's capacity for resentment but none of his fear. They wore machetes as big as naval cutlasses in their belts. For a moment they blocked the doorway eyeing the company with suspicion and distaste, then one of them spotted the juke-box, which was still a rarity in this part of the world. His expression softened and he made for our table putting each foot down carefully as if afraid of blundering into quicksands. He bowed. 'Forgive me for addressing you, sir, but are you familiar with the method of manipulating the machine over there?'

I said I was.

'Perhaps then you could inform me whether the selection of discs includes a marimba?'

I went over to the juke-box. These ladinos, I thought, would still be living the frontier life of the last century; a breed of tough, illiterate outcasts, picking up a livelihood as best they could, smugglers and gunmen if pushed to it, ready, as it seemed from the frequent newspaper reports, to hack each other – or the lonely traveller – to pieces for a few dollars, and yet with it a tremendous, almost deadly punctiliousness in ordinary matters of social intercourse. I studied the typewritten list in Spanish. There were several marimbas. The ladino looked relieved. He conferred in an undertone with the other two fugitives from justice, came back, bowed again, and handed me a Guatemalan ten-cent piece. 'If you could induce the machine to play "Mortal Sin" for us, we should be much indebted.'

I returned the ladino 5 cents change, found a U.S. nickel – which is fairly common currency in Guatemala – and put it in the slot, while the three ladinos edged forward, studiously casual but eager to watch the reptilian mechanical gropings by which their choice was singled out and manœuvred into the playing position. 'Pecado Mortal' turned out to be a rollicking *son* – a kind of paso doble – executed with the desperate energy of which the sad music-makers of Central America are so prodigal. Calmo and I were half-way through the door when I felt a tap on the shoulder. The principal bandit was insisting that we join him for a drink. 'Otherwise, my friends and I would feel hurt, gentlemen.' He laid bare his teeth in a thin, bitter smile. We went back and sat down again. While he was getting the drinks Calmo said, 'In the education of our people the most important thing taught after religion is *urbanidad* – good manners. Even those who have no schooling are taught this. I do not think that we should risk offending these men by showing a desire to leave before they do.'

A moment later our bandit was back with double aguardientes and a palmful of salt for us to lick in the proper manner, between gulps. The music stopped, and his face clouded with disappointment. Behind him a lieutenant loomed, swaying slightly, eyes narrowed like a Mongolian sage peering into the depths of a crystal, mouth tightened by the way life had gone. He was holding a coin. 'Might I trouble you to perform the same service for me, sir?' he asked politely.

It turned out that the second *mestizo* wanted to hear 'Mortal Sin' again. 'It is remarkable,' he said, 'and most inspiring. I do not think it can be bettered.' The three tough hombres moved away uncertainly towards the juke-box again, simple wonderment struggling beneath the native caution of their expressions. The needle crackled in the ruined grooves, and we heard the over-familiar overture of ear-splitting chords. Someone found the volume control and turned it up fully. Every object in the room was united in a tingling vibration. The second bandit drew his machete with the smooth, practised flourish of a Japanese swordsman, and scooped the cork out of a fresh bottle of aguardiente with a twist of its point. Two more members of the band stood waiting, coins in hand.

'Mortal Sin' had been played five times, and we were still chained by the polite usage of Central America to our chairs, still gulping down aguardiente and licking the salt off our palms, when it suddenly occurred to me that it was unreasonable that an electric train should be rumbling through a subway immediately beneath us in Huehuetenango. I got up, grinning politely at our hosts, and, balancing the liquid in my glass, went to the door. The lamps in the plaza jogged about like spots in front of my eyes, and then, coming through the muffled din from The Little Chain of Gold, I heard a noise like very heavy furniture being moved about in uncarpeted rooms somewhere in space. The world shifted slightly, softened, rippled, and there was an aerial tinkling of shattered glass. I felt a brief unreasoning stab of the kind of panic that comes when in a nightmare one suddenly begins a fall into endless darkness. Aguardiente from my glass splashed on my hand, and at that moment all the lights went out and the music stopped with a defeated growl. The door of The Little Chain

opened and Calmo and one of the ladinos burst through it into
the sudden crisp stillness and the moonlight. Calmo had taken
the ladino by the forearm and the shoulder – 'And so my friend
we go now to buy candles. Patience – we shall soon return.'

'But in the absence of electricity,' the ladino grumbled
sadly, 'the machine no longer functions.'

'Perhaps they will restore the light quickly,' Calmo said.

'In that case we shall play the machine again. We will spend
the whole night drinking and playing the machine.' The
ladino waved in salutation and fell back through the doorway
of The Little Chain.

We moved off quickly under the petrified foliage of the
plaza. Nothing stirred. The world was solid under our feet
again. A coyote barked several times sounding as if it were in
the next street, and a distant clock chimed sweetly an incorrect
hour.

'A quiet evening,' I remarked. 'With just one small earthquake thrown in.'

'A tremor, not an earthquake,' Calmo said. 'An earthquake
must last at least half a minute. This was a shaking of secondary importance.'

There was a pause while he translated his next sentence into
English. He then said: 'Sometimes earthquakes may endure
for a minute, or even two minutes. In that case it is funny . . .
No, not funny, I mean very serious.'

2

A Letter from Belize

Someone in Merida said that a good way to go to Belize was from Chetumal in south-east Mexico by a plane known in those parts as 'El Insecto', that did the twice-weekly run. My informant pointed out that this route was cheaper and more direct than going via Guatemala, as well as giving anyone the chance to get away from the insipidities of air travel with the big international lines. I agreed with him, and went down to Chetumal on a veteran D.C.3 that was the last surviving plane of a small tattered fleet once possessed by this particular company. Chetumal turned out to be a nicely painted-up little town with a wonderful prison, like a Swedish sanatorium. There were seven people at the airport seeing other people off for every one that was travelling, and going through the customs and emigration was a purely family affair. I found 'El Insecto', which was a four-seated Cessna, in a field full of yellow daisies, and helped the pilot to pull it out on to the runway. When it took off he leaned across me to make sure that the door was properly shut. There were a few cosy rattles in the cabin, of the kind that most cars develop after some years of honourable service. These added to the pleasantly casual feeling of the trip. Duplicate controls wavered a foot or two from the tip of my nose, and the pilot cautioned me against taking hold of them to steady myself in an air pocket. 'These small planes take more flying than an airliner,' he said. But apart from fiddling with the throttle lever, probably out of pure habit, and an occasional dab at the joystick, he did nothing to influence our course as we wobbled on through the air currents.

Beneath, the not very exuberant forest of the Orange Walk district of British Honduras unrolled itself. As the Cessna flew at about 2000 feet, the details were clear enough. Even birds were visible. A pair of flamingos parted company like a torn

23

flag, and a collection of white maggots, that were egrets, were eating into the margins of a pool. We were following the coast-line, a mile or two inland, with the horizons wrapped up in turbans of cumulus cloud, and a few white thorns of fishing-boats' sails sticking up through the sea's surface. Approaching Belize, swamps began to lap through the dull, dusty green of the jungle. They were gaudy with stagnation; sulphurous yellows, vitriolic greens and inky blues stirred together like badly mixed dyes in a vat. The pilot pointed out some insignificant humps and thickenings in the forest's texture. These were Mayan remains; root-shattered pyramids and temples. Around them would lie the undisturbed tombs, the skeletons in their jade ornaments. The pilot estimated that only ten per cent of these sites had ever been interfered with.

The airport at Belize was negatively satisfying. There were no machines selling anything, playing anything, or changing money. Nor were there any curios, soft drinks or best-sellers in sight. Under a notice imparting uninteresting information about the colony's industries, a nurse waited, ready to pop a thermometer into the mouth of each incoming passenger. The atmosphere was one of somnolent rectitude. A customs officer, as severely aloof as a voodoo priest, ignored my luggage, which was taken over by a laconic taxi-driver, who opened the door of his car with a spanner and nodded to me to get in. We drove off at a startling pace down a palmetto-fringed road, by a river that was full of slowly moving, very green water. Presently the road crossed the river over an iron bridge, and the driver stopped the car. Winding down the window he put out his head and peered down with silent concentration at the water. Although he made no comment, I subsequently learned that he was probably admiring a thirty-foot-long saw-fish, which lived on the river bed at this spot, and was claimed locally to be the largest of its species recorded anywhere in the world.

From a view of its outskirts Belize promised to live up to the romantic picture I had formed of it in my imagination. There were the wraiths of old English thatched cottages (a class of structure pleasantly known in Belize as 'trash'), complete with rose gardens with half the palings missing from the fences. Some of their negro occupants were to be seen shambling about aimlessly, and others had fallen asleep in the attitudes of

24

victims of murder plots. Pigeons and vultures huddled amic-
ably about the roofs. Notices on gates which hung askew from
single rusty hinges warned the world at large to beware of non-
existent dogs.

Disillusionment came a few minutes later when we pulled
up at the hotel. Here it was that I realised that what information I had succeeded in collecting about Belize before leaving England was out of date. According to an account
published in the most recent book dealing with this part of the
world, the single hotel had possessed all the seedy glamour one
might have looked for in such a remote and reputedly neglected colonial possession. But I had arrived eighteen months too
late. Newcomers are now conducted, without option, to a resplendent construction of the kind for which basic responsibility
must rest with Frank Lloyd Wright – a svelte confection of
pinkish ferro-concrete, artfully simple, and doubtlessly
earthquake-resistant. As the Fort George turned out to serve
good strong English tea, as the waiter didn't expect to be
tipped after each meal, and as you could leave your shoes outside the bedroom door to be cleaned without their being
stolen, there were – even from the first – no possible grounds
for complaint. But it soon became clear that besides these considerable virtues the Fort George had many secondary attractions which peeped out shyly as the days went by. Little by
little the rich, homely, slightly dotty savour of British Honduras seeped through its protective walls to reach me. I began
to take a collector's pride in such small frustrations as the im-
possibility of getting a double whisky served in one glass. Two
single whiskies always came. Also, the architectural preten-
sions were much relieved by such pleasing touches as the
show-cases in the vestibule which displayed, along with a fine
Mayan incense-burner in the form of a grotesque head, a few
pink antlers of coral, odd-shaped roots, horns carved into
absurd birds and a detachable pocket made of pink shells,
recommended as 'a chic addition to the cocktail frock'.

Part of the Fort George's charm arose from the fact that the
staff, who spoke among themselves a kind of creole dialect,
sometimes had difficulty in understanding a guest's requirements. This went with a certain weakness in internal liaisons,
and from the operation of these two factors arose many de-
lightfully surrealistic incidents. At any hour of the night, for

example, one might be awakened by a maid bearing a raw potato on a silver tray, or be presented with four small whiskies, a bottle of aspirins and a picture postcard of the main façade of the Belize fish market, dated 1904. The Fort George, incidentally, must be one of the very few hotels in the world where the manager is prepared to supply to order, and without supplementing the all-in charge, such local delicacies as roast armadillo, tapir or paca—the last-mentioned being a large edible rodent, in appearance something between a rabbit and a pig, whose flesh costs more per pound than any other variety offered for sale in the market. Of these exotic specialities I was only able to try the paca, and can report that, as usual in the case of such rare and sought-after meats, the flavour was delicate to the point of non-existence. The fascination of life at the Fort George grew steadily. It was a place where any beginner could have gone to get his basic training in watching the world go by, and many an hour I spent there, over a cold beer and the free plateful of lobster that always came with it, listening to the slap of the pelicans as they hit the water, while doves the size of sparrows fidgeted through the flowering bushes all round; and the rich Syrian – part of the human furniture of such places – drove his yellow Cadillac endlessly up and down the deserted hundred yards of the Marine Parade.

Among the many self-deprecatory reports sponsored by the citizens of Belize is one that their town was built upon a foundation of mahogany chips and rum bottles. True enough the mahogany, which is the principal source of the colony's income, is everywhere. It is a quarter of the price of the cheapest pitch-pine sold anywhere else, and everything from river barges to kitchen tables are made from it. Local taste, however, which has become contemptuous of a too familiar beauty, prefers to conceal the wood, where possible, beneath a layer of fibre-glass, or patterned linoleum. As for the rum, it costs thirty-five cents a bottle, tastes of ether, and is seriously recommended by local people as an application for dogs suffering from the mange. It is drunk strictly within British licensing hours, which take no account of tropical thirst, and plays its essential part in the rhythm of sin and atonement in the lives of a people with a nonconformist tradition and too much time on their hands.

Although of almost pure negroid stock, the citizens of Belize

26

have succeeded in creating a pattern of society – if due allowance is made for their economic limitations – modelled with remarkable fidelity upon that of their colonial overlords. From their vociferous nonconformity, as well as the curiously Welsh accent underlying the local creole, it is tempting to theorize that the lower-grade colonials they came most in contact with hailed from the Principality, and in Belize it is sometimes possible to imagine oneself in a district of Cardiff settled by coloured people. The evangelism of the chronically depressed area flourishes. There is always a chapel just round the corner; commercial enterprises give themselves such titles as The Holy Redeemer Credit Union; and one is constantly confronted by angry notices urging repentance and the adoption of the Good Life. Even the prophetic books are unable to supply enough warning texts to satisfy the Honduran appetite for admonition. An eating-house, which advertises the excellence of its cow-heel, observes enigmatically at the foot of its list of plats du jour, 'The soul, like the body, lives on what it feeds.' Not, by the way, that one Englishman in fifty thousand had ever tasted cow-heel – a variety of soup which as far as I know is indigenous to the neighbourhood of Liverpool, in the country of its origin. This was only one of a number of intriguing gastronomic survivals: 'savoury duck' – a rude but vigorous forefather of the hamburger, once eaten in Birmingham; 'spotted-dick' – rolled suet-pudding containing raisins; 'toad-in-the-hole' – sausages baked in batter: both the latter dishes once a feature of popular eating-houses all over England, but now usually disregarded.

One constantly stumbles upon relics of provincial Britain preserved in the embalming fluid of the Honduran way of life, and often what has been taken over from the mother country is strikingly unsuitable in its new surroundings. The minor industries, for instance, such as boat-building, are carried on in enormous wooden sheds, the roofs of which are supported by the most complicated system of interlacing beams and girders I have ever seen. One thinks immediately of hurricanes, but on second thoughts it is clear that all this reinforcement would be valueless against the lateral thrust of a high wind. It turns out that such buildings were copied from originals put up by Scottish immigrants, and were designed to withstand the snow-loads imposed by the severest northern storms.

Many of the Scotsmen themselves lie buried in the city's cemeteries, both of which are located in the middle of wide roads, just where in Latin America the living would have taken their nightly promenade in formal gardens. Many of the dead, the inscriptions tell us, were sea-captains. They came here to die of fever, or were sometimes murdered, and in this case the inscription supplies the exact time of the tragedy, but no more than this and an affirmation of the victim's hope of immortality. The tombstones serve conveniently for the drying of the washing of the neighbours on both sides of the road. It is not a bad place at all to lie, for those who were confident of the body's resurrection – by the white houses, and the lemon-striped telegraph poles, with the constant bustle and chatter of bright-eyed crows in the trees above, and the eternal British-Sunday-afternoon strumming of a piano in a chapel just down the road.

Death took these captains by surprise. It was never old age or a wasting sickness, but always the mosquito or the dagger that struck them down. No Britisher ever wanted to lay his bones anywhere but in the graveyard of his own parish church in the home country. In this lies the key to all the unsoundable differences between the Spanish and the British colonies. The Spaniard took Spain with him. The Briton was always an exile, living a provisional and makeshift existence, even creating for himself a symbol of impermanence in his ramshackle wooden house.

One of the first things that strike the newcomer to Belize who has seen anything of life in the West Indies is the mysterious absence of anything that might come under the heading of Having a Good Time. There are no calypsos, no ash-can orchestras, no jungle drums, no half-frantic voodoo devotees gyrating round some picturesque mountebank. The Hondurans sacrifice no cocks to the old African gods, and feuds are settled by interminable lawsuit or swift machete blows, but in either case without recourse to the black magic of the obeah-man. This in some ways is a pity, because by virtue of the fact that timber extraction, the main occupation, ceases with the wet season, people are left with several months to fill in, and with not the faintest idea of what to do with themselves, apart from chapel-going, playing dominoes, and suffering the afflictions of love. This highly un-African existence, with its complete ineptitude for self-entertainment, is probably the result of certain historical factors. The colony was founded by an English buccaneer called Wallace – Belize is a corruption of his name – who turned from piracy to the more dependable profits of logwood extraction. The slave-owning Wallace and his successors were very few in number. They were exposed to frequent attacks by the warlike Indians of southern Yucatan, and to the constant threat of action by the Spanish, who never recognised the legality of their settlement. The interlopers could only hope to defend themselves, and to keep their foothold, by arming their slaves, who would certainly have taken the first opportunity of pistolling their masters in the back, had their servitude been unduly oppressive. In those days the English in Jamaica produced a formidable breed of mastiff which they trained not only to track down but to devour black runaways, and such dogs were in great demand in the neighbouring French and Dutch colonies. One supposes that the atrocious treatment meted out to the blacks whose masters felt themselves secure from outside attack had the effect of drawing them together in their compounds, conserving all that was African in their lives, and uniting them in their hate for all that was white. Meanwhile the negroes of Belize, with their musketry drill, their smallholdings and their Sunday holidays, would have been encouraged to turn their backs on their African past and to struggle ever onwards and upwards towards the resplendent human ideal of the suburban Englishman.

The test of this democracy *malgré-soi* came on September 10th, 1798, when a Spanish flotilla commanded by Field-Marshal Arthur O'Neil, Captain-General of Yucatan, appeared off Belize. The field-marshal was carrying orders to liquidate the settlement once and for all, and the baymen, as the English settlers called themselves, being forewarned, mustered their meagre forces for the defence. Reading of the remarkable disparity in the opposing forces one realises that here was the making of one of those occasions that are the very lifeblood of romantic history. The captain-general's fleet consisted of thirty-one vessels carrying 2000 troops and 500 seamen. The defenders numbered one naval sloop, five small trading or fishing vessels, hastily converted for warlike purposes, plus seven rafts, each mounting one gun and manned by slaves – a total defensive force of 350 men. The resultant passage of arms has provoked a fair measure of armchair bloodthirst, flag-waving, and orotund speechifying on the annual public holiday which has commemorated it. In 1923 a Mr Rodney A. Pitts wrote a prize-winning poem called 'The Baymen', an ode in thirty-one verses, which, set to music, has become a kind of local national anthem. A sample stanza plunges us into an horrific scene of carnage:

> Ah, Baymen, Spaniards, on that day
> Engaging in that fierce mêlée –
> Ah, never such a sight before,
> They are all dyed in human gore –
> Exhausted, wounded, some are dead,
> They're sunken to their gory bed.

The cold facts of the case, supplied by contemporary records, paint a less murderous picture of the encounter. There were no casualties whatever on the British side, in an engagement which lasted two and a half hours, and the few bodies interred later by the Spanish on one of the cays were as likely to have been those of fever victims as of grapeshot casualties. One thinks of the dolorous quavering of generations of school-children through such passages as:

> All died that this land which by blood they acquired
> Might give you that freedom their brave hearts inspired.

As usual, history turns out to be a fable agreed upon.

Modern times have brought with them a slackening in the idyllic master-and-faithful-serving-man relationship of the past. A People's United Party has emerged, whose aim is total independence for British Honduras, and which, by way of a kind of psychological preparation for this end, urges the substitution of baseball for cricket, and the abolition of tea-drinking. The party's creator and leader is a Mr Richardson, a weathy creole – as citizens of non-white origin are officially described. Mr Richardson's antipathy for Britannia and all her works supposedly originates in a grievance over some matter of social recognition – a familiar colonial complaint, and one that has cost Britain more territory than all her other imperial shortcomings put together. When recently the Government of

Guatemala renewed its claim to Belize, the outside world speculated on the possibility of the P.U.P operating as a fifth column in support of the Guatemalan irredentists. The answer to this, I was told, is best expressed by the local proverb, 'Wen cakroche [cockroach] mek dance 'e no invite fowl.'

The party's official organ, the *Belize Billboard*, is a journalistic collector's item, combining the raciness of a scurrilous broadsheet with the charm of a last-century shipping gazette. It is particularly strong on crime-reporting, pokes out its tongue at the British whenever it can, and carefully commemorates the anniversaries of such setbacks in the nation's story as the sinking of the Ark Royal. It is regarded with sincere affection by the white members of the colony, many of whom keep scrapbooks bulging with choice examples of its Alice-in-Wonderland prose – full of such words as 'doxy' and 'paramour'. The trade winds blow right through the advertisement section of the *Billboard*, with its bald details of goods 'newly arrived', as if they had been listed in order of unloading on to the quayside: clay pipes, lamp chimneys, apricot bats (?), Exma preparations for the bay sore and ground itch, beating spoons, cinnamon sticks, bridal satin, colonial blue-mottled soap and – in the month of March – Christmas cards. Dropped like a dash of curry into this assortment from the hold of a ghost ship are the announcements of the Hindu gentleman with an accommodation address in Bombay who promises with the aid of his white pills to add six inches to your height, 'if not over eighty'.

In whatever direction the political destiny of Belize may lie, its economic future is dubious. In the past it has depended upon its forests; but ruinous over-exploitation in the half of the total land area of the colony which is privately owned has depleted this source of income and seriously mortgaged the future. The logical remedy would seem to lie in the switching over of the colony's economy to an agricultural basis. But it seems that the rhythm of seasonal, semi-nomadic work in the forest, sustained for centuries, has created what a government handbook politely describes as 'an ingrained restlessness'. In other words the Hondurans tend to become bored with a job that looks like being too steady.

The eventual solution to this problem probably lies in the

tourist industry, with a glamourised and air-conditioned Belize emerging as another Caribbean playground of the industrial north – and anyone who has seen what has happened to the north coast of Jamaica in the last year or two will know what to expect. All the ingredients for a colonial Cinderella story are present. Being just beyond the reach of the Cuban and Mexican fishing fleets, the Bay of Honduras is probably richer in fish – including all the spectacular and inedible ones pursued by sportsmen – than any other accessible area in the northern hemisphere. The average aficionado will lose all the tackle he can afford in a week's tussle with the enormous tarpon to be found in the river running through Belize town itself. The forests, too, abound with strange and beautiful animals, with tapir, jaguars and pygmy deer, which await extermination by the smoothly organised hunting parties of the future. The Fort George, with its deep freeze, and its swimming pool in course of construction, marks the closing of an era. I was given to understand that even this year a tourist organization calling itself The Conquistadors' Caravan was dickering with the possibility of including Belize in one of its 'Pioneer Conquistadors' itineraries, and was dissuaded only by the news that there was no night-club, no air-conditioning anywhere, no Mayan ruins within comfortable reach, absolutely no beach, and that jaguars' tracks are seen most mornings on the golf course. May other travel agents read these words and be equally dismayed.

In the meanwhile, for the collector of geographical curiosities, there is still time, although probably not much time, to taste the pleasures of a Caribbean sojourn in the manner of the last century. As a matter of fact I cannot think of any better place for someone seized with a weariness of the world to retire to in Gauguin fashion, than Belize. The intelligent recluse could even protect himself from the chagrins of the tourist era to come by renting an island, which can be had complete with bungalow and bedrock conveniences, for a few dollars a week. Here he would be in a position to knock down his own coconuts, ride on turtles, collect the eggs of boobies in season, put on a pair of diving-goggles and pick all the lobsters he could eat out of the shallow lagoon water, perhaps even note in his journal the visit of a transient alligator. Each time he crossed to the mainland to collect supplies or to see an appalling Mexican film, his eye would be delighted by the prospect of Belize from the sea, resembling an aquatint from a book I possess descriptive of Jamaica in 1830. It shows white houses with pink roofs, lying low among the thick, mossy trees; listless figures gathered at the base of an elegant, tapering lighthouse; fishing boats asprawl in the heavy water at the harbour's mouth; a few frigate birds hanging meditatively in the lemon sky that often precedes a fine sunset.

The reverse side of the medal is hardly worth mentioning. The drains *are* uncovered, but there are no mosquitoes, not much infectious disease, only an occasional plague of locusts; and for nine months of the year the heat keeps within bounds. Perhaps the hazard of the occasional hurricane should be touched upon. The last bad one blew up on September 10th, 1931, the anniversary of the naval victory of 1798; a twenty-foot-high wall of water rolled over the town, and swept the houses off the cays, and a high percentage of the death-roll of a thousand were merry-makers who were celebrating the famous victory. But taken over the years, hurricanes are a very minor risk. And while on the topic of winds, it might be considered reasonable, from an intending resident's viewpoint, to bear in mind that however hard they may blow, they do so from a remarkably consistent direction, and that this direction, that of the Atlantic Ocean wastes, is not one in which a cloud of radio-active particles is ever likely to originate.

33

3

Festival in Laos

The Laotian lady disposed her silks over the spare oil can in
the back of the jeep and rearranged the pearls in her hair, and
as we moved off, the French major at her side leaned forward
and said in my ear: 'She's an authentic Royal Highness, entitled to a parasol of five tiers.' Overhearing this, the police
lieutenant, who was at the wheel, shook his head smilingly.
'Three tiers, old man.' The major waved his hands in exasper-
ation. 'We've been friends for fifteen years,' he said. 'I can't
think why we never married.' This officer was in the operations branch of the G-Staff. He was thoroughly Laos-ised, a
moderate opium-smoker, gentle-mannered, and quite good at
kite-fighting. As an individualist he preferred the single-
handed manipulation of a small male kite, to joining one of the
teams it took to handle the enormous and unwieldy females.
The police lieutenant's Laotian wife, who rode in the front between her husband and myself, looked like Myrna Loy. Her
beauty had been dramatised by a recent cupping, which had
left a reddish disc in the centre of her forehead. Although she
had climbed vigorously into her seat in the jeep, her normal
walking gait was an unearthly glide. We were all off to a
pagoda festival near Luang Prabang.

   Glimpsed from the road above it, through the golden mohur
and the bamboo fronds, Luang Prabang, on its tongue of land
where the rivers met, was a tiny Manhattan – but a Manhattan with holy men in yellow in its avenues, with pariah dogs,
and garlanded pedicabs carrying somnolent Frenchmen
nowhere, and doves in its sky. Down at the town's tip, where
Wall Street should have been, was a great congestion of mon-
asteries. Even in 1950, although the fact went unnoticed in the
Press, the Viet-Minh moved freely about the Laotian countryside, and Luang Prabang was accessible only by rare convoys
and a weekly plane. But every French official dreamed of a

posting to this place, thought of as one of the last earthly paradises – a kind of Aix-les-Bains of the soul.

The festival for which we were bound, the lady of the five-tiered parasol assured us, was quite extraordinary. She had sat on its organising committee, and to make quite sure that it excelled in the friendly competition that existed between pagodas over such arrangements, a mission had been sent across the border into Siam in search of the most up-to-date attractions. As this wealthy, independent, and highly Westernised state was regarded in Indo-China as the Hellas of South-East Asia, we could expect singular entertainment.

Within the pagoda enclosure, indeed, East and West met and mingled like the turbulent currents of ocean. Monks tinkered expertly with the wiring of amplifying systems over which, that night, they would broadcast their marathon sermons on Pain, Change and Illusion. Dance hostesses from Siam, dressed as hula girls, with navy-blue panties under their grass-skirts, traipsed endlessly round a neon-illuminated platform, to the moaning of a Hawaiian orchestra. They were watched, a little doubtfully, by a group of lean-faced young men with guitars on their backs, who, the police lieutenant assured us, were Issarak guerrillas who had joined forces with the Viet-Minh. The Issaraks, he said, had probably come down for the festival from a near-by village they had occupied some days before.

Loudspeakers howled in space, like disembodied spirits, and then were silent. A few outdoor shows attracted early audiences. Thai-style boxers slogged and kicked each other – breaking off to bow politely between the showers of blows. A performance of the Manohara, the bird-woman of the Tibetan lake, had drawn a circle of country-people in gold-threaded silks, rustics whose untainted imagination still showed them the vast range of the Himalayas in a sweep of a player's hand, and a rippled lake's surface in the fluttering of fingers. Many flower-decked stalls attended by lovely girls displayed the choice merchandise of the West: aspirins and mouth-wash, purgatives, ball-pointed pens, alarm-clocks – the spices and frankincense of our day. For those who dared to defy the abbot's ban on the traffic in intoxicants within the holy precincts, there were furtive bottles of black-market Guinness, which, mixed with Benedictine, had become a favourite aphrodisiac in Siam. Ignoring the major's horrified appeals, the princess bought a tartan skirt and a plastic shoulder-bag.

But the ultimate triumph of the festival, and chief testimony of the organising committee's enterprise, was concealed in a gay-striped Tartar pavilion erected in the centre of the enclosure. Towards this the ladies now led the party, and having bought the candles and posies of champa flowers which served as admission tickets, we took our seats on a bench facing a low stage with footlights, curtained wings, and a back-cloth painted with battle scenes between humans and javelin-armed apes.

A young man in a shirt decorated with Flying Fortresses blew a trumpet, and five thin girls dressed in beach suits came tripping on to the stage. They were well-known ballet dancers, the ladies whispered. Their whitened faces, set in tranquil death-masks, obeyed the convention imposed by the performance of the Hindu epics. Their hands were tensed to create an illusion of passion and incident. While the audience sat in silent wonder, the young man blew his trumpet again, and as the eloquent fingers fumbled swiftly with zips, hooks and eyes, garments began to fall. '*Regards-moi-ça!*' exploded the major. '*Un strip-tease!*'

The trumpet was heard for a third time, and the five thin girls placed their hands, palms together, and bowed to the audience. Then, gathering up their clothing, they turned and tripped daintily from our sight. Outside, night had fallen, and we walked in a fluorescent glare that leeched our cheeks, and painted on us the lips of vampires. The ladies were subdued and thoughtful from the cultural experience they had undergone, as they might have been after a visit to an exhibition of abstractionist art. The major said: 'If you wish to suggest that, in the sense of building railways and roads, France did little or nothing for Laos, then I agree. In other ways – and I say this proudly – we preserved it with our neglect. As you've observed tonight, we can't keep progress out for ever. It was a wonderful country; and if you want to see what it will be like in a few years' time, just go and have a look at Siam. Of course, the Viets may take it over. In any case, the charm we've known is a thing of the past. As for the future, you might say it's a toss-up between the strip-tease and the political lecture.'

The Manohara, as we passed it again, had reached a

moment of supreme drama, when the wandering prince, having stolen up behind the unsuspecting bird-woman, is about to snatch off her wings. A gasp of intolerable suspense went up from the crowd. At that moment the steel guitars began a rumba, and the supposed Issarak guerrillas plucking up courage at last, clambered on to the stage, and went grinning and posturing in the wake of the hula girls. There was one small member of the band who hung back, it seemed from shyness, but with the rest he had bought his ticket, and a girl came and knelt at the edge of the stage and sang to him – probably about a dream land far away.

4

The Bullfight Revisited

When I first lived in Spain, I went occasionally to a bullfight.
It used up an afternoon in one of the big vociferous cities when
I had nothing better to do with my time, and although I saw
the leading bullfighters of the day go through their smooth,
carefully-measured-out performances, I never witnessed any
sight that nailed itself in my memory. The bulls came,
shrewdly chosen for weight, horn-breadth and ferocity, (not
too much or too little), and they died in the correct manner at
their appointed time; and the bullfighters, borne on the
shoulders of their supporters to their waiting Cadillacs, went
off with the stars of the nascent Spanish film industry. The
bullfights used up some of the sad afternoons for me, but I
never became a regular. I missed all the fine points, and in still
shamefully enjoying seeing the man with the sword tossed,
although not injured, I demonstrated a lack of natural passion
for the art of tauromachy.

After that I moved to Catalonia, where the natives are
seriously addicted to football but do not care for gladiatorial
spectacles; so until the spring of 1957, when I found myself at a
loose end on a Saturday in the southern town of Jerez de la
Frontera, a period of many years had passed since I had sat on
the sharp-edged *tendido* of an amphitheatre and witnessed, a
little uncertain of myself, and with incomplete understanding,
this ancient Mediterranean drama of men and bulls.

I went to Jerez to arrange a visit to Las Marismas, the great
area of desert and marsh at the mouth of the Guadalquivir,
where the last of the wild camels, presumed to have been
brought in from the Canary Islands, but first recorded in 1868
by a naturalist called Saunders, have only recently been captured and subdued to the plough. At Jerez it happened that the
man who owned most of Las Marismas was away for two days
on his country estate, so while waiting for his return I went on

to Sanlúcar de Barrameda for the annual *feria* of the Divine Shepherdess. Sanlúcar is twelve miles south-west of Jerez, at the mouth of the Guadalquivir. It was the Las Vegas of Spain in the Middle Ages before the completion of the Christian reconquest, famous in particular for its homosexuals – a tradition which lingered until the Civil War, when the puritans on both sides used machine-guns to suppress entertainment by male dancers, who went in for long hair, women's clothing, and false breasts. Across the river from Sanlúcar there is nothing but desert and marshes almost all the way to the Portuguese frontier. The half-wild fighting bulls roam in the wasteland beyond the last house, and its men are fishermen and bull-herders as well as producers of splendid sherry. It is one of the many mysteries of the wine trade that an identical vine, growing in identical soil at Jerez de la Frontera, should produce a fino sherry, while at Sanlúcar it produces the austere and pungent manzanilla.

The road to Sanlúcar went through the whitish plain of the frontierland between the ancient Moorish and Christian kingdoms. A few low hillocks were capped bloodily with poppies; there was a distant sparkle of solitary adobe huts; some bulls were moving quietly in the grassy places on short, stiff legs; and storks planed majestically overhead in the clean spring sky. The peasants, holiday cigars clenched in their teeth, were coming out of their fields for the fiesta; hard, fleshless men in black serge and corduroy who bestrode the rumps of their donkeys with the melancholy arrogance of riders in the Triumph of Death. The countryside smelt of the sweet rankness of cattle, and the villages of dust, saddlery and jasmine. Sometimes, as the car passed a scarlet thicket of cactus and geraniums, a nightingale scattered a few notes through the window.

Sanlúcar was a fine Andalusian town laid out in a disciplined Moorish style, white and rectangular, with high grilled windows and the cool refuge of a patio in every house. The third evening of the feria, which is spread out over four days, was flaring in its streets. There had been a horse show, and prizes for the best Andalusian costumes; and now family parties had settled round tables outside their house doors to drink sherry and dance a little in a spontaneous and desultory fashion, for their own entertainment and that of their neighbours. It was the time of the evening when handsome and impertinent gipsies had appeared on the streets with performing dogs, and a street photographer with the fine, haunted face of an El Greco saint had already taken to the use of flash bulbs. In the main square, where a great, noisy drinking party was in progress, trees shed their blossom so fast that it was falling in the sherry glasses, so that sometimes a glass of sherry was thrown out on the decorated pavement, and a gipsy's dog rushed to lick at the sweetness, and sometimes a little white blossom remained on the lip of the drinker. Down by the waterside, where eight hundred years ago the first English ships arrived to buy wine from the abstemious Moors, a catch of fish had been landed and spread out with orderly pride on the sand. A hunchback chosen for his mathematical ability was Dutch-auctioning the fish at a tremendous speed, intoning the sequence of numbers so quickly that it sounded like gibberish. Girls frilled at the shoulders and flounced of skirt strolled clicking their castanets absently through the crustacean fug, and distantly the dancers clapped and stamped in all the water-front taverns.

In Andalucia a spirited impracticability is much admired, and Sanlúcar had squandered on its fiesta in true patrician style. Tens of thousands of coloured electric bulbs blinked, glared, fused, and were replaced, over its streets, and every mountebank in this corner of the ancient kingdom of El Andalus had gathered to sell plastic rubbish, penicillin-treated wrist-straps, 'novelties from Pennsylvania and Kilimanjaro', hormonised face-creams and vitamin pills. Only music and the dance were tenacious redoubts in the creeping uniformity of the modern world. The ancient orient still survived in the pentatonic shrilling of panpipes bought by hundreds of children, and although the professional dancers engaged to entertain the rich families in their private booths went in for sweaters and close-cut hair, in stylish reproof of the frills and curls of their patrons, they gyrated with snaking arms to Moorish pipe music and deep-thudding drums. The gestures of the dancers too, that trained coquettish indifference, that smile, directed not at the audience but at an inward vision, were inheritances from the palace cantatrices of Seville and Granada, not yet discarded with contempt.

The bullfight of Sanlúcar which was held at five in the afternoon of Sunday, the next day, was a *novillada*; a typical small-
town affair of local boys and local bulls (which happened in
this case to be formidable enough), fought in a proper ring and
watched by a critical, expert, and indulgent public unable to
afford stars but determined to have the real thing. Besides the
formal *corrida de toros* – the bullfight seen by most foreigners –
Spain offers many spectacles involving the running, the bait-
ing, and even the ritual sacrifice, of bulls. At one end of the
scale are the corridas, which are a matter of big towns, big
names and big money, and at the other end are the Celto-
Iberian Bronze Age ceremonies of remote villages of Castille
and Aragon, sometimes involving horrific details which are
properly left for description to scientific journals. In between
come the capeas and the novilladas. The capeas are village
bullfights, where the bull is rarely killed, for the village cannot
afford its loss, but is played with capes by any lad who wishes
to cut a public figure in a ring formed by a circle of farm-carts.
The amateurs with the capes fight not for money but for the
bubble reputation, sometimes receiving the bull's charge
seated in a chair or in another of a dozen facetious and suicidal
postures, and so many aspiring bullfighters meet their deaths
in this way that often the newspapers do not bother to report
such incidents. The small towns possessing a real bull-ring
hold novilladas in which apprentice bullfighters, who are
badly paid by bullfighting standards, fight bulls which have
not reached full maturity. In theory these should be inferior
spectacles to the corrida, but often enough this is not so, owing
to the dangerous determination of the young bullfighter to dis-
tinguish himself, and the fact that the bulls, although perhaps
a year younger, are often larger and fiercer than those
employed in the regular corrida, where they prefer the bulls
not to be too large or fierce. There is less money for everyone in
a novillada and therefore less temptation for behind-scenes
manipulations; but on a good afternoon you can see inspired
fighting, and plenty of that kind of madness sent by the gods,
and most of those who meet their end in the bull-ring do so at
this particular kind of fight.

Sanlúcar's novillada held the promise of unusual interest.
In the home town of the breeders of the great bulls of Andalucia – which dwarf those of northern Spain and of Mexico – it

would have been audacious to present any but outstanding bulls; and these, fresh from the spring pastures, would be at the top of their condition. Moreover, the first of the five superlative bulls looked for by well-informed local opinion was to be fought by a *rejoneador* – a horseman armed with a lance instead of the matador's sword, and mounted on a specially trained horse of the finest quality, and not a broken-winded picador's hack supplied by a horse-contractor. The rejoneador in action is itself a rather rare and interesting spectacle, surviving from the days of the old pre-commercial bullfight, and in this case there was an additional interest in the fact that the horseman was a local boy, who it was supposed would be out to cover himself with glory on his home territory. Finally, one of the two *novilleros* who would fight the remaining four bulls on foot was already considered an undiscovered star, equal to any of the much-advertised and top-grade matadors and certain to become one himself very shortly – if he did not push his luck too far and get himself killed in the present apprentice stage.

I spent the morning correctly, as all visitors to Sanlúcar are supposed to, tasting sherry in the different *bodegas*, and after a siesta, was driven stylishly in a victoria to the bull-ring, timing my arrival for half an hour before the fight began. The bull-ring was a small, homely structure of pink-washed brick, in the heat at the far end of the town. There was little refuge from the sun, which kept the storks, nesting on the thatched huts all round, rising stiffly to let their eggs cool off, and watersellers with finely-shaped jars were waiting at the entrances. When I arrived, a pleasant confusion was being caused by the three picadors, who were riding their horses at a creaking, shambling gallop into the crowd waiting outside, and practising bull-avoidance tactics on convenient groups of citizens. A woman protesting at being charged admission for a beautifully dressed little girl of five cried out with such passion that ripples of emotion and fury, dissociated from their origin, were stirring the fringes of the crowd a hundred yards away. Over to one side of the plaza, small boys were running about under some pine trees, clapping their hands and uttering inhuman cries, in an attempt to dislodge the doves sheltering in the foliage above, and drive them over the guns of a number of Sunday sportsmen whom we could see crouching like bandits in ambush wherever they could find cover. Occasionally one of the old sporting pieces was discharged with an enormous blast, and the girls screamed prettily, and the picadors, struggling to calm their horses, swore those terrible Spanish oaths denounced ineffectively in wall posters all over the country.

In due course the promising novillero arrived, in a veteran Hispano-Suiza with a tremendous ground clearance and lace on the seats. He was in full regalia, and accompanied by three aged woman in stiff black, and his manager. One of the old women was clutching what looked like a missal. The manager was a fat, gloomy and nervous-looking man, and wore a grey Sevillian hat. He and the driver lifted down the worn leather trunk containing the tackle for the fight, the swords and the capes, and the manager opened the trunk and began to forage in its contents while the others stood by, the novillero smilingly indifferent and the women with practised resignation. Something was missing from the trunk. 'I told you to count them before you put them in,' the manager said fussily. 'I don't see why you couldn't have checked them from the list. It would have been just as easy.' He closed the trunk clicking his tongue, and the old woman with the religious book said, 'I made sure of the cotton. I brought it myself.' After that they went away to their special entrance. The promising novillero, who had the rather fixed serenity of expression of a blind man, and who smiled into the sky, didn't look in the least like a bullfighter (bullfighters on the whole are dark, and a trifle saturnine in a gipsy fashion); he looked perhaps more like a cheerful and promising hairdresser's assistant. Inside the bull-ring the crowd had separated into its component castes. The townsmen in stiff, dark, bourgeois fashions, with their regal wives, had massed in the best shade seats. The cattlemen, drawn together, each on his hard foot of bench, were a solemn assize of judges in grey sombreros, ready to deliver judgment on what was to come. A hilarious clique of fisherfolk in gaudy shirts and dresses kept their own slightly tipsy company. Above them all, in the gallery, a posse of civil guards under their black-winged hats, brooded down on the scene, rifles held between knees. Only the girls in their splendid Andalusian costumes were missing. It turned out that they had gone off to watch the bicycle race, which was the competing attraction of the day and something of a novelty in the bullfighting country.

43

Fifteen minutes after scheduled starting time, encouraged by the trumpetings of municipal band music and the exasperated slow-handclapping of the spectators, the novillada got under way. The rejoneador, Cayetano Bustillo, aged nineteen, handsome, pink-cheeked and open-faced, dressed in the Sevillian manner in short waistcoat, leather chaps and a flat-brimmed hat, made his entry on a superb horse, executing a graceful and difficult step known to the haute école as the Spanish Trot. Bustillo's mount was all fire, arched neck and flying mane, an almost mythological creature, and it would have needed only a background of fallen Grecian columns and sea, in place of the dull blood-red barrier fence and the sun curving on the wet sand, to turn this scene into a picture by Di Chirico come to life. Bustillo made a circuit of the ring, went out and returned on his working horse, a black Arab, spirited, more nervous than the first, with several small pink crescents left by old horn gashes on flanks and chest. The bugle was blown and bull number one came through the open gates of the *toril*, shattering the tensed silence of the crowd, and a kind of great contented grunt went up as they saw its size and speed. The bull came out in a quick, smooth, leg-twinkling run, at first not going dead straight but weaving a little as it looked from side to side for an enemy. Bustillo was waiting, his horse turned away, side-stepping nervously across the ring and a little to the one side; his three peons who were to work to his orders with their capes had been placed equidistant at the edge of the ring by the barrier-fence, watching the animal's movements and trying to learn quickly from what they saw. The bull appeared not to see the horse, and selecting one of the peons it went for him, tail out stiff, shoulder muscles humped and head held up until the last moment when it lowered it to hook with its horns. The peon thus chosen, Torerito de Triana by name, stood his ground instead of taking refuge behind the protective barrier, the *burladero*, which screens the entrance to the passageway, received the bull with what looked to a layman like an exceptionally smooth and well-measured pass with his cape, and turned it so sharply that the animal lost its balance and almost fell. He then proceeded to execute three more stylish and deliberate movements with the cape. The hard-faced experts all round me exchanged looks, and there was some doubtful applause from the better seating positions. The critic of La Voz *del Sur* in his somewhat sarcastic account of the fight appearing in next day's issue of the paper said: 'Four imposing passes by Torerito – who was of course quite out of order in making them, as he had appeared solely in the capacity of a peon. But then, what can you expect? The poor chap can never forget the day when he was a novillero himself.' Torerito and the other two peons were middle-aged men with worried eyes, blue chins, and fat bellies straining grotesquely in their tight ornamental breeches. You saw many of their kind sitting in the cafés of Jerez drinking coffee and shelling prawns with a quick skilful fumble of the fingers of one hand. These men had failed as bullfighters, remaining at the novillero stage throughout their long undistinguished careers. Now when their sun had set it was their task to attract and place the bull with their capes, to draw it away from a fallen bullfighter or picador, to place a pair of banderillas in the bull's neck, but not to indulge in performances competitive with that of the star of the moment.

Bustillo, who took this side-show good-humouredly enough, now called '*Huh huh*!' to attract the bull, which at last seeming to notice the horse, left the elusive Torerito and went after it with a sudden, scrambling rush. This charge Bustillo avoided by kicking his horse into an all-out gallop that took him in a flying arc across the lengthening and curving line of the bull's attack, and then when, from where I sat, it seemed certain that the bull had caught the horse, although its horn-thrust had in fact missed by inches, Bustillo leaned out of his saddle and planted a pair of banderillas in its neck.

Bustillo repeated this performance several times, using more banderillas, and then the *rejón*, which is the javelin with which the rejoneador tries – usually without success – to kill the bull. The rising tension and the suspense every time this happened was almost unbearable. Bustillo, racing away at a tangent from the bull's line of attack, his gallop slowed to the eye by the curvature of the ring, would seem to be forcing his horse into a last desperate spurt, and you saw the bull go scrambling after it over the sand as smoothly as a cat, the enormous squat bulk of head and shoulders thrust forward by the insignificant hind-quarters, short-paced legs moving twice as fast as those of the horse. After that the two racing masses would appear to fuse, the bull's head reaching up and the white crescent horns showing for an instant like a branding mark in the fluid silhouette of the horse slipping by. At this second everyone got up, moved as if by a single muscular spasm, and you found yourself on your feet with all the rest, keyed up for an intolerable sight – at the very moment when the two shapes fell apart and the tension snapped like the breaking of an electrical circuit, and everyone let go his breath and sat down. Judging from his report, the *La Voz* man remained immune from nervous strain. 'As for Cayetano Bustillo,' he wrote, 'let me say at once that as a horseman he appealed to me, but as a rejoneador – no. He was content to plant his weapons where best he could in an animal that soon showed signs of tiring. And what a slovenly trick he has of throwing down the hafts of the rejóns wherever he happens to be in the ring! Has no one ever told him that the proper thing to do is to give them to the sword-handler?'

In the end Bustillo's bull, tired though it may have been, had to be killed by a novillero substituting for Bustillo on foot. In the course of his action he gave what the critic described as several exhibitions of 'motorless flight', being caught and butted a short distance by the bull without suffering much apparent discomfort. The bull, which was too much for this novillero, died probably from fatigue and loss of blood resulting from several shallow sword-thrusts, of the kind delivered by a bullfighter nervous of over-large horns. Bustillo was accorded the mild triumph of a tour on foot round the ring, and several hats were thrown down to him, which he collected and tossed back to their owners, showing great accuracy of aim. The bugle then blew again, the doors of the toril were thrown open, and in came the second bull.

Bull number two was prodigious. It was the largest bull I had ever seen in the ring and it brought with it a kind of hypnotic quality of cold ferocity that produced a sound like a gasp of dismay from the crowd. The three peons who were waiting for it worked in the *cuadrilla*, or troupe of the novillero Cardeño, a man in his thirties, whose face whenever I saw him was imprinted with an expression of deepest anxiety. The peon's function in this preliminary phase of the fight is to try, by the simplest possible passes, the bull's reactions to the lure of the red cape. Torerito, whose flamboyant behaviour with the first bull had caused unfavourable comment, was present again, and it was perhaps lucky for him that the bull decided on one of his colleagues, thus relieving him of the temptation to indulge in any more of the stylish bull-ring pranks of his youth. The peon chosen by bull number two, who was also a middle-aged man of some corpulence, was prudent enough to hold his cape well away from his body. The bull ripped it from his hands, turned in its own length, and went after the man who had started to run as soon as the bull passed him, and with a remarkable turn of speed for a man of his years and weight, reached the barrier fence and vaulted it perhaps a quarter of a second before the bull's horns rapped on the wood. Each peon in turn tried the bull, but taking great care to keep very close to the burladero, behind which the man skipped as soon as the bull had passed. Five minutes were spent in this way, and the bugle sounded for the entry of the picadors.

'The Luck of Spears', as this business with the picadors is picturesquely called in Spanish, is one of the three main phases in every bullfight conducted in the Spanish style in any part of the world; the other two concerning the work of the banderilleros, and of the man with the sword whether novillero or full matador. It is the part of the fight which upset most foreigners as well as many Spaniards in the past, although in the last twenty-five years the horse has been fairly effectively protected by padding, so that the spectacle so repellent to D. H. Lawrence, and in a defensive way so amusing to Hemingway, of a horse completely eviscerated trotting obediently from the ring, is no longer seen.

The purpose of the picador on his aged steed, and of the banderilleros who followed him, is to tire and damage the bull's neck muscles in such a way that, without his fighting impetus being reduced, he will hold his head low and thus eventually permit the swordsman, lunging forward over the lowered horns, to drive home to the bull's heart. These picadors are placed at more or less equal intervals round the ring, and each of them, if things go as they should, sustains one or more charges which he does his best to hold off by leaning with all his strength on the *pica*, jabbed into the hump of muscle at the base of the bull's neck. A metal guard a few inches from the pica's point prevents this from penetrating far and inflicting a serious injury.

In this particular case, bull number two, supplied by the

Marqués de Albaserrada, when lured by the capes to the first horse, showed no inclination to attack. When finally it did, it turned off suddenly at the last moment, ripping with one horn the horse's protective padding, in passing, and completely avoiding the pica's down-thrust. This sent up a shout of astonishment which became a continuous roar when the bull performed the same manœuvre a second and a third time. A short discussion on strategy followed between Cardeño and his men, after which the bull, enticed once again to the horse and hemmed in by the four men with capes, charged for a fourth time, this time, however, changing its previous tactics and swerving in again when it had avoided the pica, to take the horse in the rear. Horse and rider went over, carried along for a few yards by the impact and then going down stiffly together like a toppled equestrian statue. Cardeño rushing into the mêlée to draw off the bull with his cape was tossed into the air with a windmill flailing of arms and legs. He picked himself up and straightened immediately, face emptied of pain. Great decorum is maintained in the ring in moments of high drama. The bullfighters accept their wounds in silence, but the crowd screams for them. As Aeschylus witnessing a boxing match remarked to his companion, 'You see the value of training. The spectators cry out, but the man who took the blow is silent.' It was at this point the man from *La Voz* seems to have realised that he had something on his hands justifying a report twice as long as the regular bullfight opening the season at Jerez was to get next day. 'This bull turned out to be an absolute Barabbas', he wrote, '... one of the most dangerous I have seen in my life. *It gave the impression of having been fought before.*'

This sinister possibility also appeared to have suggested itself to the public, and to the unfortunate men who had to fight the bull. The first picador was carried off to the infirmary with concussion, a limp and broken figure on a board; while the others, refusing to play their part, clattered out of the ring – an almost unheard-of action – receiving, to my surprise, the public's full support. Most of the two or three thousand spectators were on their feet waving their handkerchiefs in the direction of the president's box and demanding the bull's withdrawal. The bull itself, monstrous, watchful, and terribly intact, had placed itself in front of the burladero, behind which Cardeño and his three peons had crowded wearing the kind of expression that one might expect to see on the faces of men mounting the scaffold. Occasionally one of the peons would dart out and flap a forlorn cape, and the bull would chase him back, groping after him round the corner of the burladero with its horn, without violence, like a man scooping unhopefully with blunt finger after a whelk withdrawn into the depths of its shell. The crowd was on its feet all the time producing a great inarticulate roaring of mass protest, and the bullfight had come to a standstill. A bull cannot properly be fought by a man armed only with a sword until it has been pic-ed and has pranced about a great deal, tiring itself in its efforts to free itself from the banderillas clinging to the hide of its neck. The sun-cured old herdsman at my side wanted to tell all his neighbours, some of whom were mere townspeople, just how bad this bull was. 'I knew the first moment I set eyes on him in the corral. I said someone's been having a game with that brute, and they've no right to put him in the ring with Christians ... Don't you fight him sonny,' he yelled to Cardeño. 'You're within your rights in refusing to go out there and have that devil carve you up.' That was the attitude of the crowd as a whole, and it rather surprised me. They were sympathetic to the bullfighters' predicament. They did not want the fight to go on on these terms; and when the four men edged out from behind the burladero and the bull charged them and they threw their capes in its face and ran for their lives, the girls screamed and the men cursed them angrily for the risks they were taking. The crowd hated this bull. Bullfight regulars, as well as most writers on the subject, are addicts of the pathetic fallacy. Bulls that are straightforward, predictable, and therefore easy to fight, are 'noble', 'frank', 'simple', 'brave'. They are described as 'co-operating loyally' in the neat fifteen-minute routine which is at once the purpose, climax and culmination of their existences, and they often receive an ovation – as did bull number one on this particular afternoon – from an appreciative audience as the trio of horses drag them, legs in air, from the ring. Hemingway, a good example of this kind of thinker, tells us in *Death in the Afternoon* that an exceptionally good bull keeps its mouth shut even when it is full of blood – for reasons of self-respect, we are left to suppose. No one in a Spanish audience has any affection for the one bull in a thousand that possesses that extra grain of intelligence. The ideal bull is a character like the British Grenadier, or the Chinese warrior of the last century, who is supposed to have carried a lamp when attacking at night, to give the enemy a sporting chance.

In the next day's newspaper report this bull was amazingly classified as 'tame', although it was the most aggressive animal I have ever seen in my life. When any human being appeared in the line of its vision, it was on him like a famished tiger, but tameness apparently was the professional name for the un-bull-like quality of calculation which caused this bull not only to reject the cape in favour of the man but to attempt to cut off a man's flight by changing the direction of its charge. This sinister and misplaced intelligence provoked many furious reactions. I was seated in the *barrera* – the first row of seats behind the passageway. Just below me a Press photographer was working with a Leica fitted with a long-focus lens, and this man, carried away by his passion, leaned over the barrier fence and struck the bull on the snout with his valuable camera. A spectator, producing a pistol, clambered down into the passageway, where he was arrested and carried off by plain-clothes policemen and bull-ring servants. The authorities' quandary was acute, because the regulations as laid down prevented their dismissing a bull on any other grounds than its physical inability to fight in a proper manner, or the matador's failure to kill it within fifteen minutes of the time when he takes his sword and goes to face it. But physically this bull was in tremendous shape, and although half an hour had passed, the third episode of the fight, sometimes referred to in Spanish as 'the Luck of Death', had not yet begun.

The outcome of this alarming farce was inevitably an anticlimax, but it taught me something I had never understood before: that bullfighters – at least some of them – can be brave in a quite extraordinary way. Black banderillas had been sent for. They are banderillas of the ordinary kind, wrapped in black paper, and their use imposes a kind of rare public degradation on the bull, like the stripping of an officer's badges of rank and decorations before his dishonourable discharge for cowardice in the face of the enemy. The peons, scampering from behind cover, managed to place two of the six banderillas, one man hurling them like enormous untidy darts into the bull's shoulders while another distracted its attention with his cape. After that, Cardeño, shrugging off the pleadings of the crowd, took the sword and muleta – the red square of cloth stretched over wooden supports that replaces the cape when the last phase of the drama begins – and walked towards the bull followed by his three obviously terrified peons. Although Cardeño had been standing in the shade for the last ten minutes, his forehead and cheeks were shining with sweat and his mouth was open like a runner's after a hard race. No one in this crowd wanted to see Cardeño killed. They wanted this unnatural monster of a bull disposed of by any means, fair or foul, but the rules of the bull-ring provided no solution for this kind of emergency. There was no recognised way out but for Cardeño to take the sword and muleta and try to stay alive for fifteen minutes, after which time the regulations permit the president to order the steers to be driven in the ring to take out a bull which cannot be killed.

Cardeño showed his bravery by actually fighting the bull. Perhaps he could not afford to damage his reputation by leaving this bull unkilled, however excusable the circumstances might have made such a course. With the unnerving shrieks of the crowd at his back he went out, sighted along the sword, lunged, and somehow escaped the thrusting horns. It was not good bullfighting. This was clear even to an outsider. Good bullfighting, as a spectacle, is a succession of sculptural groupings of man and beast, composed, held, and reformed, with the appearance almost of leisure, and contains nothing of the graceless and ungainly skirmishing that was all that the circumstances permitted Cardeño to offer. Once the sword struck on the frontal bone of the bull's skull, and another time Cardeño blunted its point on the boss of the horns. Several times it stuck an inch or two in the muscles of the bull's neck, and the bull shrugged it out, sending it flying high into the air. The thing lasted probably half an hour, and, contrary to the rules, the steers were not sent for – either because the president was determined to save Cardeño's face, even at the risk of his life, or because there were no steers ready as there should have been. In the end the too-intelligent bull keeled over, weakened by the innumerable pinpricks that it had probably hardly felt. It received the coup de grâce and was dragged away, to a general groan of execration. Cardeño, who seemed suddenly to have aged, was give a triumphant tour of the ring by an audience very pleased to see him alive.

After that the novillada of Sanlúcar went much like any other bullfight. The stylish young novillero who had arrived in the Hispano-Suiza killed his bulls, who were big, brave and stupid, in an exemplary fashion. This performance looked as good as one put on by any of the great stars of Madrid or Barcelona, and it was pretty clear that the old Hispano would soon be changed for a Cadillac. The bulls did their best for the man, allowing themselves to be deluded by cape flourishes and slow and deliberate passes of supreme elegance, and the novillero tempted fortune only once, receiving the bull over-audaciously on his knees and being vigorously tossed as its swung round on him for the second half of the pass. Miraculously all he suffered was an embarrassing two-foot rent in his trousers, and was obliged to retire, screened by capes from the public, to the passageway, for this to be sewn up, probably with the very cotton the old lady in black had remembered to bring. The crowd did not hold this against the bull, and it was accorded a rousing cheer, when five minutes later it was removed from the ring.

With this the fight ended, to the satisfaction of all but the critic of *La Voz*. The two novilleros were carried back to their hotel on the shoulders of their supporters, followed by a running crowd of several hundred enthusiasts. Just before the hotel was reached they unfortunately collided with another crowd running in the other direction who were honouring the winner of the bicycle race; but the bicycle racing being an alien importation with a small following in this undisturbed corner of Spain, the bull-ring crowd soon pushed the others into the side streets, smothered their opposition, and fought on to reach their objective. When I passed the bull-ring half an hour later the old Hispano-Suiza was still there. The enthusiasts had pushed it about twenty yards and it had broken their spirit; a man with a peaked cap and withered arm stood by it waiting to collect a peseta from whoever came to drive it away. Otherwise the place was deserted, and the circling storks had come down low in the colourless evening sky.

5

Rangoon Express

Punctually at 6.15 a.m., to the solemn ringing of hand-bells, the train steamed out of Mandalay station and headed for the south. Its title, the Rangoon Express, was hardly more than a rhetorical flourish, since among the trains of the world it is probably unique in never reaching its destination. It pushes on, carrying out minor repairs to the track as necessary, unless finally halted by the dynamiting of a bridge. Usually it covers in this way a distance of about 150 miles to reach Yamethin, before turning back. Thereafter follows a sixty-mile stretch along which rarely less than three major bridges are down at any given time, not to mention the absence of eleven miles of permanent way.

Here at Yamethin, then, passengers bound for Rangoon are normally dumped and left to their own ingenuity and fortitude to find their way across the sixty-mile gap to the railhead, at Pyinmana, of the southern section of the line. The last train but one had even ventured past Yamethin, only to be heavily mortared before coming to a final halt at Tatkon; but our immediate predecessor had not done nearly as well, suffering derailment, three days before, at Yeni — about ninety miles south of Mandalay.

Against this background of catastrophe, the Rangoon Express seemed invested with a certain sombre majesty, as it rattled out into the hostile immensity of the plain. Burma was littered with the vestiges of things past: the ten thousand pagodas of vanished kingdoms, and the debris of modern times; smashed stone houses with straw huts built within their walls, and shattered rolling-stock, some already overgrown and some still smelling of charred wood, as we clattered slowly past. In this area, the main towns were held by Government troops, but the country districts were fought over by various insurgent groups—White Flag Communists of the Party line,

53

and their Red Flag deviationist rivals; the P.V.O.s under their *condottieri*, the Karen Nationalists, and many dacoits. All these battle vigorously with one another, and enter into bewildering series of temporary alliances to fight the Government troops. The result is chaos.

Our train was made up of converted cattle-trucks. Benches which could be slept on at night had been fixed up along the length of each compartment. Passengers were recommended to pull the chain in case of emergency, and in the lavatory a notice invited them to depress the handle. But there was no chain and no handle. The electric light came on by twisting two wires together. Protected by the religious scruples of the passengers, giant cockroaches mooched about the floor and clouds of mosquitoes issued from the dark places under the benches. According to the hour, either one side or the other of the compartment was scorching hot from the impact of the sun's rays on the outside. This gave passengers sitting on the cooler side the opportunity to demonstrate their good breeding and acquire merit, by insisting on changing places with their fellow travellers sitting opposite.

With the exception of an elderly Buddhist monk, the other occupants of my carriage were railway repairs officials. The monk had recently completed a year of the rigorous penance known as '*tapas*', and had just been released from hospital, where he had spent six weeks recovering from the effects. Before taking the yellow robe he too had been a railwayman, and could therefore enter with vivacity into the technicalities of the others' shop-talk. He had with him a biscuit tin commemorating the coronation of King Edward VII, on which had been screwed a plaque with the inscription in English: 'God is Life, Light and Infinite Magnet.' From this box he extracted for our entertainment several pre-war copies of *News Digest*, and a collection of snapshots, some depicting railway disasters and others such objects of local veneration as the Buddha-tooth of Kandy.

Delighted to display their inside information of the dangers to which we were exposed, the railway officials kept up a running commentary on the state of the bridges we passed over, all of which had been blown up several times. It was clear that from their familiarity with these hidden structural weaknesses a kind of affection for them had been bred. With relish they

54

disclosed the fact that the supply of new girders had run out, so that the bridges were patched up with doubtfully repaired ones. Similar shortages now compelled them to use two bolts to secure rails to sleepers instead of the regulation four. Smilingly, they sometimes claimed to feel a bridge sway under the train's weight. To illustrate his contention that a driver could easily overlook a small break in the line, a permanent-way inspector mentioned that his 'petrol special' had once successfully jumped a gap of twenty inches that no one had noticed. That reminded his friend. The other day *his* 'petrol special' had refused to start after he had been out to inspect a sabotaged bridge, and while he was cleaning the carburettor, a couple of White Flag Communists had come along and taken him to their H.Q. After questioning him about the defences of the local town, they expected him to walk home seven miles through the jungle, although it was after dark. Naturally he wasn't having any. He insisted on staying the night, and saw to it that they gave him breakfast in the morning. The inspector, who spoke a brand of Asiatic-English current among minor officials, said that they were safe enough going about their work unless accompanied by soldiers. 'They observe us at our labours without hindrance. Sometimes a warning shot rings out and we get to hell. That, my dear colleagues, is the set-up. From running continuously I am rejuvenated. All appetites and sleeping much improved.'

These pleasant discussions were interrupted in the early afternoon, when a small mine was exploded in front of the engine. A rail had been torn by the explosion, and after allowing the passengers time to marvel at the nearness of their escape, the train began to back towards the station through which we had just passed. Almost immediately, a second mine exploded to the rear of the train, thus immobilising us. The railwaymen seemed surprised at this unusual development. Retiring to the lavatory, the senior inspector reappeared dressed in his best silk *longyi*, determined, it seemed, to confront with proper dignity any emergency that might arise. The passengers accepted the situation with the infinite good humour and resignation of the Burmese. We were stranded in a dead-flat sun-wasted landscape. The paddies held a few yellow pools through which black-necked storks waded with premeditation, while buffaloes emerged, as if seen at the

55

moment of creation, from their hidden wallows. About a mile from the line an untidy village broke into the pattern of the fields. You could just make out the point of red where a flag hung from the mogul turret of a house which had once belonged to an Indian landlord. With irrepressible satisfaction the senior inspector said that he knew for certain that there were three hundred Communists in the village. Going by past experience, he did not expect that they would attack the train, but a squad might be sent to look over the passengers. When I asked whether they would be likely to take away any European they found, the old monk said that they would not dare to do so in the face of his prohibition. He added that Buddhist monks preached and collected their rice in Communist villages without interference from Party officials. This, he believed, was due to the fact that the Buddhist priesthood had never sided with oppressors. Their complete neutrality being recognised by all sides, they were also often asked both by the Government and by the various insurgent groups to act as intermediaries.

And in fact there was no sign of life from the village. Time passed slowly and the monk entertained the company, discoursing with priestly erudition on such topics as the history of the great King Mindon's previous incarnation as a female demon. A deputy inspector of waggons, who was also a photographic enthusiast, described a camera he had seen, with which subjects, when photographed in normal attire, came out in the nude. The misfortunes of the Government were discussed with much speculation as to their cause, and there was some support for a rumour, widespread in Burma, that this was ascribable to the incompetence of the astrologer who had calculated the propitious hour and day for the declaration of Independence.

With much foresight, spare rails were carried on the train, and some hours later a 'petrol special' arrived with a breakdown gang. It also brought vendors of *samusa* (mincemeat and onion patties in puff pastry), fried chicken, and Vim-tonic—a non-alcoholic beverage in great local demand. Piously, the Buddhist monk restricted himself to rice, baked in the hollow of a yard-long cane of bamboo, subsequently sucking a couple of mepacrine tablets, under the impression that they contained vitamins valuable to his weakened state.

Quite soon the damaged rail ahead had been replaced, and we were on our way again, reaching, soon after nightfall, the town of Yamethin. Yamethin is known as the hottest town in Burma. It was waterless, but you could buy a slab of ice-cream on a stick, and the Chinese proprietor of the tea-shop made no charge for plain tea if you bought a cake. With traditional magnificence a burgher of the town had chosen to celebrate some windfall by offering his fellow-citizens a free theatrical show, which was being performed in the station yard. It was a well-loved piece dealing with a profligate queen of old, who had remarkably chosen to cuckold the king with a legless dwarf. The show was to last all night, and at one moment, between the squealing and the banging of the orchestra, there could be heard the thump of bombs falling in a near-by village.

It was only here and now that the real problem of the day arose. Since we were to sleep in the train, who was to occupy the upper berths, now fixed invitingly in position? Whoever did so would thus be compelled to show disrespect to those sleeping beneath them; a situation intolerably aggravated in this case by the presence of the venerable monk who was in no state to climb to the higher position. Of such things were composed, for a Burman, the true hardships of travel in troublous lines. The perils and discomforts attendant upon the collapse of law and order were of no ultimate consequence. What was really important was the unswerving correctness of one's deportment in facing them.

6

Ibiza

I spent five consecutive summers in Spain, migrating farther
south every year before the tourist invasion from the northern
countries, which by 1954 had provoked the building of thirty-
two hotels in my favourite Costa Brava village, with its native
population of about one thousand.

In 1955 I crossed the hundred miles of sea separating Ibiza,
the smallest and southernmost of the Balearic Islands, from
the mainland, and took a house for the season in the coastal
village of Santa Eulalia, about fifteen miles from the island's
capital, also called Ibiza. By a stroke of luck of the kind that
turns up occasionally in the lotteries in which life involves us,
this was the house I had always been vainly looking for, a stark
and splendidly isolated villa, on the verge of ruin, with an
encroaching sea among the rocks under its windows. I paid instantly, and without question, the extortionate price of 3000
pesetas (about £23) demanded for a season's tenancy – I never
dared admit to my Spanish friends to paying more than half
the sum – and settled down to my annual courtship of the brilliant and infallible Spanish summer.

The Casa Ses Estaques (House of the Mooring-posts) happened also to be the port of Santa Eulalia – or at least, its
garden was. Its original owner had been allowed to build in
this superb position among the pines on a headland commanding all the breezes, only by providing in the rear of the
premises, as a quid pro quo, several small well-built shacks in
which the fishermen stored their tackle. This house turned its
back on the basic amenities. The water supply came from an
underground *deposito*, normally replenished from rain-water
collected on the roof, but now dry, and the alternative to the
clogged and ruined installation in the lavatory was a broken
marble throne among the rocks overhanging the sea.

In spite of this it offered many advantages from my point of view, not the least of these being a unique vantage-point for the study of the ways of Ibizan fishermen. These were a sober and softly-spoken breed – quite unlike the boisterous hearties of the Catalan coast – who expected the stranger to make the first move when it came to opening diplomatic relations, and only occasionally indulged in an accumulated craving for violence and noise by ritually exploding one of a store of oil drums they had recovered from the sea.

The House of the Mooring-posts had been built in the 'thirties to foster, it was said, the adventures of a gallant bachelor from the mainland, and it was full of the grandiose vestiges of a thwarted ambition. There were ten rooms, all fitted with basins and taps through which water had never run. Wires, undoubtedly intended to connect the lamps in elaborate chandeliers, curled miserably from the centre of every ceiling, although the only illumination provided was by four oil lamps of the kind carried by the Foolish Virgins in children's illustrated Bibles. Of the original furniture, stated by the fishermen to have been sumptuous, only a colossal gilt mirror remained, which must have been placed in position before the roof went on, since it would have been impossible for it to pass through the door. For the rest, there were ten simple beds, all broken in the middle, a table which could only have served for a dwarfs' tea-party, or for reclining orientals, because it was impossible for normal human beings to get their legs under it, and a country auctioneer's collection of wicker-work chairs, which sprayed the beautiful, polished-stone floor with the fine white powder of their decay whenever they were sat in. The only pictures left on the walls were seven framed engravings of early steamships, and three damp-stained lithographs of the predicaments of Don Juan. When the windows were first opened – they opened inwards – a number of nestlings which had been hatched in the space between the glass and the exterior shutters flew in and perched on the pictures. The garden was thickly coated with pine needles, and in certain lights it glistened as if gem-strewn with the fragments of the gin bottles which the fishermen claimed the last tenant – a Turkish princess – had hurled from the flat roof-top at imaginary enemies. The princess, they said, had never thought much of the place, and friction had arisen between her and them as a result of their practice of drying their nets on the front doorsteps and stringing fish up to be sun-cured between convenient pine-trunks in the garden.

The Turkish princess's tenancy, which had preceded mine, with an interval of six months, had provided an episode certainly destined for incorporation in the permanent folk-lore of the island. About nine months before I arrived the princess had gone off on a jaunt to Madrid, leaving her beautiful seventeen-year-old daughter in the charge of a trusted maid. The daughter had promptly fallen in love with a young fisherman, and in keeping with the traditions of the house, which had been architecturally designed with this kind of adventure in mind, she had succeeded in receiving him in her room at night, without the maid's knowledge. Returning from Madrid to learn the worst, the mother had placed her daughter in a convent in Majorca, and given up the house. But in the course of time the girl suddenly turned up again in Santa Eulalia and went to live with the young fisherman's parents. The civil guard were called up to intervene, but in Spain a romance is never abandoned as hopeless on the mere grounds of an extreme disparity in the social position of the parties involved, and eventually, notwithstanding her mother's wrath, the marriage took place. The couple are now in the process of living happily ever after – their first child has already arrived – on a fisherman's average income of 25 pesetas (or about 4s.) a day.

One of the pleasures of Ses Estaques was the contemplation of archaic modes of fishing, which were always graceful and unhurried, and not very productive. Soon after dawn every day a boat would be visible from the terrace of the house, gliding very slowly over the inert water, with an old man rowing, who stood up facing the bow. This was one of the six Pedros of the port, known as 'he of the octopuses'. At intervals he would lay down his oars, pick up a pole with a barbed iron tip, jab down into the water, and snatch out an octopus. He appeared never to miss. Pedro, a gaunt, marine version of Don Quixote, had dedicated his whole life to the pursuit of octopuses, which he sold to the other fishermen to be cut up for bait. He had developed this somewhat narrow specialisation to a degree where every man who fished with a hook depended upon him, and he could see an octopus lurking where another would have seen nothing but rocks and seaweed through the wash and flicker of

60

surface reflections. Pedro, whose daily activities were circumscribed by the light-shunning habits of his prey, also gave a spookish flavour to the early hours of the night – particularly when there was no moon – by moving afreet-like about the black-silhouetted rocks with a torch with which he examined the pools and shallows.

Another picturesque adjunct to the scene was Jaume, an artist in the use of the *raï*. The raï is a circular, lead-weighted net, in use in most parts of the world, which in the Mediterranean is thrown from the shore over shoals of fish feeding in the shallows. Usually these are *saupas*, a handsome silver fish with longitudinal golden stripes, considered very inferior in flavour, but highly exciting to stalk and catch. Jaume's routine was to patrol the shore when, in periods of flat calm, certain flat-topped rocks were just covered by the high tide. Schools of saupas would visit these to graze like cattle on the weed which had recently been exposed to the air and, as there were only a few inches of water, would thrash about in a gluttonous orgy, their tails often sticking up right out of the water, and completely oblivious of Jaume's pantherish approach. Jaume had been doing this for thirty years, and, just like Pedro, he never missed. At the moment of truth his body would pivot like a discus-thrower's, the net launched on the air spreading in a perfect circle, then falling in a ring of small silver explosions, Jaume's arm still raised in an almost declamatory gesture in the second before he sprang forward to secure his catch. Sometimes he caught as many as thirty or forty beautiful fish at one throw, but they were worth very little in the market. Jaume also fished with a kind of double-headed trident with a twelve-foot haft called a *fitora*, usually at night, spearing fish by torchlight as they lay dozing in the shallows after rough weather. This kind of fishing too was unprofitable, depending, as it did, too much on time and chance, and the fishermen who went in for it were usually bachelors, without mouths at home to feed, who had an aristocratic preference for sport as opposed to profit. The great aesthetic moment of any day was when, all too rarely, Pedro and Jaume appeared together in the theatrical seascape laid out under our windows, Pedro passing like an entranced gondolier while in the foreground Jaume stalked, postured, and invoked Poseidon with a matador's flourishes of his net.

These were the dedicated artists in our community. Besides them there were others who fished with hook and net, and thereby wrested a slightly more abundant living from the sea within the limits imposed by their antiquated methods and tackle, their superstitions, their hidebound intolerance of all innovation, and their lack of a sound commercial outlook. Even the hooks these men used were exact replicas of those employed by the Romans, to be seen in the local museum, and when these were in short supply nothing would ever persuade them to use others of foreign origin having a slightly different shape.

Only three of the Ses Estaques men, working as a team, made anything like a living by Western standards. They fished all night, putting down deep nets at a conflux of currents off a distant cape, and at about nine in the morning their boat would swing into sight round the headland, its lateen sail slicing at the sky. All the citizens of Santa Eulalia with a fancy for fish that day would be gathered in our garden awaiting the boat's arrival, which would be heralded by three long, mournful blasts on a conch shell. Each day this little syndicate landed between six and twenty kilograms of fish, about half of which would be of the best quality – mostly red mullet. Within a few minutes the catch would be sold, the red mullet at the fixed price of 16 pesetas a kilogram, while the rest, gurnets, bream, mackerel and dorados, fetched about 10 pesetas. In summer there was never enough fish to go round, but there was no question of raising the price to take advantage of this situation. Ibiza may well be unique in the world in that here the laws of supply and demand are without application. Whatever the catch, the price is the same. The system by which in Barcelona or Majorca, for example, prices are advanced to as much as 60 pesetas a kilogram when hauls are scanty is considered highly immoral, although this strange island morality of Ibiza can hardly survive much longer in the face of the temptations offered by the defenceless and cash-laden foreigner.

From this it will be understood that no fisherman of Ses Estaques has ever made money to free himself – even if he wanted to – from the caprices of wind and tide. There is no question of his ever rising to the bourgeois level of a steady income from some small enterprise, nights of undisturbed sleep, and a comfortable obesity with the encroaching years. If he leaves the sea at all, he is driven from it by failure, not tempted from it by success. This is regarded as the worst of catastrophes. The life of a fisherman is a constant adventure. He realises and admits this, and it is this element of the lottery that attaches him to his calling. In the long run he is always poor, but a tremendous catch may make him rich for a day, which gives him the taste of opulence unsoured by satiety. The existence of a peasant, with its calculation and lack-lustre security, and that of the generous, improvident fisherman, are separated by an unsoundable gulf. For an ex-fisherman to be condemned to plant, irrigate and reap, bound to the wheel of the seasons, his returns computable in advance to the peseta, is considered the most horrible of all fates.

The village of Santa Eulalia lay across the bay from Ses Estaques. It was built round a low hill which glistened with Moorish-looking houses and was topped by a blind-walled church, half fortress and half mosque. The landscape was of the purest Mediterranean kind – pines and junipers and fig trees growing out of red earth. Looking down from the hill-top, the plain spread between the sea and the hills was daubed and patched with henna, iron rust and stale blood – the fields curried more darkly where newly irrigated, the threshing-floors paler with their encircling beehives of straw, the roads smoking with orange dust where the farm-carts passed. From this height the peasants' houses were white or reddish cubes and the cover of each well was a gleaming egg-shaped cupola, like the tomb of an unimportant saint in Islamic lands. The course of Ibiza's only river was marked across this plain by a curling snake of pink-flowered oleanders. Oleanders, too, frothed at most of the well-heads. A firm red line had been drawn enclosing the land at the sea's edge. Here the narrow movements of the Mediterranean tides seemed to submit the earth to a fresh oxidation each day, and after each of the brief, frenzied storms of midsummer, a bloody lake would spread slowly into the blue of the sea, all along the coast. The sounds of this sun-lacquered plain were those of the slow, dry clicking of water-wheels turned by blindfold horses, the distant clatter of women striking at the tree branches with long canes to dislodge the ripe locust beans and the almonds, the plaintive cry, 'Teu teu' – like that of the redshank – with which the farmers'

63

wives enticed their chickens; and everywhere, all round, the switched-on-and-off electric purr of the cicadas. The whole of Santa Eulalia was scented by great fig trees standing separated in the red fields, each spreading a tent of perfume that came not only from the ripe fruit, but from the dead leaves that mouldered at their roots.

Down in the village, life moved with the placid rhythm of a digestive process. The earliest shoppers appeared in the street soon after dawn, although most shops did not close before midnight. By about 9 a.m. the first catch of fish was landed, and the fisherman who sold it arrived on the scene blowing a conch shell, a solemn, sweet and nostalgic sound, provoking a kind of hysteria among the village cats, who had grown to realise its significance. After that, nothing much happened in the lives of the non-productive members of the population until 1.30 p.m., when the day's climax was reached with the arrival of the Ibiza bus amid scenes of public emotion as travellers who had been absent for twenty-four hours or more were reunited with their families. Between three and five, most village people took a siesta. Shutters were closed, filling all the houses with a cool gloom redolent of cooking pots and dead embers. The venerable taxis, Unics, De Dions, Panhards, crowded into the few pools of shade by the plaza. The only signs of life in the streets were a few agile bantam cocks which appeared at this time, to gobble up the ants, and some elderly men of property who, preferring not to risk spoiling their night's sleep, gathered pyjama-clad on the terrace of the Royalti bar to play a card game called 'cao'. At seven o'clock in the evening the water cart which came to replenish my drinking tank at Ses Estaques with what was guaranteed to be river water, and usually contained one or more drowned frogs, used to fill up its ex-wine-barrel at the horse-trough in the square. Then, with sprinkler fitted, it would pass up and down the only street that mattered, spraying the roseate dust. The horse's name was Astra – by which name most goats are also called in Santa Eulalia – and the driver, who was very proud and fond of it, used to urge it on with gentle, coaxing cries in what was just recognisable as an Arabic which had become deformed by the passage of the centuries.

At the week-ends things brightened up. Saturday evening saw an invasion from the countryside of farm-labourers and their heavily-chaperoned girls. The farm-labourers worked cheerfully all the hours of daylight for 18 pesetas – or about 3s. – a day. On Saturday nights they paraded the principal street of Santa Eulalia, which does not possess a single neon sign, until it was time to go and dance at Ses Parres – Ibicenco for The Vineyards. Drinks at Ses Parres cost only 3 pesetas and the purchase of a round entitled the patron to watch the floor show and to dance all night. About a third of the girls still sported the local costume, which is voluminous in an early-Victorian way, a matter of many petticoats and an abundance of concealed lace, worn with a shawl like Whistler's mother, pendant ear-rings, and long-beribboned pigtails. Many still wear the *paesa* costume because it is insisted upon by their husbands or future husbands. A friend, a prosperous small farmer, told me that of a family of eight girls, only his wife retained the paesa dress, the pigtail and the tight side curls. He had insisted on this and made it a stipulation of the marriage, as he thought it improper that another man should see his wife's legs. Women dressed in paesa style are allowed to wear 'modern' *ciudadana* clothes and rearrange their hair style if they leave the island – usually on a visit to a medical specialist in Palma.

Sunday mornings in Santa Eulalia always produced a curious spectacle. As the growth of the village away from its defensive position on the hill had left the church rather at a distance from the centre, people had taken to going to mass in the chapel of a tiny convent away among the grocers' shops and the bars in the main street. The sixty women, or thereabouts, who attended seven o'clock mass filled this building to overflowing, so that the men – who in any case were separated from them by custom – were obliged to form a devotional group on the other side of the road. Here, divided from the rest of the congregation by the flow of morning traffic, they followed the service as best they could. There were usually about twenty of them, and, as in Catalonia, I noticed that no fishermen were present. The fishermen of Ibiza are, and have probably always been, almost savagely anti-Catholic. This antagonism does not arise merely from recent conflicts over attempts to compel fishermen to attend mass or to join in religious processions, but appears to be rooted in some ancient resistance never completely overcome, to Christianity itself. It is unlucky to see a priest, or to mention the name of God unless coupled with an obscenity, and fatal, indeed, to the day's luck with the line or nets to overhear Christian prayer. One of my fisherman friends told me that his daughter, whom he had been obliged to send to the nuns to be taught her three r's, took advantage of this fear of his, to blackmail him into taking her fishing. If he refused, all she had to do was to threaten him with the Lord's Prayer. The Lord's Prayer for him was a malefic incantation of terrible power which would bring the dolphins to ruin his nets.

'And then of course,' Vicente said, 'you'll have heard of the Inquisition. They used it to try to get the better of us. All this happened somewhat before my time, fifty or sixty years ago. It was our wives they were after. Every priest's house had a hole dug in it with iron hooks on the sides and a trap door. If they took a fancy to your wife they ordered you to take her to their house for some reason or other, and you can be sure that it wasn't many minutes after you got there, before the priest had your wife, and you were down the hole.'

Ses Parres bar, dancing and cabaret, functioned on both Saturday and Sunday nights. The floor show was innocent entertainment, intended to provide something typical for foreign visitors, and usually consisted of a group of local artists performing Ibizan dances. However unexciting this might have been for the peasants in the audience it at least did nothing to dissatisfy them or endanger their cultural integrity by potentially corruptive spectacles from the outside world. In these dances of Ibiza – so unlike the bouncing jotas and sardanas of the neighbouring regions of Spain – anything that is not Moorish is pre-Moorish, or perhaps even Carthaginian, in origin. The woman twists, turns, advances, recedes, eyes cast down with resolute unconcern, body uncompromisingly stiff, feet twinkling invisibly beneath the sweeping skirt. The effect is that of an oriental doll moved by an exceptionally smooth clockwork mechanism. Her partner is more active. He postures at a distance, arms raised, hands clacking castanets, and swoops deferentially to the rhythm of flute and drum. Sometimes the rhythmic beat may be accentuated by striking a suspended sword. Occasionally the entertainers at Ses Parres are persuaded to sing those strange songs – the *caramel-*

les – each line of which ends in a sobbing, throaty ululation. The caramelles are properly sung before the altar on high feast days, and nobody knows anything about them, except that there is nothing to be heard like them anywhere in the world, and that their antiquity is so great that they no longer sound like music even to the most imaginative ear.

Ibiza's un-European flavour is, simply enough, the product of the island's geographical position, of which its history has been almost the automatic consequence. It is on the nearest sea route between Spain and the two conquering North African civilisations of the past – those of Carthage and of the Moors. It was taken and colonised by Carthage only 170 years after the foundation of the mother city herself in 654 B.C. For the Moors it was the indispensable half-way port of call – in the days when a fair proportion of galleys never reached their destination – between Algiers and Valencia, the richest city of Moorish Spain. These were the two civilising influences in the island's early history and the thousand years in between were full of the pillagings of Dark Age marauders: Vandals, Byzantines, Franks, Vikings and Normans. In 1114 Ibiza was considered by Pope Pascual II a sufficiently painful thorn in the Christian side to justify the organisation of a minor crusade in which five hundred ships were necessary to carry the loot-hungry adventurers normally employed on such expeditions. But after Ibiza's final recapture from the Moors in 1235 its strategic importance was at an end. It was no more than a remote and inaccessible island, with no natural wealth to attract Spanish settlers, and soon deteriorated into a hideout for corsairs, pillaged indiscriminately by Christians and Arabs. Within a few years of the recapture, the population had declined to five hundred families.

Much of the island's distinctive style, and those special and subtle flavourings which differentiate it from the other Balearic islands, and also from the adjacent mainland, are likely to have been formed in the two breathing spaces of peace and plenty of antiquity. The Carthaginians taught the natives almost all they knew about agriculture, including such basic Mediterranean techniques as how to grow olives. They also instructed them in the making of garum, the most famous of Carthaginian dishes, which consisted of the entrails of the tunny fish beaten up with eggs, cooked in brine and left for several months to soak in wine and oil – a modern version of which, *estofat del buche del pescado* (tunny-fish stomach stew) is still prepared. They struck enormous quantities of coins bearing the effigy of their god Eshmun, shown as a bearded, dancing dwarf, and built cave temples for the worship of Tanit, the Carthaginian Venus, who in spite of her appearance, which in her statuettes is as sensible as a Dutch barmaid's, had a sinister reputation for demanding young children as sacrifices in time of national stress. The Carthaginians were extremely systematic in the disposal of their dead, which they buried in vast necropolises, as standardised in all their details as a modern block of flats. Although most of these must have been ransacked in the past, a few still remain intact, and one or two, with their inevitable yield of ivory charms, figurines and lachrimatories, are opened every year.

During and after the Carthaginian period, the island manufactured and exported great quantities of amphorae. The Ibizan product was esteemed throughout Europe for certain magical properties attributed to the clay from which it was made, including the talismanic power of driving away snakes. Many galleys laden with them foundered in storms when outward bound along the island's excessively rocky coast, and a minor modern industry has arisen as a result of the large number of amphorae which have been salvaged intact in the fishermen's nets. These amphorae fetch between 500 and 1000 pesetas apiece in Ibiza, according to their size, shape, and the secondary interest of the marine encrustations with which they are covered. The industry consists in 'improving' genuine amphorae with interesting arrangements of shells, which are cemented in position – it took me several hours to remove those that had been stuck on a wonderful 2600-year-old pot I bought – and submerging modern amphorae in the sea until enough molluscs have attacked them to deceive the would-be buyer of a genuine antique.

The Arab contribution to the Ibizan scene is obvious and dominant. It persists in the names of all the most essential things of life – which tend to be prefixed with the Arabic definite article '*Al*'; in the cunning systems of irrigation with which the Ibizan farmer sends water coursing in geometrical patterns all over his fields; in the semi-seclusion of the women;

and above all in the architecture. An Ibizan farmhouse, which is as Moorish-looking as its counterpart in the Atlas mountains, is in its simplest form a hollow cube, illuminated only by its door. With the family's growth in size and prosperity, more cubes and rhomboid shapes are added, apparently haphazardly, although the final grouping of stark geometrical forms is always harmonious, and perfectly suited to its natural setting.

In recent years poor communications and austere standards of comfort on the island have fostered Ibiza's individuality. An air service was inaugurated in 1958, but when I was there the most direct route from Spain was by a grossly overcrowded ship sailing once weekly in winter and twice weekly in summer from Barcelona. It required long foresight and a fair amount of luck to obtain a passage on this; sailing times were sometimes changed without notice, and in my experience letters to the Compania Transmediterranea, who are the owners, were rarely answered. One's best hope of getting to Ibiza in the summer season was to arrive in Barcelona on the day previous to sailing, and to be ready to queue at the company's office soon after dawn on the following morning. The sea crossing still takes all night, and conditions probably parallel those of a pilgrim ship plying between Somaliland and the port of Jeddah. Decks are packed with the recumbent but restless forms of passengers doing their best to doze off under the harsh glare of lights, installed with the intention of reducing contacts between the sexes to their most impersonal level. This concern for strict morality gives the ships of the Compania Transmediterranea, as they pass in the night, an appearance of gaiety that is deceptive.

Island transport is by buses of a design not entirely free from the influence of the horse-drawn vehicle, by taxis which until recently were impelled by what looked like kitchen stoves fixed to their backs, and by spruce-looking farm-carts without much springing. The choicest spots in the island are only to be reached on foot, or with the aid of a bicycle, which has to be carried across flowery ravines. Once, when I was temporarily interested in spear-fishing, I asked a Spanish friend on the mainland where to go with a reasonable chance of seeing that splendid Mediterranean fish, the mero, which has practically disappeared from the coastal waters of France, Spain and

Italy. He said, 'That's easy enough. All you do is to look out for a place without things like running water and electric light ... a dump with rotten hotels, where no one in his right mind wants to go.' He thought for a moment, 'Ibiza,' he said. 'That's it. That's the place you're looking for.'

The description was most exaggerated and unjust. You can find a bleak, clean room in a *fonda* anywhere in the island, and if it happens to be in Ibiza town itself, or in San Antonio or Santa Eulalia, there may be a piped water supply, and almost certainly a small, naked electric bulb that will gleam fitfully through most of the hours of darkness. What can you expect for 30 pesetas a day, including two adequate – often classical – Mediterranean meals? Ibiza is very cheap. (I know of people who still pay rents, fixed in the early years of last century, of one peseta a month, for their houses.) Resourceful explorers have found that by taking a room only, at 5 pesetas a day, and buying their food in the market, they can live for a third of this sum. The standard price for drinks in back-street bars – whether beer or brandy – is 2 pesetas, as compared to 5 pesetas in Barcelona. The strong wines of Valencia and of Tarragona are sold at 6 pesetas a litre. The proper drink, though, of Ibiza, is *suisse* – pronounced as if the final 'e' were accented. This is absinth mixed with lemon juice, and costs one peseta a glass. At the *colmado* of San Carlos – a village once famous for excluding as 'foreigners' all persons not born in the village – you can see the customers on Sundays line up, a glass of suisse in hand, to receive an injection of vitamin B in the left arm, administered by the proprietress, Anita. The injection costs 5 pesetas, and is supposed to ensure success in all undertakings, especially those of the heart, during the ensuing week. These economic realities make Ibiza the paradise of those modern remittance men, the free-lance writer who sees two or three of his pieces in print a year, and the painter who sells a canvas once in a blue moon.

Every year the Spanish police decide that they must cut down on the floating population of escapists, who regard the island as a slightly more accessible Tahiti, and a purge takes place. Deportation is usually carried out on grounds of moral insufficiency. A fair amount of laxness in the private life is tolerated in Spain so long as an outward serenity of deportment is maintained. A departure from this, whether it be a matter of habitual drunkenness in public places, or brawling, or obvious sexual nonconformity, becomes officially '*un escándalo publico*', and the perpetrator thereof receives a visit from the Commisario de Policia, who if it is a lady who is concerned will kiss her hand, before begging her to depart on the next boat. Annually, Ibiza's bohemian plant is pruned back to the roots, and with each new season it produces a fresh crop. Most of these Gauguins are both harmless and picturesque. In 1955 the beard came in again and was adopted by all nationalities except the Spanish. It was no longer the furious growth inherited from naval service but a sensitive and downy halo worn on, or under, the chin in true *fin de siècle* style. The female of the species looked as if she might have woven her own clothes.

A fair number of these refugees from the left-bank cellars of the northern cities drifted up the coast to Santa Eulalia. Our prize specimen, of whom we were very proud, was an English actor who had embraced a strict yoga discipline, and who regularly reached phases of reintegration in our open-air café, El Kiosko. On one such occasion he sank to his knees, eyes lifted heavenwards, in the path of a bus just about to depart for Ibiza, and remained in this position for about five minutes, while the bus awaited his pleasure with the engine ticking over and a pair of civil guards sat at a near-by table eyeing him with a kind of grim connoisseurship. We also had with us for a short time, until he was removed to a madhouse, a genial American who in his less lucid moments believed himself to be Ernest Hemingway, while any evening after five it was unusual not to be accosted in one of the two popular bars by a Russian nobleman anxious to explain his solution of the problem of perpetual motion. Native – or perhaps I should say Spanish – eccentrics were comparatively rare, but they included a massive Catalan who strode through the streets perpetually cracking a stock whip, and a fair-only bullfighter who had found a summer asylum in the house of a local lady of quality and used to accompany her on long walks holding an iron bar in his extended right arm to develop the muscles employed in skewering his bulls.

These were some of the transients who brightened our lives. We also had our small colony of permanent foreign residents who sometimes acted strangely by Spanish standards. The only American resident, for example, a charming lady who loved animals, built a tower just across the water from Ses Estaques to shelter a pony she had found with a broken leg. The tower, in fautless local style, harmonised with the several others that had survived in this majestic panorama from the Middle Ages, but the quixotry of the action was complicated by the fact that it had inadvertently been built on someone else's land. But the Spanish were as tolerant of all such foibles as if they had been Buddhists of the Hinayanist canon. No extravagances ever produced so much as a raised eyebrow. If they'd had the chance to travel, they'd probably have cut a comic spectacle in the foreign country too. That was how the man in the street saw it. The police sat and pondered whether or not yoga trances in the main thoroughfare constituted a public scandal, shrugged their shoulders and decided to refer the matter to higher authority.

The interest I developed in Ibiza's eccentrics, both of the present time and of the past, actually provoked me into making a pilgrimage, to the highly inaccessible village of San Vicente, where Raoul Villain – most notable of them all – spent his last years.

In July 1914, Villain succeeded in concealing himself in the French Chambre des Députés, and there shot dead the Socialist leader Jean Jaurès, who opposed France's entry into the First World War. This action was committed by Villian in the sincere belief that he was a reincarnation of Joan of Arc, charged with the mission of protecting France from the shame of a craven retreat. He spent a few years in a lunatic asylum, after which he was quietly released and smuggled out of the country by his relatives, who sent him to San Vicente on the north-east corner of the island. Here he lived quietly enough until the outbreak of the Spanish Civil War in 1936, when he was killed by the anarchists.

San Vicente is about eight miles up the coast from Santa Eulalia, and as it was said to be in surroundings of extraordinary beauty, I decided one day to make a trip there. When Villain's influential kinsmen had picked out San Vicente as being, so far as Europe went, the end of the world, they were undoubtedly well-informed. The hardiest of our *taxistas* excused himself from taking me in his 1923 Chevrolet, so I hired a bicycle – as usual, devoid of brakes – which I hauled most of the way through a landscape of infernal grandeur. Peasant women robed like witches passed with a slow gliding motion over fields that were stained as if with sacrificial blood. Ancient isolated fig trees hummed and moaned mysteriously with invisible doves sheltering in their deep pools of foliage. The stumps of watch-towers stood up everywhere half strangled with blue convolvulus, and the air was sickly with the odour of locust beans. This was a scene that had not changed since Gimnesia, the Island of the Naked, was written about in *Periplus* – except that in the matter of clothing the people had gone from one extreme to the other.

I lost my way several times and was redirected by signs and gestures by the aged women who were permitted to appear at the doors of their houses, from one of whom I received a bowl of goat's milk. San Vicente proved to be a sandy cove, deep-set among mouldering cliffs, with a derelict house, a farm, a fonda, and a shop. The beach, which was deserted, had been carefully arranged with antique wooden windlasses and a frame like a miniature gallows, from which huge, semi-transparent fillets of fish hung drying against a violet sea. The quality and distribution of these objects in this hard, clear light, had clothed them in a kind of vitreous surrealism. This may have been the chief Carthaginian port in Ibiza. About a mile inland lies the cave temple of the goddess Tanit, called Es Cuyerám, which is only partially excavated, and from which in the course of amateurish investigations great archaeological treasures have been recovered, and most of them smuggled out of the country.

The derelict house had been built by Villain, but never finished. The walls were painted with faded fleurs-de-lis, and there were black holes where doors and windows had been. The first inhabitant of San Vicente I ran into had known the exile well, and luckily for me he spoke Castilian Spanish. Villain, he said, had been much liked by the village people, among whom he had developed a kind of gentle patriarchal authority. He had been a bit funny in the top storey, my informant said, screwing his forefinger against his temple in a familiar Spanish gesture – but then, clever people like that often were. The villagers, it seemed, had shown no desire to argue when Villain propounded his doctrine of reincarnation, and had listened with interest and respect while he described episodes from his previous existence, and told them what it felt like to be burned at the stake. When the anarchists landed there soon after the outbreak of the Civil War in 1936, they all ran away except Villain, who, in his grand role, and carrying the standard of Joan of Arc, went down to the beach to meet – and perhaps repel – the invaders. My informant's belief – which is commonly held – was that he was on the anarchists' list for liquidation. This strikes me as highly unlikely. The truth of the matter probably is that they had as little sense of humour as they had regard for human life. At all events, Villain was shot twice and left for dead, lying on the beach. Two days later, when the villagers decided to return, he was still there, and still alive – but only just, and before a doctor could be brought, he was dead.

When you have seen enough of Ibiza's foreign birds of passage, all you have to do is to move out of one of the three centres already mentioned, where they concentrate between migrations. The interior of the island, which is 26 miles long, with an average width of about 9 miles, and has a population of 36,000, is not only unspoilt but mysterious: so much so that Don Antonio Ribas, the leading authority on everything appertaining to folk-lore in Ibiza, was unable either to confirm or to deny a rumour that a mountain hamlet exists in which women are still veiled in Moorish style.

The Ibizan peasant is the product of changeless economic factors – a fertile soil, an unvarying climate, and an inexhaustible water supply from underground sources. These benefits have produced a trance-like routine of existence, a way of life that in the absence of some social cataclysm might remain in a state of cosy ossifiction until doomsday. The peasant lives, on the whole, monotonously, with calculation and without surprise. He suffers from inbreeding, which produces a great deal of baldness in the women, an addiction to absinth (which in Ibiza is the real thing), and an abnormally high incidence of syphilis. Like the industrial proletarian, the Ibizan peasant carefully separates work from play, and his many fiestas and ceremonies are the sauce for the long, savourless days of hard labour. Much of the remote past is conserved in the husk of convention, and archaic usages govern his conduct in all the crucial issues of existence.

74

Of the peasant's many customs the most singular are those associated with courting, called in the Ibizan dialect *festeig*. This has no parallel elsewhere in Spain – or probably in the world – and is at least an intelligent advance on the match-making system employed in most oriental and semi-oriental lands. A marriageable girl's state is officially proclaimed by the act of her attending mass standing between her father and mother. Eligible young men may then present themselves formally at the girl's home and apply to her father for permission to take part in the festeig, which is staged in public. The father usually appoints an hour or more on three evenings of the week – Tuesdays, Thursdays and Saturdays – for this. Courting time begins at eight o'clock, to give the girl time to prepare herself after her day's work in the fields, and in the case of a girl who has a large number of suitors it may be continued until midnight, or even one in the morning. The highest number of suitors reported by my informant was fifteen. Three chairs are placed in the centre of the principal room, one each for the girl and her father, and a third for the suitor, and this is occupied in turn and for exactly the same number of minutes by each of the young men who have entered the amorous contest. While he puts his case the others look on critically. As soon as his time is up he is expected to get up and leave of his own accord, and if he fails in this the suitor whose turn comes next is entitled to throw small stones at him as a reminder. If this warning is ignored it is taken as a deliberate insult, and in theory at least the injured party leaves the house and waits outside for his rival, with knife drawn. The festeig – now only to be found in remote parts of the island – has in the past been responsible for numerous killings.

While docile in all other things the Ibizan is traditionally pugnacious where the heart is affected. A girl who finds herself unable to accept any of the candidates presenting themselves at her festeig, or who takes too long to make up her mind, may be publicly stoned. Peasant society – though not the Guardia Civil – approves of an admirer showing his enthusiasm for a girl by firing his pistol at a point in the ground a few inches from her toes as she leaves mass. If rejected, he sometimes, and with public toleration, gives vent to his natural frustration by firing at the ground behind the girl. In either case she loses face if she displays anything but the completest indifference. This

75

amorous gunplay has given the police some trouble in the past. Even now a civil guard rarely passes a young peasant who is not at work when he should be, without satisfying himself that he is not concealing a weapon. The commonness of feuds in bygone days arising from breach of courting and other customs is attested by the fact that even now, no Ibizan *paes* greets another after dark: originally this was to avoid the possibility of betraying his identity to an enemy.

Such customs as these – the miming and buffoonery at the annual pig-killing, and the elaborate feasting and dancing which accompany the communal ploughing and the harvesting of various crops and, above all, marriages – are on the point of disappearance. They can no more survive improved education and 'standards of living', technical progress, and the example of how the rest of the world lives as demonstrated by the cinema, than similar customs could survive these things elsewhere. One other extraordinary custom survives, and in spite of the energetic disapproval of the Guardia Civil. This is the *encerrada* – which also continues to exist in off-the-beaten-track regions in Andalusia, and is described by Mr Gerald Brenan in his book *South from Granada*.

The Spaniards appear always to have felt an antipathy towards the remarriage of widows or widowers. There is evidence to suggest that in the Bronze Age the surviving partner was promptly killed off, since husband and wife appear to have been buried at the same time, squeezed into the same funeral jar. The encerrada is the public form taken by this disapproval, which varies very much and according to the circumstances of the case, between the extremes of noisy but harmless peasant horseplay and something very close to a lynching party. The Ibicencans, who are scrupulous about the forms of mourning, consider it particularly scandalous to remarry within the year, the more so if either of the contracting parties has children. The encerrada in its mildest form consists in a party of neighbours collecting to keep the newly-weds awake all night on the first night of the marriage by a raucous serenade played on guitars and accompanied by the blowing of conch shells and the beating of tin cans. When a breach of custom has been unusually shocking, the encerrada may be prolonged for four or five nights and draw hundreds of participants from other parts of the island. An atmosphere of hysteria prevails and obscene verses are improvised and screamed under the windows. At this point the civil guard usually arrives, and the violence and bloodshed start. In 1950 at the village of Es Cana the police arrested the participants in an encerrada, all of whom spent fifteen days in gaol; but the encerrada still goes on. Police permission is actually given for an encerrada, so long as no obscene verses are sung. When permission is refused, the encerrada is still sometimes organised by the women only, in the knowledge that they will receive milder treatment from the civil guard, when they appear upon the scene, than would the menfolk if they too had been involved. The object of the encerrada, when it is seriously undertaken, is clearly to force the offenders to leave the neighbourhood, and in this it is usually successful.

On the feast of the August Virgin, which occurs on the 15th of that month, I gave a little party at Ses Estaques which in retrospect strikes me as illuminating the situation. The party was for the family of the woman who looked after the house – two daughters and a son. They had been born in the town of Ibiza, although their mother was a peasant from San José who would still intone, after a great deal of persuasion, the old warbling, elusive African melodies. In one generation the young people had moved forward a thousand years or so, even though they were still not quite modern Europeans. On this occasion they spent an hour or two happily searching for sea-snails, and prising limpets off the rocks to enrich the splendid ritual *paella* their mother would cook for their midday meal. Afterwards the boy went off to watch a football match, while the girls relaxed under the pines, half absorbed in novelettes of the kind in which servant girls marry the sons of rich men with racehorses and yachts. At the same time I observed the girls giving half an eye to the antics of some French women who were disporting themselves (illegally) in bikinis on the rocks near by.

This sight appeared to provoke a certain restlessness in the young women from Ibiza. It was as if they were the not wholly reluctant onlookers at the performance of some religious rite to which they felt they owed some concession of reverence, and after a while, and following a whispered conversation, both girls removed their frocks, and sat there somewhat defiantly in their petticoats.

Our garden, at the very edge of the sea, was a thoroughfare for all fiesta excursionists, and about midday a particularly imposing couple passed through with their formal escort. There were an admiral's daughter then holidaying in Santa Eulalia, her escort of two younger sisters, and a waiter from the local restaurant – a young Apollo who was not-quite hopelessly in love with her. This was an affair which, despite the obvious disparities, could have been settled in the time-honoured Ibizan way, by a formal abduction, with the girl lodged with some female person of probity until the father's consent could be obtained. Perhaps in this case a marriage by capture would be arranged, or perhaps Santa Eulalia was already too civilised. It remained to be seen.

Later that day, too, I saw the rather astonishing sight of one of our Pedros taking his wife for a pleasure trip in his boat. This, by local standards, was definitely taboo. Wives stayed at home, and women in boats were almost as unlucky as priests. But Pedro had been taking out mixed parties from the local hotel, so his wife had probably told him that if it was all right for him to take out foreign females, then he could take her too. At this time, the height of the season, Santa Eulalia was crowded with fair strangers, many of them unattached. Their admiration for the hard-muscled, sun-bronzed fishermen, who took them out for boat rides at 25 pesetas a time, was sometimes manifested indiscreetly, and a few were said to have gone so far as to make advances when the time and place was right. One of the young fellows thus favoured had only recently confided his doubts in me. Was it not a fact that foreign ladies usually suffered from syphilis?

And so this golden day passed with its contrasts and its confrontations. The French ladies came and went, happy daughters of that full turn of the wheel where sophistication joins hands with innocence, oblivious of the Bishop of Ibiza's pastoral fulminations on the subject of decency in dress. Pepita and Catalina got badly sunburned in spite of the markedly olive undertone of their Mediterranean skin, and were thus chastened for their first cautious step forward into the full enlightenment of our times. The tide moved up a few inches and licked at the ruins of our private sea wall. This would be the last season that the house of Ses Estaques would embellish this shore with its patrician decay, because the land along the sea-front had now gone up to 40 pesetas a square metre, so the house was to be pulled down and replaced with the stark white cube of an hotel.

Just outside the fine ruin of the archway entrance to what was left of the garden, a family of peasants were gathered round their cart. They lived in a fortified farmhouse in the mountains in the centre of the island, which sheltered several families and was in reality a hamlet in its own right. At this time they were relaxing after a late meal of goat's flesh and beans. One of the men had invoked the holiday spirit by blackening his face and dressing up like a woman, and the other, sitting apart, was playing a wistful improvisation on his flute. The sister had left them. She had been studying the French women, and the Ibizan girls, and she had pinned back her skirt from the waist so that it fell behind in a series of dressy folds, to show an orange silk petticoat, and was gleefully dabbling with her toes in the edge of the tide.

The men spoke Castilian, and one of them told me that it had taken them half the morning to get down to Santa Eulalia, which, because of the difficulty of the journey, they only visited once a year – on this day. But next year, he said, things would be a lot better. The roads were going to be made up, and the piles of flints were already there, awaiting the steamroller. With a good surface on the roads they could cover the distance in half the time, which meant they would be able to come more often. They all agreed with me that Santa Eulalia was a very wonderful place.

7

Assassination in Ibiza

Any foreigner who installs himself for the summer in Ibiza is
certain sooner or later to be approached by an extraordinary
dog. This will be an Ibicene hound on the look-out for temporary adoption. At first sight it may seem ludicrous to the visitor
to the island that he could ever be induced to cherish such an
animal. The Ibicene hound is admittedly of ancient lineage.
Many local savants believe that the Phoenicians introduced
the breed when they had an important settlement in Ibiza, and
there is even some romantic nonsense talked about its being related to the sacred dog of the ancient Egyptians. But aestheti-
cally it is hard to accept. There is something haphazard and
unplanned about its general outlines, suggesting the result of a
union between a greyhound and the most depraved-looking
Indian pariah. In colour it is brown and white. Its long,
pointed face ends in a pale tan muzzle, and it possesses large,
pink up-pricked ears, pink toes, and amber eyes. Until one
gets to know the dog better its expression, which is really mild
and speculative, appears to be charged with a shifty imbecil-
lity. But above all the dog's condition is usually appalling. It
will almost certainly be dreadfully emaciated, as a result of the
local belief that to feed a hunting dog is to reduce its keenness.
Most Ibicene hounds are kept tied up during the daytime, or
at best chained to a heavy log which they drag painfully
behind them. Only at night are they released, to hunt for rabbits. Despite this absence of immediate charm, the extraordinary fact is that the few dogs that make their escape and turn
to beachcombing soon find someone to look after them. The
secret may lie in the Ibicene hound's quiet tenacity of purpose,
and the natural tact with which it finally wears away the
repugnance engendered by its hideous presence. A ceremonial
offering of food is all that is necessary to attach one of these
wanderers to one's person and one's house. Thereafter the

summer visitor never again feels himself a complete stranger. He has been formally adopted by a dog which will guard him and his possessions in the most unobtrusive way, and which will keep its distance and know its place. In fact a natural aristocrat of a dog.

This year, as usual, I passed the summer by the shores of an Ibizan bay round which five small stark Moorish-looking cottages had been put up by local enterprise for holiday occupation. By the time I arrived four of the five cottages had already been taken by miscellaneous foreign families, and each family had already acquired its dog. Within twenty-four hours I had mine too, an errant bitch known locally as Hilda, after the star in a recently shown film who had unknowingly given her name to about one-third of the female animals of Ibiza. Hilda was a normal Ibicene hound, silent and self-effacing in her disposition. Her only drawback consisted in her insistence on trotting in front of my car about twenty yards ahead – a custom carried over from the old days of the vendetta when the watch-dog had to be on the look-out for enemies lying in ambush. This reduced my speed when we made excursions together to eight miles per hour. Otherwise I was reasonably well satisfied.

The local farmer too had got himself a new dog – a six-months-old puppy – but this had turned out to be far from satisfactory. It had what was known as '*el vicio*' – that is to say it had never become resigned to its hunger – and this had caused it to devour several hens, as well as the farmer's cat, when it had been released at night. It now spent its days tied up miserably in the thin shade of a locust-bean tree fifty yards from my door. It was roped to a bough over its head in such a way that it could just manage to lie down but not walk about. For at least half the day it was in the full glare of the sun. The farmer had left a bowl for water which was dry when I inspected it, but I doubted very much that it was being fed. Its neck was raw from straining at the rope when anyone came near it. I watched it unhappily for a whole day, and when night came I took a knife, and crept out and cut it free. I was a little nervous about this interference in local affairs, and I was afraid that the dog might give me away by barking, or might even attack me as I groped towards it in the darkness. These fears turned out to be groundless. It probably took me three minutes to saw through the enormously thick, home-twisted rope. While I did so the dog licked every exposed part of my anatomy it could reach, and as soon as it was free it streaked off into the night.

Alas, I awoke next morning again to the sound of its forlorn yapping. It seemed that at dawn it had surrendered itself to its master, and was now tied up even more dreadfully than before, in a tumbril-like cart standing just by the farmhouse door. At about 6.30 a.m. a woman called Pepa, who went round the cottages doing the odd chores, came and knocked on my door. Pepa was a fisherman's daughter, now middle-aged, who worked eighteen hours a day to bring up and to pay for medical treatment for the spastic child that had been left on her door-step in the town twelve years before. She had a request to make on behalf of the farmer. Was there any chance of my making a trip shortly to Portinaix? Because if so the farmer would be glad to know if I would oblige him by taking the dog with me and abandoning it there. Portinaix was a lonely beach at the other end of the island to which I made occasional fishing trips. She added innocently that someone – certainly a foreigner – had cut the dog loose in the night, and it had slain more chickens. In that case, I suggested, what objection could there be to putting the animal out of its misery? Why not, for example, shoot it, rather than abandon it to starve?

The reply taught me how much after four summers of life in Ibiza I still had to learn about the island mentality.

'The peasants don't like to kill these dogs.' There was a hint of contempt in her voice when she spoke of the peasants.

'Not even the vicious ones?'

'No, they're too superstitious. They're afraid to kill a dog. If a peasant wants to get rid of a dog he takes it across to the other side of the island and lets it go.'

'And we get the dogs from San Miguel and Portinaix?'

'That's right. That's where Hilda came from. Mind you, if a farmer happens to be on good terms with a fisherman he usually asks him to take the dog out to one of the islands and let it go. In that way he can be sure the dog will be all right. There are plenty of rabbits on the islands.'

The fate of this dog was now beginning to assume for me a most uncomfortable importance. I fed it several times that day, but there seemed no way of defeating its chronic and ferocious hunger. It was the poorest and most repellent specimen of its breed I had seen, with the face of a monster from a bestiary, and possessed of a kind of mad vitality. In its noisy, hysterical demonstrations, too, it was most untypical of the true Ibicene. I suddenly found that I was feeling the beginnings of an attachment for this appalling dog, and the knowledge frightened me a little. A few more days' acquaintance and I knew that I should find myself asking the farmer to give it to me. And then, what was to happen when I went back to England? I was relieved of this fear by the appearance of the only other English member of the colony: a middle-aged woman. She was on the verge of tears. 'That poor, poor animal,' she wailed. 'I haven't been able to sleep for nights, for worrying about it. And of course, it's simply ruined my holiday. All I want to do now is to get away from this dreadful island, and never set foot in it again.' What was important about this visit from my point of view was that she had come to ask me to see the farmer and find out whether he would sell her the dog.

The farmer of course hadn't the slightest objection to parting with the beast. Nor did he want any money. His only stipulation was that it must be kept tied up. So the dog was removed forthwith from its tumbril and tied to a fig tree at the back of the Englishwoman's cottage. The Englishwoman put penicillin ointment on its sores and bound the loop of the rope, where it touched the dog's neck, with soft cloth. While she was tending it the dog struggled to lick her hands. It gulped down the quart of milk she gave it, and the moment it was left to itself it started its mournful barking again.

Next day Pepa brought incredible news. 'You won't believe this – the Englishwoman's going to have the dog killed!' It was the first time I had seen her shaken out of her stolid acceptance of the behaviour of foreigners in general. 'She says that the dog's hers now, so she has the right to have it killed. Please don't ask me to understand the mentality of people like that.' Pepa had shrugged off the berserk drunks, the betrousered women, the artists with their beards and sandals, the occasional nudist on the beach, and the actor who practised yoga exercises in the village square. But this was too much. To ask to be given the dog, only to have it destroyed!

But the intended mercy-killing turned out to be a harder project than the Englishwoman had expected. None of the local males could be persuaded to undertake the execution, and the village veterinary surgeon – under the pretext that he had run out of chloroform – succeeded in excusing himself too. Undismayed by this setback she took the seven o'clock bus next morning to Ibiza town, nine miles away, where she finally discovered a vet who had emancipated himself from local superstition. He promised to come out next day on his motor cycle, and said that he would arrive at about one o'clock.

Next morning a shadow had fallen upon our little colony. The atmosphere was charged with mass emotion – a kind of mob-hysteria in reverse – that made us shrink from meeting one another. The dog leaped about in the shade of the fig tree as the foreigners, French, Germans and Catalans, slunk up with their last offerings of food.

Pepa, who was to cook lunch for me that day, fussed about the kitchen doing nothing in particular, and then at midday appeared with a strained face to say that she was off home.

'Me pongo nerviosa.' ('I'm feeling upset.')

'Didn't you tell me that you killed the pigs at the matanza?' I asked her, referring to the great autumnal slaughter when every village in the island is full of the shrieking of pigs.

'That's different. Anyway, I don't kill my own pigs.'

Just as she was leaving she was treated to the spectacle of the dog being given its last meal by the Englishwoman. This contained a fair amount of meat, which Spanish fisherfolk can only afford to give to sick children. Pepa commented on the seeming illogicality of this, in a voice which carried at least two hundred yards.

After that began the waiting. All the foreigners had closed the shutters of their windows facing the direction where the dog sat under the fig tree digesting its enormous meal, its ugly face twisted into a smirk of crazy beatitude. The members of the farmer's family, who at this season when the harvest was in, spent most of the day doing odd jobs about the farmyard, had disappeared from the scene. Even the mule-carts seemed to have stopped coming down the road. I went into a room overlooking the sea, for no clear reason locking the door, and tried to read, but listening all the time for the executioner's arrival. I could hear the dry clicking of the distant water-wheels sounding as though the landscape on which I had turned my back were full of ancient timepieces ticking off the seconds until one o'clock. Now I knew a little of the state of mind of prisoners confined to their cells awaiting the obscene moment when, somewhere under the same roof, the trap door of the gallows will be sprung. I had caught the Spanish horror of this cool and premeditated killing, and as a foreigner, I felt myself included in their disapproval.

The blindfolded mules turning the water-wheels ticked off the seconds. One o'clock passed, then one-thirty, and I was beginning to permit myself to hope that the vet from Ibiza too might have suffered from cold feet at the last moment. But at two o'clock death approached, with the feeble puttering sound of a two-stroke motor cycle bumping slowly up the terrible road. (Later I heard that the rider had stopped at the kiosk in the village to brace his nerves with a couple of absinths.) I went through to the bathroom in the front of the house and looked out through the shuttered window. The vet had leaned his motor cycle against my wall just below, and he was unpacking the kit strapped to his carrier. The Englishwoman came out, and they talked in low voices. 'I shall require someone to control the animal while I administer the injection,' the vet said. 'Rest assured, there will be no struggle – no sensation of pain.' The woman said that she would hold the dog. 'It is just as well that it appears to possess an affectionate nature,' the vet said softly, filling his syringe, '– although perhaps excessively excitable. I say this because it is not a good thing to be bitten by an animal of this kind, which is liable to carry various infections.' The woman reassured him in her halting Spanish. 'Es muy bueno. Tiene mucho cariño.' ('It has much affection.')

They went off together, walking very slowly towards the fig tree. From my angle of vision through the slats of the shutter, I could see only the lower part of their bodies for a moment as they moved away, and then I saw no more of them, but I could hear the snuffling, whining excitement of the dog and the tug of the rope as it jumped towards them, fell on its pads and jumped again. And then I heard the woman's quietly comforting voice, in English. 'Good little doggie. Good little doggie. Now keep still there's a good boy. There's a good little chap.

Good little doggie.' After that, as Lorca puts it, a stinking silence settled down.

The farmer buried the unsatisfactory Ibicene hound, being paid for this service the sum of 10 pesetas – first, however, removing the rope, which was in good condition, and which he took away with him. In keeping with the discreet traditions of a people whose ancestors have suffered, on the whole silently, under many tyrannical regimes and alien people, I believe that he never commented again on this distasteful business. Pepa, who returned to duty that evening, also avoided mentioning the subject for some time. Several days later though, after a glass or two of wine, she was induced at the village stores-cum-tavern known as the *colmado* to discuss the foibles of foreigners – a subject on which she was considered by the villagers to possess expert knowledge. This time she had a new charge to add to her previous main objection about their lack of taste and common decency in matters of dress. 'They are frequently egotists,' she said. 'This applies in particular to the women, who are also spoiled. Take for example the case of the one who recently assassinated the dog. Do you really ask me to believe she did it out of love or consideration for the animal? What nonsense! She was suffering from bad nerves through having too much money and too little to do. The dog barked at night, she was distressed by the sight of it, and she could not sleep. Therefore the dog had to die. And, by the way, a woman possessing real warmth of heart will not think so much of dogs but more perhaps of certain children who go hungry. But because the children do not come to cry at her door this woman has no bad nerves for them.'

The last sentiment was applauded by several of the regulars, and then, perhaps remembering the shocking spectacle of a condemned dog eating good meat that it would never have time to digest, Pepa was struck by an idea. Perhaps, after all, it is because the foreigners never see the misery of the children. Perhaps we should tell our children to go and weep where nervous foreigners can see them.

8

'Tubman Bids Us Toil'

On the whole Liberia has had a poorish press. Back in the 'thirties Graham Greene gave the impression, in his travel book *Journey Without Maps*, that he found it a sad and sinister place. John Gunther, writing in 1955, summed it up as 'odd, wacky, phenomenal, or even weird'. Lesser authorities in between have produced books with supercilious titles like *Top Hats and Tom Toms*, while some of us with tenacious memories can still recall the startled headlines in 1931 when a League of Nations committee published a report proving that slavers still hunted down their human prey in the Liberian hinterland. To me in the spring of 1957, Liberia still sounded potentially a traveller's collector's piece; so on my way home by slow stages from the Ghana independence celebrations, I decided to break my journey at Robertsfield airport and see something of the country.

It happened that I was seated in the plane next to the only other passenger getting off at Robertsfield, an American rubber man who had also read John Gunther's account: he spoke of what faced us with the kind of macabre relish sometimes found in old soldiers and world travellers. 'If anything, Gunther soft-pedalled the situation,' he assured me. 'And don't, by the way, run away with the idea that this place is a kind of American colony: they push us around just like anyone else. Step out of line and you pretty soon find yourself in gaol.' I asked the rubber man if he knew Monrovia well, but he said no, they had a pretty comfortable set-up on the plantation and he'd only been down there once or twice. And that reminded him, we should be fingerprinted at the airfield. They would take our passports away, and we should have to go to the police headquarters in Monrovia to get them back. As a final warning, he recommended me to keep out of arguments with Liberian officials and to submit with good grace to the going-over that awaited us in the customs.

These predictions proved to be ill-founded. It was an hour before dawn when we touched down. The immigration officer, yawning, stamped our passports wordlessly and disappeared as if dematerialised. The customs man put his mark on our bags and waved us away. A moment later my American friend, claimed by a colleague with a waiting car, was borne off to the security of his comfortable set-up, and I was left alone in the dimly-lit customs shed until a boy of about fourteen appeared and offered to show me where I could get what he called 'morning chop'. There was a wait of three hours before the daily D.C.3 plane took off for Spriggs Payne airfield, Monrovia. So I went with him. We walked about a hundred yards before reaching a long building raised on piles, looking like an Indonesian long-house, which the boy said was the airport hotel. Here, he said, I should have to leave my luggage, which it was forbidden to take to the restaurant. I was suspicious of what seemed to me a possible manœuvre to dispossess me, but, before I could argue, a zombie came out of the hotel, took my bags from the boy, went in, and shut the door. The restaurant was a little farther on: a chink of light showing in the black shutters of the forest. The boy pointed it out and told me that he would come and fetch me when it was light. He shook hands with me and went off. At the time, this perfunctory service struck me as peculiar; but after I had been in Liberia a few days I realised that small boys preferred not to walk about by themselves in the dark.

The only other occupants of the restaurant made up a conspiratorial group, muttering in Spanish at a near-by table. I was served an American-style breakfast by a taciturn waiter. While I was busy with this, a young Liberian in a flowered shirt wearing a snub-nosed gangster's pistol in a shoulder holster came in and gave me a quick, power-saturated, policeman's stare. The muttering Spaniards looked up hopefully. I paid one dollar and twenty-five cents, and went outside again. Dawn was rising in total silence like grey smoke among the trees. A thick coverlet of mist lay along the low roofs of the airport buildings. There was a pharmaceutical smell coming out of the forest like the odour of dried-up gums, medicinal roots and benzoin. The air was flabby as if breathed in through a mask holding the moist warmth of one's last exhalation. I could see the boy squatting distantly by the door of the airport hotel, waiting for the daylight, to cross the no-man's-land between us.

It was a fifteen-minute flip in the D.C.3 across forty miles of swamp to reach Spriggs Payne airfield, on the outskirts of Monrovia. From the air, the capital looked gay and dilapidated like a Caribbean banana port. It was crowded on to a peninsula outlined in yellow beach, with a hard white line of surf on the Atlantic side. The cheerful mossy green of the bush came unbroken right up to the neck of the peninsula. There were big ships in port, and as the plane came down you could see a few vultures drift past over the roof-tops and the tangle of traffic in the central streets.

Visitors to Monrovia have complained that it is short of public transport, that the telephone system is uncertain, that there are regular breakdowns in the basic services, that most of the streets are unpaved, and that until recently the appropriation for brass bands exceeded that for public health. On the whole they have been stolidly impervious to the city's faded charm and its colour. The ex-slaves who were the original settlers here built Monrovia in the time-improved image they carried in their minds of the American South. They built with a touching and preposterous affection for Greek columns, porticoes, pilasters and decorative staircases; and a century of Liberian sun and rain has reduced their creations to splendidly theatrical shacks. The bright, slapped-on paint no longer serves to keep up pretences, although Van Gogh would have been in his element here among all the sun-tamed reds and blues and browns. There is a carnival cheerfulness about all the sagging, multicoloured façades beneath which the citizens of Monrovia promenade with the senatorial dignity of a people whose ancestors have carried burdens on their heads in a hot country. It was Monrovia that taught me the beauty and the interest of corrugated iron as a building material, when suitably painted, with its rhythmical troughs of shade. And in Monrovia it is in lavish use.

By night, especially if there is moonlight to put back a little of the colour, the effect is strikingly romantic. The city becomes fragile, its buildings cracked and seamed with the pale internal light of Hallowe'en candles. There are visions of interiors crammed with Victoriana, and walls hung with holy

89

pictures and framed diplomas. As the Liberians, although shy, are polite and sociable, one is continually greeted by a soft guttural 'How-do-you-do?' spoken by an invisible watcher behind a shutter. A little music is spun out thinly into the night from aged gramophones playing in barbers' shops: 'Bubbles', 'Alice Where Art Thou?' ... Cadillacs, festooned with fairground illumination and bearing their dark-skinned grandes dames and white-tied cavaliers, swish over the snow-soft laterite dust of the streets. A congregation of silent worshippers collects outside the Mosque – a yellow building with its walls edged with broken lager bottles, possessing a minaret like a fat section of drain-piping. Here, where the Faithful have cleared a space, they spread their personal prayer-rugs on a small oasis of clean white sand amid the urban debris. If it is Sunday there will be the sound of ecstatic hymn-singing from the direction of many nonconformist Houses of Worship. Every night at about ten the town's *belles de nuit* begin to lurk in the neighbourhood of the cinemas, where the last performances are coming to an end. They are dressed in the style introduced by the missionaries of the last century: blouses with leg-of-mutton sleeves, voluminous frilled skirts, honest calico underclothing – it is said – and they carry parasols.

It is by day that you notice the squalor bred from the problem of the relative indestructibility of modern waste. At Byblos and at Sidon the domestic debris of a thousand years may be compressed into a yard of dust. In Monrovia there are towering middens of imperishable rubbish; of iron, rubber and plastic that are the legacy of barely two generations. Most Monrovian houses are raised on piles, and the space under each house serves for the concealment of old engine blocks, back axles, radiators and batteries. In the gardens you sometimes see one car-chassis piled upon another, their members entwined with flowering convolvulus and transfixed by the saplings of self-sown tropical fruit trees. Almost every side-street is littered with abandoned vehicles, many of them recent models which may at first have been immobilised by some small mechanical failure, but then subjected to nightly piracy for spare parts until only the bare bones have remained. The citizens of Monrovia have not yet learned to clear up their debris as they go along. Even the fragments of basic rock blas-ted out over a hundred years ago to level the ground for the original buildings are still left just as they fell.

Old prints of Monrovia suggest that basically the town has changed little in its appearance from the days when over a century ago the first settlers ventured to leave their tiny stronghold on Providence Island in the Mesurado River estuary and establish themselves on the mainland. These pioneers were negro freedmen returned to Africa from the United States under a scheme promoted by a philanthropic body known as the American Colonization Society. Their first decade was precarious. They suffered from disease, semi-starvation, and the attacks of slavers who probably felt that the success of this experiment in resettlement might establish a disastrous precedent for the business. The first Liberians were supported entirely by shipments of provisions from the U.S.A. and protected by the guns of American and British warships. Their numbers were strengthened by further batches of Africans released from slave-running ships, but from 1822 – the date of the first settlement – until 1840, they were ruled by white governors appointed by the American society, and the country had no official existence in international law. In 1846 the first black president, Joseph Jenkin Roberts, prepared a constitution, and Great Britain recognised Liberia as an independent republic, although the U.S.A. did not follow until 1862. The first century of Liberia's existence has been called by Liberians 'The Century of Survival'. Considerably more territory than Liberia's present extent of 43,000 square miles was originally claimed by the settlers, but this, before the days of exact surveying, and despite the frowns of the U.S.A., was constantly nibbled at by the adjacent British and French colonies.

It is said that the Liberian pioneers included many skilled tradesmen who were in fact responsible for the building of Monrovia. This spadework accomplished, later generations seem to have been content to relax. A social order recalling that of the American plantations soon developed, with the freed slaves and their descendants playing the part of pseudo-aristocratic and leisure-loving masters, leaving all manual work to be done by such native Liberians as could be induced or compelled to do it. An elaborate social ritual was built up, from which Liberia has never fully recovered, and which some-

91

times seems to the foreign eye to achieve the opposite of the dignity at which it aims. All professions fell into social disrepute except those of the law, politics and diplomacy. Liberians developed into a race of astute politicians, but there were no native craftsmen, doctors, technicians, engineers – and there are few even today. In the meanwhile the hinterland, occupied by its twenty-odd tribes, remained roadless and neglected, and a concealed oppression of native Liberians by their African brothers returned from servitude gradually developed, until it was fully exposed by the League of Nations committee in 1931, with the ensuing world-wide scandal. The fact still remains that in spite of all reforms that have since been carried out, Liberia has been, and remains in practice, a species of colony in which about two million tribal Africans are governed by a minority of 150,000 English-speaking Americo-Liberians from which they are totally separated by barriers of race, religion, language and way of life.

At the present time there is a drive towards the integration of the tribal people into what is called 'the social life of the nation'. This unification policy is a favourite enterprise of President Tubman, Liberia's eighteenth president and probably the most able and energetic figure ever to appear on the Liberian political scene. President William Vacanarat Shadrach Tubman performs the considerable feat of leading a parliamentary democracy in which no official opposition is permitted to exist. The president was elected in 1943 to serve a term of eight years, re-elected in 1951 for a second term of four years, and in 1955 once again (although he was reluctant, the *Liberian Year Book* informs us) for a further four-year term. The national jubilation at the enormous majority obtained by the president in 1955 was marred by an attempt on his life. Since this occurrence the official opposition has ceased to exist, its members having withdrawn into exile, died suddenly, or been converted with equal suddenness to the policies of the True Whig Party of which His Excellency is the leader. It is said that President Tubman, in spite of the geniality and exuberance of his character, is resentful of criticism. When the official opposition crumbled and fell, such journalistic mouthpieces of divergent public opinion as the *Friend* and the *Independent* also collapsed. The year book tells us that they were suppressed as 'irresponsible'. The two remaining newspapers, the *Listener* and the *Liberian Age*, wholeheartedly support the president's point of view. With the object of emphasising the unanimity of the country's acclaim for the president, these papers sometimes publish eulogistic tributes from ex-opponents newly released from prison. At odd times an appreciation in poetic form may be slipped into their pages. Here is an example from a recent *Liberian Age*, which in its complete form runs to eight happy verses:

TUBMAN BIDS US TOIL
(Tune: Jesus Bids Us Shine)
By John N. George
Public Relations Officer, Sinoe County

Tubman bids us toil at the Nation's Plan,
With the Lone-starred banner building every clan
As he ever trusts us we must work,
So in your small corner don't shirk and lurk!

Tubman bids us toil in the gleeful way,
Saving every moment of the precious day;
Whether big or little we must work,
So in your small corner don't shirk and lurk!

Etc.

After a century of stagnation, in which Liberia lagged far behind the adjacent areas under white colonial domination, the country has begun to move rapidly ahead under President Tubman's firm, paternal guidance. Liberia assumed strategic importance during the last war. It could at any time provide a base in traditionally friendly territory for American armed forces defending the South Atlantic, and, along with Brazil, it is the only source of vital natural rubber bordering the Atlantic Ocean. The president's intelligent exploitation of these factors has conjured up such evidence of prosperity as the new Free Port of Monrovia, five hundred miles of new roads, a three-million-dollar bridge over the St Paul River, a sprinkling of new hospitals in the hinterland, an air-conditioned hotel with a magnificently eccentric Spanish lift, taxis, telephones, piped water and modern sewage disposal for Monrovia, and a fairly elaborate yacht for the president himself. The president's 'open door' policy has attracted foreign capital to Liberia and an assortment of American, Swiss, German and Spanish firms who now share with the Firestone Rubber Company – that great monolithic pioneer – in the considerable natural wealth of the country.

The main problem confronting these concessionaries is Liberia's acute shortage of unskilled labour. The Liberian tribesman has always been accustomed to gain the mere necessities of life with a minimum of effort. At the most he will consent to clear and burn a little virgin bush, and then leave it to the womenfolk to plant the 'dry' rice and cassava forming the basic diet. Even the women's agricultural work is very light. No hoeing, weeding or watering is done. The family simply waits for the crop to come up, and supplements its diet by harvesting a few tropical fruits. The Liberian countryman will eat anything. There are no sizeable wild animals left in the country to hunt, but the chance windfall of a serpent or a giant snail, the seasonal manna of flying ants, and palm grubs – all are joyfully accepted for the cooking-pot. The result of this catholicity of appetite is a well-balanced diet and a good physique. The amount of leisure enjoyed by a Liberian villager – especially a man of substance with a full quota of three wives to wait on him hand and foot – is quite beyond the comprehension of modern civilised man. It is natural enough that such a villager is extremely reluctant to exchange this lotus-eating existence for that of a plantation labourer working up to twelve hours a day for a wage of 30 cents, and what are called 'fringe benefits', i.e. free housing, medical supervision, and so on. When, indeed, he is driven by force of circumstances into the plantations, he will sometimes pathetically attempt to emphasise the transitory and separate nature of his life as a labourer by adopting a temporary name which often recalls the brighter side of plantation life, such as Dinner Pail, T-shirt, Pay Day, or Christmas. In these circumstances, labour is simply obtained by a system of bonuses paid to local chiefs – whose word is more than law. There is nothing furtive or shamefaced about this procedure, and the amounts paid duly figure in company balance sheets submitted for stockholders' approval.

Firestone, which controls a labour force of 25,000 men to operate its million-acre concession, and which sets the pace in these matters, pays $1.50 per man, per annum, and its 1955 balance sheet discloses a total of $90,000 expended in this way. 'In addition [I quote from *Case Study of Firestone Operation in Liberia*, published in the Nation Planning Association series] a regular scale of non-monetary gifts from Firestone to the paramount, clan, and occasionally town chiefs, has also evolved.' This regular scale of non-monetary gifts for the supply of labour goes under the dignified title of the 'Paramount Chiefs Assistance Plan', and it was developed, we are assured, with the full knowledge and consent of the Liberian Government, and has also been adopted by other foreign companies.

I learned, by the way, that it was considered highly unethical to outbid one's competitors in this extremely restricted labour market. Just as a successful tradesman may consider it a good thing to contribute occasionally to the local police benevolent fund, foreign companies operating in Liberia are also notably generous in their support of charitable, educational, cultural and religious institutions in Liberia.

The minimum wage of 30 cents a day, which is between one-third and one-fifth of wages paid for equivalent labour in the adjacent colonies of the British Sierra Leone and the French Ivory Coast, is explained in the publication already quoted, as a device for keeping inflation in check. More cogently it is argued that Liberian employers of labour could not afford substantial pay increases. Liberians have been quick, in fact, to convert themselves into plantation owners, and as soon as a new road is completed it is lined on both sides with the plantations of prominent Liberians who act as small subsidiaries of Firestone. These native plantation operators obtain free seedlings from Firestone, and as long as their labour costs remain cheap, and their land can be obtained under 'advantageous' terms from tribal communities who have never heard of title deeds, they seem to be on a very good thing. Occasionally in the current scramble for land, someone oversteps the mark, and there is a rumpus in the Liberian Press. While I was in Liberia, a tribe actually dared to take a foreign company to court for the illegal enclosure of its tribal land, and no one was more astounded than the tribesmen themselves when they won their case.

Considering the subservience of the Liberian Press, it is extraordinary how much self-criticism can be found in its pages, combined with extreme sensibility to adverse comment from anyone outside the True Whig Party family – especially foreigners. All the private scandals of Liberian government: the corruption in the judiciary, the oppression of tribal people by district commissioners, the bribe-taking by persons in high places (with the exact amount of the bribe), are ruthlessly exposed to the foreign eye. Some of these revelations, in fact, such as the account published in the *Listener* of May 14th, 1957, of organised highway robbery on one of Liberia's two main roads – which had then been in progress for over two months, and had the backing, the paper thought, of 'top interior officials' – make almost incredible reading. Yet the same papers explode with indignation on the slightest foreign comment that might be taken as injurious to national pride. Such outbursts are sometimes lacking in a sense of proportion. Recently the *Listener* came out with banner headlines: 'Stamp Dealer Says Liberia Owns Savage Cannibal Tribes'. About one quarter of the space normally allotted to news was devoted to mulling over this slander, and there was a further orgy of wound-licking in a long editorial headed 'Please Treat Us Kindly Next Time'. It turned out that an obscure stamp dealer in Boston had had the enterprising notion of printing a little geographical information on the packets he sent out. Naturally this was highly coloured stuff intended to excite the interest of the children whom one presumes would be his principal customers; but to the Liberian inflamed sensitivity it was a monstrous calumny that overshadowed any international crises, such as that of the Suez Canal, that happened to be about at the time.

There are of course no 'cannibalistic tribes' anywhere in Africa but the fact that cannibalistic practices do exist in Liberia is abundantly clear to anyone who reads the very uninhibited Liberian Press. Cases of 'medicine' murders by 'Human Elephant Men', 'Snake People', 'Water People', an organisation with the macabre official title of the Negee Aquatic Cannibalistic Society, and various other criminal secret groups, are regularly reported in the newspapers. These often contain gruesome anatomical details, and are sometimes accompanied by a journalistic-reactionary demand for the reinstitution of trial by Sassywood – which in its pure form means that the suspect drinks deadly poison, brewed from the bark of the sassy tree, *Erythrophloeum guineense*, from which he is supposed to recover if innocent. Here is an example extracted from the editorial published in the *Liberian Age* of April 30th, 1956, which incidentally explains the motive behind ritual murders.

TRIAL BY ORDEAL

In the last few weeks the *Liberian Age* reported that two men and a child have been murdered to make medicine. One was to invoke the blessings of the gods so that there will be a plentiful harvest in the rice season and the others were for reasons far more dubious.

The Government might do well in the circumstances to put a check to these unwholesome and superstitious practices by reinstating trial by ordeal, commonly known as trial by Sassywood.

Admittedly, Sassywood is a pagan cult and in a Christian State pagan cults should be frowned upon and eliminated. But the fact remains that in order to check these pagan practices we must employ the one method in which practitioners of paganism have an abiding faith, namely, the Sassywood trial.

In the Revised Statutes and in the Administrative Regulations trial by ordeal is forbidden except in minor matters and under licence of the Interior Department.

But the Constitution also provides that government should use every possible method to protect the life of the citizen and to punish the guilty of wilful murder. In such cases where life is endangered, the Government would be perfectly justified in using any legitimate method in bringing to account persons with pagan proclivities who are in the habit of so destroying life for foolish ends. The case for trial by ordeal even becomes stronger when the ordinary process of law becomes powerless in finding the guilty, due to the fact that persons who normally engage in such practices belong to some society or the other which gives them protection.

The 'medicine' referred to in this article is sometimes called 'borfina'. It is manufactured from the organs of a murdered person, and as well as being employed in the ancient magical ceremonies common to primeval humanity to promote rainfall and to influence the growth of crops, it is in brisk demand by those who dabble in witchcraft for their own ends. Borfina is in common use, not only in Liberia, but in most of West Africa, and it is reported that rich men will offer as much as 100 dollars for a scent bottle full of the grisly stuff. In Liberia it is obtained by professional 'heart-men' who usually work at night and prefer women and children for their victims. It is a sinister fact that the 'heart-men' are more active at the period of the Christian festivals of Christmas and Easter, when they are believed to invade even the capital itself in search of their prey. At these times Liberian countrymen go armed and in pairs along the jungle paths, and the women working in the fields keep in touch by calling to each other at frequent intervals. It is practically unknown for a white man to be the victim of a medicine murder, as it is believed that medicine obtained from a white man is of little or no value.

Trial by ordeal, I soon discovered, although not practised by colonial regions of Africa, is an everyday occurrence in Liberia, and I had only been in the country about a week before I had the opportunity of seeing how it worked. Wanting to learn as much as I could of the interior – a little of which had become accessible in the last few years by the completion of new roads – I hired a taxi in Monrovia and drove across country to the frontier of French Guinea and back, a journey taking three days. I carried with me a letter of introduction to Mr Charles Williams, District Commissioner of Bgarnba, where I hoped to stay the first night, and it was at Bgarnba that I encountered this survival of medieval justice.

Mr Williams was in court when I arrived. I sent in my letter, and in a few minutes the commissioner came out to welcome me. He was a tall handsome man, with a reserved, almost melancholic expression. He mentioned that he still had a large number of cases to try, and asked whether I would be interested in seeing the district court in operation. I was naturally more than interested. As we strolled back to the courthouse Mr Williams softly whistled a bar or two of 'Through the Night of Doubt and Sorrow'. I later discovered that he was a devout Episcopalian, with a great affection for *Hymns Ancient and Modern*.

The court was held in a large circular hut. About fifty members of the public were present, seated on rows of benches. The atmosphere was relaxed and informal. Most of the women had their babies with them, which they fed intermittently at the breast. The soldiers who bought in petty offenders from time to time hung about in wilting attitudes until they were dismissed. A pair of counsels, nattily dressed in sports clothes, kept up a crossfire of legal repartee. Seated behind his desk Mr Williams looked mildly judicial and perhaps a trifle sardonic. Once in a while he picked up his mallet and brought it down with a crash, sometimes to restore order, sometimes to deal with a tsetse fly that had alighted on his desk. Most of the complainants and defendants did not speak English, and as Mr Williams was a member of the Liberian ruling class and therefore spoke nothing but English, the services of an interpreter were often necessary. The interpreter translated from the tribal languages into a kind of Liberian pidgin, which I found completely impossible to understand. Even Mr Williams was often in difficulties, and called on the interpreter to repeat a sentence.

The examination of witnesses began with the routine question put by the commissioner, 'Do you hear English?' – followed, if the witness did in fact hear English by a second question, 'You Christian man?' Three out of four of those appearing before the court were not Christian men, and in these cases Mr Williams ordered the administering of an oath by 'carfoo' – a liquid concoction, or medicine, prepared by a witch-doctor, which although normally innocuous, is supposed to be fatal to the pagan perjurer. Although restrained in his manner at most times, Mr Williams seemed unable sometimes to control an outburst of genial contempt when he noticed a tendency on a witness's part to hang back at this moment of the oath-taking. 'Come, drink carfoo and lie, so that you may die tonight,' was a typical invitation roared at a minor chief who showed some reluctance when the witches' brew was put into his hands. When a Christian witness avoided touching the Bible with his lips, the commissioner leapt to his feet and pushed the book into his face. 'Come on, man. Kiss the holy book, unless you are determined to lie.'

Most of the civil cases arose out of what is known in Liberia as 'woman palaver'. Mr Williams explained to me that no man of standing would have less than three wives, each having been purchased for the standard bride-price of 40 dollars, paid to the girl's father. A rich man bought wives as an investment. They worked his land for him without expecting to be paid, and they produced valuable children into the bargain. The local paramount chief, he mentioned, had a hundred wives – each one decently housed in her separate hut in his compound. Unfortunately the tendency was for a man's wives to increase in number as he himself advanced in years, and – well – you knew what it was – the women sometimes found themselves with a fair amount of time on their hands. This meant that they were inclined to get into hot water, and although most possessors of large harems took a pretty civilised view of wives forming subsidiary friendships, there were a few narrow-minded and litigious husbands who went to court, particularly to sue for the return of the 40 dollars paid, when a wife ran off with some other man. In dealing with these 'woman palaver' cases, one of Mr Williams's chief difficulties was his evident distaste for coarse language. When a man complained that his wife refused to sleep with him, Mr Williams winced and put this blunt statement into the more elegant and evasive English of Monrovia. 'Your husband alleges that you refused to accord him the privilege of meeting with you,' was how he reworded this delicate circumstance, when cross-examining the wife. The only European to appear in court that day was the Italian overseer in charge of a gang of labourers working on a bridge-construction project near by. His offence was that in dismissing one of his men for malingering he had referred in a burst of anger – as Italians will – to the man's wife, using at the same time a four-letter word. This was a grave matter indeed in a country where a European can be heavily fined and deported for calling a man a 'nigger', and all work on the bridge stopped while the whole gang of workmen were brought to the court to testify. Mr Williams, after first ordering English-hearing women to leave the court, asked for the actual word complained of to be repeated. It was spoken in a stunned silence. The Italian spread his palms and smiled apologetically. One English word was like another to him. He genuinely didn't understand what the fuss was about. In the end Mr Williams read him a long lecture on vulgarity and let him off with a caution, and the Italian went away still mystified, shaking his head.

Shortly after this a woman was brought in by her husband, who charged her with infidelity. She had confessed to five lovers – or as Mr Williams put it, to granting intimate favours to five men other than her lawful husband – and in accordance with Liberian law the husband had been awarded damages of 10 dollars against each man. The trouble was that he now claimed that the names of other lovers had been concealed. Witnesses and counter-witnesses were produced, there were charges of perjury, and it was quite clear that this had all the makings of a lengthy and endlessly complicated case, when the woman agreed to submit to trial by ordeal. With evident relief Mr Williams ordered this to take place next morning immediately after dawn.

I slept the night in the commissioner's house, and at the appointed hour next morning I went over to the local lock-up, outside which the trial was to be staged. I found the calabozo of Bgarnba to consist of a long thatched hut, on the veranda of which several female prisoners, faces plastered with white cosmetic clay, were reclining in hammocks, under the apathetic guard of a soldier of about sixteen years of age. A witch-doctor – previously referred to by Mr Williams as 'a mystical man' – had arrived, and was lighting a small fire of twigs. He was a foxy-looking old fellow dressed in a fairground mountebank's purple robe. Mr Williams was not present.

As soon as the fire was well alight, the mystical man produced from the folds of his robe a metal object like a large flattened spoon, engraved with Arabic characters, and put this to heat in the heart of the fire. This was to be a version of the ordeal by the burning iron. In another variant of this type of ordeal, a heated sabre is brought into contact with one of the limbs. Other ordeals in common use involve the insertion of small pebbles under the eyelids, or the thrusting of needles into the flesh.

A few minutes later the wronged husband and the errant wife came on the scene. Both had dressed very carefully for the occasion – the man in a sort of yellow toga and the girl in a bright cotton frock printed with a pineapple design. They were accompanied by the clerk of the court, who wore a sports blazer with a crest on the breast pocket, and had a pencil stuck in his thick, woolly hair. A young soldier carrying a rifle trailed behind them. No one spoke or showed the slightest interest in the preparations. Liberians, other than the citizens of Monrovia, are trained by their long and rigorous years of initiation in the bush to maintain an attitude of formal unconcern in the face of all such crises. Later, I discovered that the woman had not been held in custody overnight, and may have had the opportunity to visit the head of the local women's secret society, the Sande, then in session, who might have prepared her with some 'bush-medicine' for what she had to face, or even have induced a protective hypnotic state.

Chairs were fetched, and the couple took their seats facing the fire, which was now burning briskly. They sat a few feet apart, stolidly oblivious of each other, like bored life-partners awaiting the serving of an uninspiring meal. The mystical man pulled out the iron, tested it with his spittle, and pushed it back into the fire. There was a short wait, and at a nod from the witch-doctor the girl put out her tongue. He bent over her and there was a faint sizzle. The witch-doctor went closer, peering at the girl's mouth like a conscientious dentist. He dabbed again with the iron. Nothing moved in the girl's face. Her husband looked glumly into space. The witch-doctor picked up a mug that stood ready, containing water, and handed it to the girl, who filled her mouth, rinsed the water round, spat it out, and thrust out her tongue again for inspection. The witch-doctor, the clerk and the soldier then examined it closely for condemnatory traces of burning. 'Not guilty,' said the clerk in a flat voice. He took the pencil out of his hair, wrote something in a notebook, and the whole party, their boredom in no apparent way relieved, began to move off. Justice had been done.

The bush society which may well have taken a surreptitious hand in these proceedings is probably the feature of Liberian life which has most impressed – or appalled – foreigners who have visited the hinterland. African tribal life from the southern limits of the Sahara Desert to the borders of the Union of South Africa is dominated more or less by secret societies, but it is in Liberia, where European influence has been least felt, and the original fabric of tribal life therefore best preserved, that the secret societies are most strongly entrenched. There is a society for the men called the Poro, and one for the women, the Sande. These are in session alternately, each for several years. Every member of the tribe must enter the society and the prestige of the society is so great that, outside the control exercised by government officials, it is the *de facto* ruler of the country, with the grand-master of the society as a kind of under-cover opposite number of the government-appointed district commissioner. When the women's society – the Sande – takes over from the Poro for its normal session of three years, actual power passes to the women. All major decisions relating to tribal life are decided by them, and it is customary for men to dress in symbolical homage as women, and in this guise to apply for admission to the Sande – which is of course refused.

Exact information about African secret societies is extremely difficult to obtain, even by anthropologists, but it is clear that their real purpose is to perpetuate the tribe's highly complex way of life, by the communal education of its youth, which at the same time is physically and mentally prepared for the hard life of savannah and jungle. Both societies impose a Spartan, even terrifying, discipline on their initiates. The boys must in theory – even if the practice has fallen into disuse – be transformed into warriors, must learn to defend themselves against savage animals, to take part in successful raiding parties, and to frustrate the attacks of tribal enemies. To achieve this result they are subjected to a more than military discipline; starved, flogged, made to sleep in the rain, to take part in gladiatorial combats, attacked and wounded superficially by human beings disguised as wild beasts, finally 'swallowed' by the totemic animal of the tribe, after which they are 'reborn' – in theory with no memory of their past lives – as fully initiated tribal members. The training of the girls is less arduous, but may be even more painful since it includes processes of beautifying by cicatrising, tattooing, and sometimes actually carving the flesh with knives, and finally that scourge of nearly all African women: clitoridectomy – performed with crude surgery, and without anaesthetics.

All the African races seem to have decided that only supernatural sanctions can induce human beings to submit to such a course of self-improvement: so teachers in the bush schools are masked and regarded by their pupils as spirits. These are the celebrated 'bush-devils' of Liberia, who vary in their importance according to their function, and who are presided over by a kind of super-devil who is a combination of head-master, sergeant-major and ghost – as well sometimes as judge, and even executioner – and who projects a power so devastating that merely to catch sight of him as he walks in the moonlight is death to an African. Not all this aroma of terror is consciously a disciplinary device. The devils, who are high-ranking members of the bush society, are believed by adepts to be controlled at certain times by powerful spirits, including the tribal ancestors – a belief which may well be shared by the devils themselves. Anthropologists in neighbouring French Guinea, where such aspects of tribal life are more easily observed than in Liberia, believe that masked dancers often pass into a kind of trance, on ceremonial occasions – or some-times as soon as they put on their masks, which in themselves are supposed to possess a kind of separate life, and to require 'feeding' with blood.

Remarkably enough, the life of the bush-school is popular with Africans. After initiation – which corresponds to gradu-ation in the West – people frequently return to the bush on a voluntary basis to take further courses, and success in these 'post-graduate courses' is recognised as a stepping-stone to ad-vancement in the hierarchy of the secret societies, and carries with it at the same time much social prestige.

African art is seen at its best in the production of cult objects and masks for the Poro and the Sande, and Liberia is one of the last strongholds of vigorous, untainted African art. As the masks worn by the principal bush-devils possess a kind of sanctity, it is not easy for a foreigner even to inspect one, let alone purchase one. The men who carve the sacred masks – who are usually high-ranking adepts of the Poro – say that they do so only when under the influence of an inspirational dream. While I was staying in one of the villages in the bush with an American anthropologist I shall call Warren, the local tribe's best carver dropped in to pay one of the formal calls which are a part of the complex social ritual of African village life. The carver came in smiling, shook hands, with the characteristic Liberian snap of thumb and finger, accepted a glass of cold beer, and picked up an illustrated book on African art that had just arrived from the United States. 'Why you no come before, man?' Warren asked him. 'I'm vexed with you because you no come.' The mask-carver said he hadn't been able to dream for weeks, and as his inspiration seemed to have dried up, he'd gone off to look for diamonds – a popular occupation at present in the area adjoining the Sierra Leone frontier. Warren was relieved. He was afraid that he had unwittingly offended the man in some way. The elaboration of Liberian tribal etiquette makes it quite bewildering to a white man, and although Africans will make intelligent allowances for a foreigner's ignorance of good manners, it is sometimes difficult to avoid giving offence.

The mask-carver turned over the pages of the book, giggling slightly, and Warren asked him what he found funny. It was the African's turn to tread warily now. He'd probably done a six-months course in the bush-school, learning, the hard way, how to avoid hurting people's feelings, and he clearly didn't want to tell Warren that he found this collection of master-pieces chosen from the whole African continent pretty poor stuff. In the end Warren got him to express his objection – the mask-carver by the way had picked up a fair amount of English, working on the plantations. 'I no see the use for these things.' Non-Liberian African art, in fact, was as extravagant – as grotesque even – to him, as African art as a whole tends to appear to the average untutored Westerner. He just couldn't see what purpose these distorted objects could serve. The idea of art for art's sake was completely foreign to him. He flipped over the pages of the book, making a well-bred effort to disguise his contempt. None of these objects could be used in his own tribal ceremonies, so they were useless – and ugly. He was like a die-hard admirer of representational painting asked to comment on the work of, say, Braque. The point was that his own work, which both Warren and I readily accepted as great African art, was as exaggerated and distorted in its own way as were all the rest in this book: except of course that all these diversions from purely representational portraiture had some quasi-sacred meaning for him. Warren had managed to buy a single mask from this man. He had made it to be worn by a woman leader of society, who for some reason had not taken delivery. The mask was kept out of sight, covered with a cloth. It was dangerous because it was sacrilegious to have it in the house, and it was destined for an American museum unless the Liberian Government suddenly decided to clamp down on the export of works of art – which this certainly was.

The village of the mask-carver was the cleanest 'native' village I have ever seen in any part of the world, as well as being very much cleaner than the average village of southern Europe. Silver sand had been laid between the neatly woven huts, and there were receptacles into which litter – including even fallen leaves – had to be put. While I was there, a tremendous hullabaloo arose because a stranger from another village had relieved himself in a near-by plantation instead of taking the trouble to go to the proper latrine creek in the bush. This was an exceedingly grave offence by Liberian country standards. The man was haled before the town chief, and as he had no money and therefore couldn't be fined on the spot, he was sentenced to ignominious expulsion from the village – a sentence which was carried out by a concourse of jeering children.

It was in this village too that I heard the eerie sound of the head woman bush-devil coming out of the sacred bush for a rare public appearance. We could hear the cries of her female attendants, first faint and then coming closer, as she came down the jungle path leading to the village, and a neighbour popped in to tell us that she was on her way to supervise the clearing of a creek by the women's society. Then something happened and she failed to appear. Perhaps she had been informed of the insalubrious presence of a stranger in the village, and we heard the warning cries of her attendants grow fainter again, and then stop. The men pretended to be relieved. The devil's attendants acted as female lectors, and administer mild beatings to anyone who happens to cross their path.

It was while I was in Liberia that an economic use in the modern scheme of things was found for the bush-devil, and the sophisticates of Monrovia were as happy as if they had hit upon a method of extracting cash from some previously discarded industrial by-product.

Liberia possesses two predominant flourishing industries: rubber, and the mining of the extremely high-grade iron ore. Business heads on the look-out for further sources of national income recently thought of the tourist trade, which has been the economic salvation of far less viable countries than Liberia, and there was some talk even of developing tourism as a third industry. Accordingly plans were laid, and in March this year Monrovia received its first visit from a cruising liner, the *Bergensfjord*, a luxury Norwegian ship carrying 350 passengers, most of whom appeared from the passenger list to be presidents of U.S. banks and insurance companies, and their womenfolk.

Unfortunately the *Bergensfjord* docked on a Sunday, which in Monrovia is surrendered to a zealous nonconformist inactivity, the silence only disturbed by the chanting of hymns and the nostalgic quaver of harmoniums in mission halls. The town was shut up – 'like a clam' – as the *Listener* put it. Liberia's new industry was in danger of dying stillborn, when someone thought of the bush-devils, and a few fairly tame and unimportant ones were hastily sent for. Even when the tourists finally landed, the situation was in the balance. Although they had already been given handbills describing the traditional Liberian entertainment that awaited them, they found their path barred by a large and determined matron in a picture hat who was determined to protect them from such pagan spectacles as they had been promised. When asked where the devil-dancing was to take place, she smiled indulgently and said, 'In Liberia we do not dance on Sunday. We remember the Sabbath day, to keep it holy.' She would then recommend various places of interest which might be visited by taxi, such as the Capitol building, the lighthouse, the near-by Spriggs Payne airfield, and the Trinity Pro-cathedral.

Most of the passengers succeeded in escaping the clutches of this well-intentioned lady, and led by an organiser of the Bureau of Folklore in a jeep, they were taken in a taxi-caravan to the vacant lot behind a garage, where the dancing was to take place. There were half a dozen assorted devils in not very good masks and all-concealing mantles of raffia, and three little bare-breasted girls who had just finished their initiation and who, despite the presence of a mob of camera-brandishing tourists, were still plainly timid of the devils. It all went off very well. The little girls did a rapid, sprightly dance, and the devils whirled and somersaulted diabolically in their manes and skirts of flying raffia. When the dancers stopped, the tourists clapped enthusiastically. They lined the girls up, took close-up portraits of them with miniature cameras, asked them their ages, shook hands, and gave them silver coins.

Next morning the Liberian Press wallowed in its usual self-criticism. Hadn't the town's lights failed and the telephone system gone dead last time a distinguished party of foreigners, headed by none other than Vice-President Nixon, had visited Monrovia? There were stories of tourists being carried off on enormous purposeless drives by taxi-drivers who didn't understand English and who charged them extortionate fares, and of others stuck in the City Hotel's Spanish lift. 'We did it again', wailed the *Listener*. '... Here was a chance to impress some of these big business tycoons and draw their capital here some day – but we did it again.'

In the paper's next edition, however, the situation wasn't looking quite so black. The wife of a president of a Boston safe deposit and trust company was reported to have said she loved the country and wanted to come back. Liberia's latest industry had got off to a hesitant start perhaps, but at least it was on the move.

9

Goa

Soon after dawn the Goa shore lifts itself out of the sea, a horizon of purplish rocks and palms sabred by the dark sails of dhows. The Indian trippers who came aboard at Bombay, fashionably scarfed, in tweeds and corduroys, have accepted a mood of southern lassitude, and now gather in pyjama-clad groups to gaze respectfully shorewards. As the ship swings into a river-mouth, the shores close in, a red watch-tower on every headland, and baroque chapels gleaming through the greenery. Over the starboard-bow Nova Goa is painted brilliantly on the sky, a hubbub of colour with bells chiming in the churches built on its high places. A few minutes later the gangplank goes down, and as the passengers are released into the smiling apathy of the water-front, a flock of mynahs settle on the ship's rigging. A line of golden omnibuses wait to bear the voyagers away to distant parts of the territory. The town itself is served by calashes of skeletal elegance, drawn by ponies who, even while dozing in the shafts, are unable to relax their straining posture. For foreigners there are taxis of reputable old Continental make, such as De Dion Bouton. They are decorated with brass-work and advertisements for German beer. Although their owners are usually Christians, Hindu gods, considered as more effective in purely routine matters of protection than, say, St Christopher, squat amongst the artificial flowers over the dashboards.

The quayside, which is really the heart of the town, is presided over by a statue, not – as one would have expected – of the great Albuquerque, founder of the colony, but of one José Custodio Faria, who, the inscription relates, 'discovered the doctrine of hypnotic suggestion'. Faria, who is not mentioned in short textbooks on the subject, is dressed in a wicked squire's cloak of the Wuthering Heights period, and is shown strikingly in action. His subject – or victim – a young lady with a Grecian hair-style, has been caught in the moment of falling, one trim foot in the air, left hip about to strike the ground, while Faria leans over her, fingers potently extended. Her expression is rapt; his intense, perhaps demoniacal. The background to this petrified drama is a row of shops and taverns, coloured like the wings of tropical birds and decorated with white plaster scrollwork, seemingly squeezed out of a tube.

A stranger, newly landed, is whisked quickly beyond the range of Faria's ardent gaze. Ahead of him strides the porter, carrying on his shoulder the luggage which several small boys, running on either side, reach up to touch with their fingertips, as if it contained relics of extraordinary curative virtue. This attendance entitles them to claim a reward of one anna apiece. The baggage is then placed in the taxi, and the newcomer is driven to the Hotel Central, because it is a long way from the centre of the town and therefore a worthwhile taxi-fare. All this happens to be to the good. The Central is a precious repository of the atmosphere of Goa, and worthy of mention not on account of its advertised attraction – the small tiled dungeon, called a bathroom, available with every room – but of many less tangible charms unappreciated by the management. The fine old Portuguese colonial building growing naturally from the red earth of Goa is the colour of Spanish oxide, with its main façade covered in green tiles and a white make-believe balcony moulded on one wall. Coconuts and frangipani blossoms float down a jade-green stream at the back of the house, and burnished bright-eyed crows come hopping into the front rooms and try to fly away with the guests' sunglasses. The beach is just across the road, and you can sit and watch Goans prowling about it in search of the nacreous discs with which they repair their old-fashioned mother-of-pearl windows. A cab-driver sleeps on his seat under a banyan tree just outside the dining-room, and when any guest wants to go, the waiter leans out and wakes him up by pulling the end of his whip.

Old Goa is eight miles away up the river. With the exception of five great churches standing impressively isolated in a jungle clearing, it is a Carthaginian ruin. The Bom Jesus, vast and superbly baroque, houses the principal treasure of the old Portuguese Indies in the shape of the mortal remains of St Francis Xavier, the great evangelist who was not quite successful in the conversion of the Japanese. Owing to its world-wide reputation for miracle-working the mummified body has undergone a gradual decrease in size. Inspired by the example of a Pope who asked for an arm to be severed and sent to him,* pilgrims have succeeded, under an osculatory pretence, in gnawing small portions off the saintly anatomy and carrying them away in their mouths. Sometimes these were recovered, and the phalanx of a thumb is kept in a silver reliquary, which, after it has been wrapped in a protective cloth, is placed in the visitor's hand.

St Francis Xavier, although of indisputable sanctity, was partly responsible for the bringing to Goa of the Inquisition, which he believed to be essential for the survival in the Indies both of the Portuguese influence and the Christian religion. In Goa, the Inquisition functioned as more of a political than a religious instrument; an efficient security service, supreme in jurisdiction and secret in procedure. Its prisoners, well fed and housed in two hundred hygienic cells, were subjected to constant psychological pressure in accordance with the most modern practice. The object was their reduction to an utter and unquestioning conformity to the discipline which the Portuguese, as a small community surrounded by vast hostile forces, believed necessary to their survival. In this the Inquisition was rarely unsuccessful, and during the century and a half of its active mission only about eight hundred and fifty of the incorrigibly independent were burned to death on the open space which has now become a football field. Even such a modest exercise of disciplinary action, however, was enough to shock the tolerant East, and render almost hopeless the task of evangelisation.

As a weapon of self-defence the Inquisition was less successful than others, such as the social equality offered to all converts to the Christian religion. This was a colony with no 'Natives'. A Christian, whether of Portuguese or of Indian birth, was a Goan, and distinctions soon became unthinkable in the face of the intermarriage policy, which has bequeathed to so many admirable P. & O. stewards the purposeful faces of *Conquistadors*.

A mellowed authoritarianism still pervades the Goanese air and constitutes a provocation to the nascent democracy across the frontier. For example, everything printed in the local

* It was subsequently put to use as a curative application for his haemorrhoids.

Marathi language – even a marriage invitation – must be submitted to the censor. Such pin-pricks set off explosions in the Indian Press. In January *Filmindia* – not the kind of journal, one would have thought, to bother itself with the problems of India's remaining pockets of colonial rule – emitted almost a Hitlerian scream of exhausted patience, under the heading 'Portuguese Pirates in India!' This article, provoked by an order under which all Indian films shown in Goa must bear Portuguese sub-titles, began by the declaration that 'a White man is always a nuisance to the rest of the human race', and went on to describe Goa as a place where a small crowd of white-skinned Portuguese rulers practised colonial imperialism over eight million coloured Indians. The truth is that one can walk about all day in Goa without seeing a white skin, and that the fifty per cent of the Goanese population which professes Christianity would exceedingly resent being described as Indians. There is in fact less colour prejudice in Goa than in India, and no Goanese paper would be allowed to publish the matrimonial advertisements for brides of fair or 'Jewish' colour which are a regular feature of the Indian Press. It is indeed unlikely that Goa would return to India in the event of a plebiscite being held. The Christian Goans would certainly vote to remain as they are, while many of the Hindus believe that they are better off economically under Portugal; for Goa shows few signs of the really appalling poverty common throughout the Indian countryside.

Certainly *Filmindia* was on firmer ground when it accused Goa of large-scale smuggling activities, although it did not add that this was done through the connivance of corrupt Indian frontier officials. Across the border flows a torrent rather than a stream of those things for which the hunger of the East is insatiable: fountain-pens, watches, and patent medicines. A more important traffic is that of gold, carried not in lorries but in the bodies of the smugglers themselves, and whole human caravans, thus strangely burdened, are regularly marshalled for the trek across the frontier. Herein lies the source of Goa's present prosperity, and on the strength of it half a street of delightful old buildings has been torn down and replaced by a miniature Karl Marxhof in grey cement, housing shops which sell nothing but American goods. Thus perishes the charm which poverty protected.

Goa's other immediate commercial advantage depends on the fact that it is an alcoholic oasis in a largely dry subcontinent – a paradise for the Indian week-ender who has been unable to wangle a doctor's certificate classifying him as an addict and therefore entitled to a ration of costly liquor. In Goa he can sit and drink all day, so long as he succeeds in concealing obvious intoxication, for at the slightest disorder a policeman will appear, to conduct the celebrant to a cell, which is likely to be less well-arranged than those provided in the Inquisition building of old.

Goa prides itself on the sobriety of its pleasures. There are no popular amusements beyond an occasional snake-charming and a well-censored cinema show. Night-clubs do not exist. If you want to listen to music, you must go down to the water-front to the Café Praia, where Arabs, pious and withdrawn – who are supposed to do a little gold-smuggling on their own account – sit pulling at their hookahs and drinking *qishr*, a decoction made to their own specification from the husk of the coffee-bean. Sometimes they tell the owner of the place to switch off Radio Cairo, and begin to hum nasally and to pluck at the strings of archaic instruments. At ten o'clock a paternal authority sends all citizens home to bed by turning out the city lights. Obediently the Arabs get up from their table and grope their way down to their canoes. The dhows are anchored in mid-stream, with the silhouettes of ancient ships on decorative maps. Even if there is no moonlight you can follow the path of the canoe by a ripple of phosphorescence as the spoon-like oars stir the water, or by the declining notes of a flute.

10

A Few High-Lifes in Ghana

The important thing to bear in mind when visiting what was once the Gold Coast and is now Ghana is that the advice liberally proffered by old Gold Coast hands in retirement will be designed to perpetuate a nostalgic legend. You are warned to prepare yourself for a scarcely tamed White Man's Grave, where you do not omit to take Sensible Precautions, stick to sundowners, keep your possessions in an ant-proof metal box, and wipe the mildew off your boots at regular intervals. I fell a victim to this propaganda to the extent of buying a pair of mosquito boots before I left London. They were made of soft, supple leather, fitted very tightly at the ankle, and they reached almost to the knee, beneath which they could be drawn tight with tapes. I put them on once only, in the privacy of a hotel bedroom, noting that worn with khaki drill shorts they made me look like some grotesque Caucasian dancer. After that I packed them away. It was a symbolic act. I had observed that in Accra, Europeans in these days seemed to make it a point of honour to go bareheaded in the noonday sun. The sundowners seemed to have gone out with sola topis. You popped into a bar and drank a pint of good German or Danish lager whenever you felt like it. It was hot in Accra, but not so hot as New York at its worst and – in the dry season – not so humid either, and down by the shore there was usually a cool breeze blowing in from the Atlantic.

Accra turned out to be a cheerful, vociferous town with an architectural bone-structure of old arcaded colonial buildings – some of them vaguely Dutch or Danish in style. The streets, in the English manner, had been cut in all directions. There were corrugated-iron shack warrens right in the heart of the town, a wide belt of garden suburbs, and isolated slabs of modern architecture looking like enormous units of sectional furniture. As usual, the English had thrown away the chance –

ELAND BOOKS

53 ELAND ROAD
LONDON SW11 5JX
01 - 228 5450

We are enclosing a review copy for
the publication date of 2nd June, 1986.

It would be kind if you could send us
a copy of any review.

Please contact us if you require
any further information.

always seized by the French in their colonies – of turning the sea-front into a pleasant, tree-shaded promenade. The surf crashing on the beaches was out of sight behind the warehouses, put up at a time when trade was all and the merchants were content to put off their gracious living until they had made their pile on the Coast and could get away with it back to England before malaria or the Yellow Jack finished them off. The streets were crowded with a slow-moving mass of humanity: the men in togas, the women in the Victorian- and Edwardian-style dresses originally introduced by the missionaries but now transformed by the barbaric gaiety of the material from which they are confected. The designs with which these cottons are printed demand some comment. They are produced in Manchester, in Brussels and in Paris, from African originals, and although they recall the most striking Indian saris, there is something fevered and apocalyptic in the vision behind the drawing itself, that seems to be purely African. The best results are supposed to be produced by West African artists as the result of dreams, and the artist may mix abstract symbols and careful realism in a single design, with a result that often has a drugged and demonic quality, like a descriptive passage from *The Palm Wine Drinkard*. Dark blue birds flit through an ashen forest of petrified trees; silver horses with snake-entwined legs charge furiously into a sable sky; huge metallic insects glint among the lianas of a macabre jungle; the black bowmen of Lascaux pursue griffins, fire-birds and tigers over fields of gold, with autumn leaves the size of shields tumbling about their shoulders. Why do European women rarely if ever wear these materials, although there are a few out-of-the-way shops in London and Paris where they are stocked? Perhaps because to do so would be to risk extinguishing themselves.

Amazingly an Englishman can be at home in this atmosphere, which somehow, in defiance of the genial African sun, the colour, and the seething vitality, succeeds in reproducing a little of the flavour of life in England. The African citizen of Ghana, for example, is reserved in his manner compared, say, with his counterpart in Dakar. It is hard to believe, in fact, that a century of independence will be long enough to expunge the essentially British odour of life in the Gold Coast: the cooking (Brown Windsor soup and steak-and-kidney pie), the class

observances, the flannel dances, the tea-parties, and the crick-
eting metaphors in the speech. Even the paint on the fences in
a suburb of Accra is of a kind of sour apple green never found
outside Britain and her dominions. The middle-class African
of Accra, too, lives in home surroundings indistinguishable
from those favoured by his equivalent in the London suburbs.
There is the same affection for whimsy and humorous pretence: china ducks in flight up the wallpaper, Rin-Tin-Tin
book-ends, toby jugs, telephones disguised as dolls, poker-
work mottoes, and jolly earthenware elves in the back garden.

It is generally believed that fraternisation between whites and
blacks is less complete in African territories colonised by the
British than in those colonised by the French. This does not
apply in West Africa. In Dakar the colour bar is officially non-
existent, but it is extraordinary to see an African in a good
hotel or a fashionable restaurant. The reason one is given is
that they do not feel comfortable in such surroundings. The
natives of Accra are not overawed in this way, and there is a
fairly proportional colour representation – say ten Africans to
one European – in all public places of entertainment. It was in
fact quite the normal thing that my first experience of Accra
night-life should be in the company of Africans.

This was in early March. Ghana was just about to receive its
independence. There had been a week of celebrations, and the
streets were awash with restless, slightly jaded revellers. My
host was a minor political figure we will call Joseph, and he
had brought with him his secretary, Corinne. We started the
evening at the new Ambassadors Hotel, which is said to be one
of the three best hotels in Africa. At this time there was no hope
of staying there, as the Government of Ghana had filled it with
foreign V.I.P.s invited for the celebrations. We sat in the bar
and admired the photomontage on the wall, which included a
dancing scene from *Guys and Dolls* and the towers of the Kremlin. Behind the palms a pianist in tails was striking soft, rich
chords on a grand piano. Joseph and Corinne ordered Pimms
No. 1, which was currently *de mode* in Accra. I noticed that the
V.I.P.s present included firebrands from British Guiana and
Tunisia – temporarily tamed and transformed in glistening
sharkskin – and a berobed African chief who wore ropes of
beautiful ancient beads, and who waved genially and said

'Ta-ta' as we came in. There was no hope of a table for dinner at the Ambassadors, so we went on to another restaurant, and there, in the sombre and seedy surroundings of an English commercial hotel in a small Midland town, we made the best of a highly typical meal of fried liver, tomatoes and chips.

After that we visited a night-club called A Weekend in Havana, outside which Joseph got into an altercation with a policeman over parking his car. There is often a fine Johnsonian rumble about such exchanges in Accra. 'You were attracted by the glamour of your profession. Now you must work,' was Joseph's parting shot. Later in the evening when a cabinet minister offered him an extremely stiff whisky he said, 'I am not, sir, a member of your staff, and am not, therefore, accustomed to more than singles.' Still later when an enormous Nigerian emir, gathering his robes about him, joined our table, Joseph remarked, 'I hear, sir, that your people reproduce at an alarming rate,' and the emir, who took this as a compliment, grinned hugely and replied, 'You have been correctly informed.'

A Weekend in Havana turned out to be an open-air place, with the tables placed round a thick-leaved tree that gave off an odour of jasmine. A white dove-like bird circled continually overhead as if attracted by the powerful fluorescent lighting. When we arrived the band was playing 'It's a Sin to Tell a Lie', and the dancers were gliding round in a stately Palais-de-Dance manner. About half those on the floor were in national costume and the rest in evening dress. The few European women to be seen were outclassed by the African girls with their splendidly becoming gowns and their majestic carriage. Corinne sat happily commenting on the private lives of those present, and closing my eyes and listening to her remarks I could hardly believe I was not sitting in a similar night-spot in London, although Corinne's voice was somewhat richer and deeper than that of any conceivable English counterpart. 'Good heavens! Isn't that Dr Kajomar with Mrs Chapman? Had *you* any idea that show was still going on, Joseph?' A girl swung past in the arms of her partner wearing one of the new slogan dresses with 'JUSTICE AND LIBERTY' printed across her ample posterior, and Corinne looking away as if pained said, 'Do you know – I do think people should draw the line somewhere!' Soon after this the band played a high-life – a dance of

Gold Coast invention – which resembles a frenzied and individualistic samba. A party of British sailors from a naval vessel helped themselves to partners from the local girls and joined in this to the best of their ability, and were much applauded by the Africans. The trouble about the British – Corinne had just commented – was that they never let themselves go. Her ex-boss had been a Scotsman who had made her blood run cold by his habit of concealing his anger.

This gave me an opening to indulge in a favourite pastime, when in regions that are slipping, or have slipped, through the colonialist fingers – that of carrying out a post-mortem on the relationship between the two peoples involved, in the full prior knowledge that the findings – allowing for local variations – will be the same. Getting right down to bedrock objections, Joseph said, it amounted to the fact that the Englishman had never learned to stop complete strangers in the street, shake hands with them warmly, and ask them where they were going, and why. What was even worse, they had almost succeeded in breaking the people of the Gold Coast of such old-world African displays of good breeding, inculcated in all the bush-schools before the European came on the scene with his version of education and his insistence on the formal introduction. I knew this to be true. Only a few weeks spent in Africa – especially if not too much time is wasted in big towns where the real flavour of the country is subdued – are enough to convince one of the extreme and innate sociability of the African. Africans, as one discovers them in travelling in the villages of the interior, are never stand-offish, rude or aggressive; always ready to receive the visitor in a courteous and dignified way. This is the tradition of the country, and even in such Europeanized areas as the Gold Coast, where a boy no longer spends four years or more under the strict discipline of the bush-school learning the ideals of manhood, a stern semi-Victorian training is usually carried out in the home, with what to me are excellent results. It might even be reasonable to suggest that there are strong temperamental and emotional factors behind the façade of politics, which are in reality helping to strip the Briton of his colonies. Even in the Gold Coast, where the Englishman had learned to become a better mixer than his French neighbour, there remained a trace of that aloofness, that inability to get together with the African on a footing of absolute social equality, which makes it so difficult for him to be loved as well as respected. Here, as in India and in Burma, the European clubs defended their exclusiveness to the last ditch. The Englishman was received socially by the educated African without any reserve whatever, but the African's civility was not fully returned, and there was an offensive flavour of patronage in this lack of reciprocity. The Accra Club admitted no African members or guests. At Cape Coast only two influential chiefs had ever succeeded in joining the white man's club. The Kumasi Club underlined its determination to hold out to the last by posting a notice which informed the members that 'due to the development of events' they would be permitted on and after Independence Day to introduce guests of 'any nationality' – although the names of such proposed guests had first to be submitted to the secretary. To these pinpricks, to which Africans submit cheerfully and without rancour, more serious wounds are added when they come to England as students and find that under some dishonest excuse – since the colour bar in England has no admitted existence – 85 per cent of hotels and boarding houses will refuse to admit them.

No demonstration of the virtues of imperialism – the high-minded incorruptibility, and the like, of the white overlords – could quite compensate the new, nationalistic African for his being treated, whether overtly or not, as a member of an inferior race. Thus many Africans who have been hurt by the coolness of their reception in England have returned to Africa carrying the germ of a disease that is fairly new in that continent – anti-white racial feeling. Now the whites were on the point of surrendering their domination in the Gold Coast. The European clubs would open their doors to all. Dr Nkrumah's portrait would – despite the protests of the parliamentary opposition – replace that of Her Majesty Queen Elizabeth, on both stamps and coinage, and shortly the British Governor-General, Sir Charles Noble Arden-Clarke, would be asked to surrender his impressive apartments in Christiansborg Castle to Dr Nkrumah, and to retire to the modest accommodation previously prepared for Dr Nkrumah in the State House. But already, on the eve of independence, the newspaper editorials sounded a little less dizzy with success. There would be no colonial scapegoats about, when things went wrong in the future.

The Ghanaians would have only themselves to blame if the much-publicised corruption in their public men brought about their undoing as a nation, or if the disputes with the Ashanti and Togoland minorities were allowed to deteriorate until they exploded into civil war.

Many members of the newly freed colony regarded the victory of Kwame Nkrumah and his followers as the victory of an energetic political clique which had been able – sometimes by dubious means – to impose its will upon the politically lethargic general masses. Such disgruntled opponents of the regime, who did not expect to participate in the fruits of the victory, were on the whole unhappy to see their white rulers depart, and there were refusals in several parts of the country to put out flags. That the English could pull out as they did with so little apparent reluctance, and so many protestations of good will all round, is due to the nature of their stake in the country, which does not in reality demand their physical presence. Ghana has been saved from the tragic situation of Algeria, and the almost equally unhappy situations of Kenya and South Africa, by the fact that it has never been considered suitable for European settlement. West Africa as a whole has been protected from white ownership by malarial mosquitoes, an inexorable rainy season, and an absence of salubrious highlands where European farmers could have established themselves. When the demand for independence came, there was no reason not to accede to it. As things were, only British traders, technicians and colonial officials got a living from the country, and these would not be compelled to leave. The only conceivable losers might be certain African underlings with a preference for the devil they knew to the devil they didn't know and a suspicion they might be exchanging King Log for King Stork: these and the 300,000 small farmers of the Ashanti, who between them produce the cocoa that forms the country's wealth, and who in the long run – and at present with little political representation – must foot the bills run up by the politicians at Accra.

From the very beginning it has been commerce that has drawn the European to the Gold Coast, and from this commerce developed one of the gravest social cancers that have cursed the human race – the slave trade. All the maritime European nations, with the exception of the Spanish – Portuguese, Dutch, Danes, British, Swedes and Prussians – at one time or another established strongholds in the Gold Coast, and squabbled among themselves over the rich loot in captives. The English proved to possess most staying power. In recognition of their straightforward and efficient business dealings, they finally secured the much sought-after contract for the supply of slaves to the Spanish colonies, held previously by the French and then the Dutch. In the end, over one-half of the total slave trade fell into British hands. It has been estimated that between 1680 and 1786, 2,130,000 slaves were exported from the Guinea Coast, as it was then called. The wastage of life was tremendous. Livingstone believed that ten lives were lost for every slave successfully shipped, and even at sea the carnage continued. French ships' stores, for example, included corrosive sublimate, with which slaves were poisoned when the ship was becalmed in the Middle Passage and supplies ran low (the French defended the practice as being more humane than the British and Dutch one of simply tossing the starving slaves into the sea).

From the very beginning the slave trade was carried on in a shamefaced manner, and contemporary accounts by those who took part in it are full of conscience-salving devices. Much was made of the slave's happy opportunity to be brought into contact with Christianity. Slavers piously presented themselves as the rescuers of prisoners taken in African wars who would otherwise have been slaughtered, making no mention of the fact that it was they, the slavers, who encouraged or even organised the wars. The slave merchants could be tender, too. 'I doubt not', says William Bosman in a letter written in 1700 from the castle of St George d'Elmina, 'but that this trade seems very barbaric to you, but since it is followed by mere necessity it must go on; but yet [in branding the slaves] we take all possible care that they are not burned too hard, especially the women, who are more tender than the men.' I have visited this castle and seen the rooms where the slaves were confined and where they were auctioned. What particularly struck me was the delicacy of feeling shown in the old days in the arrangement by which heads of families who had brought some dependant to be auctioned were permitted to watch the proceedings from a chamber overlooking the auction room, where they themselves would not be exposed to the reproachful gaze of their victim.

Bosman, despite his name, was a Dutchman, a man of severe morality and regular habits, who much deplored the intemperance of his English trade rivals entrenched at Cape Coast Castle some thirty miles away: '... The English never being better pleased than when the soldier spends his money in drink ... they take no care whether the soldier at pay-day saves gold enough to buy victuals, for it is sufficient if he have but spent it on Punch; by which excessive tippling and sorry feeding most of the Garrison look as if they were Hag-ridden.' The English, Bosman observed, were also much given to a plurality of wives, particularly the chief officers and governors of the castle, while two of the English company's agents had married about six of the local ladies apiece. This enterprise was the Royal African Company, promoted under a charter granted by Charles II. His Majesty was the principal shareholder in the venture, in which the whole of the royal family invested money. In spite of Bosman's poor opinion of the garrison a dignified protocol, as befitted a royal enterprise, was observed in all the company transactions. Slaves were branded, as a compliment to the Duke of York, the company's governor, with the letters 'D.Y.' – and the brand used was of sterling silver.

Denmark was the first European power to abolish the slave trade, by a royal order in 1792. The British followed in 1807, although a general European agreement was delayed for another twelve years by the French, who hoped in this way to gain time to be able to crush the rebellion in Haiti and restock the colony with fresh slaves. The century that followed saw the gradual adjustment of the Gold Coast to legitimate trade, based at first principally on the extraction of gold (the guinea was originally coined from the gold secured from the Gold Coast), and then the cocoa bean. The first cacao tree to be grown is supposed to have been brought from Fernando Po in the 'eighties of the last century, as the result of the enterprise of a native blacksmith, and each pod is said to have sold for £1. By 1949 the Gold Coast was producing as much cocoa as all the rest of the world put together. It is now one of the richest areas in Africa, and its total revenue from all sources is about ten times that of the neighbouring republic of Liberia, which has never been under colonial domination. It is a curious illustration of the mentality of nationalism that the politically educated citizen of Ghana now tends to play down the importance of the slave trade in the history of his country. The subject when raised is likely to be changed or to be brushed aside as historically insignificant. The memory is clearly considered derogatory to the dignity of a modern nation.

The emergence of this modern nation could never have been delayed more than a few years, but the fact that the Gold Coast became Ghana in March 1957, and not perhaps twenty years later, is largely due to the energy and the tactics of its leader, Dr Kwame Nkrumah. Dr Nkrumah was born in 1909, said by some to be the son of a market woman, and by others, of an artisan. After a few years spent in the teaching profession he went to America and gained the degree of Bachelor of Sacred Theology of Lincoln University, Pennsylvania, which a few years later granted him an honorary doctorate. When he returned to Accra, Nkrumah took over the nationalist movement, founded a new party, the Convention People's Party, with its slogans 'S.G.' (Self Government) and 'Freedom' (the two syllables are pronounced in Ghana as two separate words). Nkrumah's tactics began with a boycott on European goods, and from this, rioting and looting developed. Two short prison sentences followed, both of them invaluable to the progress and propaganda of the C.P.P., and Nkrumah was released from the second of them to become officially first 'Leader of Government Business' and then Prime Minister over a predominantly African team of ministers.

Democracy is liable to be transmuted by the old tribal tradition of government into a parody of what is understood by that word in the West. Political issues are decided not so much by party programmes – which are quite beyond the comprehension of village electors – as by the political personalities involved, and the crowds swarm to the support of the energetic and flamboyant leader. The enfranchisement of the black masses spells the end of the white man's domination – not because there is any solidarity in colour except an artificial one in the course of creation at this moment – but because the white man cannot compete with the African's knowledge of native psychology, and cannot in our time, even if he would, play on the African electors' hopes and fears with the deadly expertness of an ex-tribesman. As an illustration of what is happening all over those parts of Africa where the electoral system has been introduced, a party will often choose as its emblem an animal known for its sagacity and strength – say the elephant – while the opponents may decide on the lion. The election, in the unsophisticated countryside, now resolves itself into a contest between the merits of these two animals. The elephant followers will obviously be unsuccessful in districts where a herd may be running wild and trampling the crops, whereas lion supporters can have no hope of gaining ground in remote pastoral areas where lions still sometimes carry off livestock. African political parties – and this applies not only to those of Ghana, but to the whole of West Africa – change their programmes and their affiliations in such a way that not even a trained student of politics can keep up with them. Their appeal to the mainly illiterate elector must then be simplified to the point of absurdity. The standard of political advancement of the village masses may be judged from the fact that when just before the election Nkrumah and his supporters carried out a perfectly normal animistic ceremony which consisted of formally asking the support of the spirits of the Kpeshi lagoon near Accra, the rumour became general that the Prime Minister had called on the gods to kill all who voted against him. Many electors, as a result of this, abstained from voting. Again in the Ashanti country, where Nkrumah is not liked, his supporters had successfully spread the report that the Duchess of Kent when she arrived for the Ghana celebrations had actually crowned Nkrumah king of Ghana. Many people say that Dr Nkrumah would like to be not a mere prime minister but a real king – and not a king over Ghana alone, at that. French newspapers published in Dakar report that when, several years ago, he visited a celebrated witch-doctor in Kan-Kan, in the French Sudan, this was the prize foretold when the auguries were taken from the blood of a sacrificed chicken. After the independence celebrations Dr Nkrumah visited Kan-Kan again, but in the meanwhile the old witch-doctor had died, and, as his successor was not yet fully trained, no cock was sacrificed this time. A friend of mine who saw Dr Nkrumah on this occasion noted that he was carrying a copy of Machiavelli's *The Prince*.

The most frequent charge levelled against the C.P.P. is that of corruption, and even to the casual observer it would seem that many Government functionaries live in a style remote from that made possible by their salaries. By the time I visited Ghana it was said that no man could expect to get on the short list for any Government appointment without a scale payment 'to the party funds', while a British senior police official who was staying on, admitted that the length of his service probably depended entirely on how soon it was before he received an order to turn a blind eye on the misdoings of someone in a high place. This general corruption in African politics is excused, even defended, by some observers, on the ground that it is strictly in line with the ancient tradition of the country. Every formal human contact calls for its appropriate offering. When a man leaves on a journey all his friends make him a gift, however trivial, and when he returns he will be welcomed with another small offering. The successful conclusion, in the old days, of an initiatory stage in the bush-school was signalled by a shower of congratulatory presents. A girl expected to receive tributes of beads and cosmetics not only for her wedding, but when she was officially recognised as marriageable. No dispute could be brought for a chief's adjudication without a 'mark of respect' being offered by both parties in the case. One of the worst torments of African travel until very recently arose out of this necessity of 'dashing' every chief one visited on one's travels, and the problem of disposal of the livestock one was frequently 'dashed' in return. When I once paid a courtesy call on an important dignitary living in a remote part of the country where the old way of life was still followed, I was startled after we had shaken hands to be told by the chief that he could not receive me, 'without warning'. What he meant by this was that I had not given him time to find a suitable 'dash', and our meeting must therefore be considered as without official existence. It also meant that the two bottles of beer I had brought for him could not be decently handed over until I had gone. These are the usages of highly complicated civilisation; they are all-pervasive, and when – as at present – the old order breaks down and politicians take over from the chiefs, nothing is easier than the transition in almost imperceptible stages from the ceremonial gift to the outright bribe.

The official jollifications that took place in March 1957 in Accra, it should be stressed, celebrated in reality a situation virtually in existence since Nkrumah became Prime Minister in 1952, so that by the time I visited Ghana the country had been to all intents and purposes independent for several years. The formal take-over was accompanied by all the public junketings one would have expected, but as these were not particularly characteristic of West Africa, I took the opportunity two days before Independence Day to go on a sightseeing trip outside Accra. Hiring a taxi I drove to Ho, capital of Togoland, a hundred miles away. Although it had been feared that the Ashanti minority – many of them were opposed to union with Ghana – might cause trouble at this historic moment, it was in Togoland, in fact, where rioting was actually going on, and to which troops had been sent.

This particular day turned out to be a coolish one. We drove eastwards from Accra along a good asphalted road, shortly, as the road left the coast, entering the rainforest belt. Here opulent woods replaced the parched scrub-lands of the coastal areas. There were frequent giant ant-hills by the roadside, pinnacled like Rhine castles painted in the background of German old masters. I was disappointed to see no animals, no flowers except a few meagre daisies growing in the verges, and no birds but turtle-doves and an occasional lean dishevelled-looking hornbill. The African native's access to firearms has brought about the virtual extermination of all edible animal species in the Gold Coast. It turned out indeed to be a great day in the driver's life, when later in the trip a hunter offered us a large cane rat – practically the only form of game obtainable in these days. The price asked for this animal was 25s. The driver beat the man down to 15s. and told me that it was a bargain at that figure. We passed through nondescript villages plastered with advertisements for Ovaltine, Guinness, and Andrews Liver Salts. Africans it seems are easily persuaded to worry about their health. There was a decrepit shack of a restaurant called 'Ye Olde Chop Bar', and a drinking saloon called 'Honesty and Decency'. We met a great number of what are called 'mammy-lorries' coming down for the Accra celebrations. These trucks, which are owned by the world's most prosperous market-women, are famous for their names, which – following the principle used in the tabloid headlines – usually attempt to crowd too much information or comment into too few words. The result is sometimes unintelligible to the outsider. We saw trucks with such names as 'Still Praying For Life', 'Trust No Future', 'Still As If', 'One Pound Balance', 'Look, People Like These', and 'As If They Love You'. These trucks are driven with abandon, and their wrecked and burnt-out shells litter the roadside. The African brand of driver's fatalism is even more irremediable than most, due to the fact that the African tends not to believe in the existence of inanimate matter. Trees and rocks are capable of locomotion, so that after an accident a driver – washing his hands of something so completely outside his control – may simply say: 'A tree ran into me.'

We crossed the new bridge over the Volta and immediately entered a new country. This had been German colonial territory until 1919, when the country had come under League of Nations control and been divided rather crudely and purposelessly between the British and the French. There were few signs of jubilation in these villages. In the outskirts of Ho a shop still carried the title Buch Handlung, although it no longer sold books. At this point, we ran through the tail end of a rain storm and the thick spicy odour of an old-fashioned grocer's reached us from the wet jungle.

I had a letter of introduction to Mr Mead, who had been formally known as Resident of Togoland but whose official title had now for some time been modified to Regional Officer. My arrival could not possibly have been worse timed. The situation at that moment in the surrounding villages was officially described as explosive, and Mr Mead, whose job it was to see that no explosion took place, had had no sleep for several nights. A minor upset had been caused by a tornado that had ripped through the edge of the town that afternoon, torn off some roofs, and put the town electricity supply out of action. Finally the R.O.'s wife was in the last stage of a difficult pregnancy, and a car stood by, ready, in an emergency, to rush her to Lome, the capital of French Togoland, where, Mr Mead said, the medical services were better developed than the local ones.

Mr Mead faced these difficulties with an Olympian calm. We dined splendidly on the vast polished veranda of the Residency, served by white-coated, whispering stewards who moved as stealthily as Indian stranglers. Almost certainly having first discovered through the steward in charge of the

127

guest bungalow that I was travelling very light, Mr Mead had asked to be excused from dressing for dinner, and we ate in civilised, tieless comfort. Like all great administrators the R.O. seemed to admire and respect the customs of the people he ruled, although he thought that they were rather letting the side down in their violent and non-constitutional reaction to their integration with Ghana. My host was a master of magnificent understatement, and his only complaint arising from the vexations of the moment was that there was a shortage of bath water. About half-way through the meal a dispatch-rider arrived with an urgent message, and, excusing himself hurriedly, the R.O. departed for his headquarters for another sleepless night, carrying with him a copy of *À la recherche du temps perdu*.

Next day I set out to see something of Togoland. Etiquette first called for a visit to the paramount chief of Ho, but here a difficulty arose. A schism had taken place in the leadership of the Ewes of Togoland over the issue of their permanent incorporation with Ghana, and a very strong minority had asked to remain under British rule until such time as they could unite with their brothers in French Togoland to form a separate nation. When the division of Togoland had taken place in 1919 about 170,000 Ewes found themselves transferred to the British, and about 400,000 came under French control. The Ewes complained that they suffered by this change of masters. The British slice, in particular, of the ex-German colony, they said, became no more than an unimportant appendage of the Gold Coast, and from 1919 onward no Ewe had much hope of self-advancement unless he left his native country – as great numbers did – and migrated to Accra. The two political factions dividing the country – those in favour of the C.P.P. and union with Ghana, and their opponents who had lost the recent elections – now regarded each other with implacable hostility. What was perhaps the most extraordinary feature of this situation was that the original paramount chief who headed the apparently pro-British faction had come under Mr Mead's displeasure, and diplomatic relations had been broken off between him and the Residency. The British, in fact, officially supported a new pretender from the royal family – a member of the once revolutionary C.P.P. (which still talked sometimes about breaking the chains of imperialism – although in these days with no really convincing show of acrimony).

It was a problem to know which chief to visit first, as it had been hinted to me that either might feel himself slighted if it came to his knowledge that I had placed him second on the list. In the end I decided to make it the dissident chief who was notorious for his readiness to take umbrage. I found him living in a small single-storey house. From the bareness of the furnishings and the absence of comfort, I got the impression that this chief – like so many minor potentates of West Africa – was a poor man. Chiefs are elected from a number of suitable candidates drawn from the royal family and I was told later that no Ewe candidate stood much chance of election unless he was the kind of man who got up early every morning and set off, hoe over his shoulder, to work on his farm.

Chief Togbe Hodo's reception was not a genial one. I found the chief in his courtyard, wearing his working clothes and seated on a piano stool. He was a man of about sixty. According to old-fashioned local usage he affected not to notice my entry, and appeared to be absorbed in his study of the faded coronation picture which provided the room's only decoration. A 'linguist' invited me to seat myself on a worn-out sofa and whispered that the chief would answer my questions when his council of 'wing-chiefs' arrived. He then fiddled with the knobs of a radio set until he found a station broadcasting hymns, and turned this up to a fair strength. The council of wing-chiefs, who had evidently been fetched from their work, soon trooped in, and seated themselves on a miscellany of chairs that had been placed round the courtyard. There were eight of them, and one of them wore a carpenter's apron and sat clutching a plane. This was my cue, as Mr Mead had warned me, to get up and shake hands with each chief in turn, starting with the man on my right and working my way round the circle. Speaking on behalf of the paramount chief, who now appeared to have noticed my presence for the first time, the linguist now said, 'You are welcome. Pray begin your questions.' Formal palavers of this kind form a great part of African small-town life and any visitor from another country, however unimportant he may be, is expected to enter with good grace into the spirit of the thing. I don't remember what questions I asked, and these certainly only provided an excuse for the exposition by the council of their views on the burning theme of union with Ghana. Chief Togbe Hodo's Grey Eminence turned out to be a nonconformist minister, who had been hurriedly sent for. The Reverend Ametowobla had been at Edinburgh University, and he spoke with persuasion and grandiloquence in the soft accent of the Scottish capital. There had never been much hope for Togolanders, he said, since the Germans who wanted to make a show-colony of it had left. Now that they were to be delivered up to the mercies of the politicians of the Gold Coast, there would be none at all. One of the chiefs present was old enough to remember what it was like under the Germans. Herzog the German governor had wanted to outstrip the Gold Coast and had set to work with tremendous energy to develop the country. There had been compulsory schooling for all, whereas in these days there was about 85 per cent illiteracy. On the other hand the Germans had introduced forced labour. Chief Togbe Hodo made no contribution to this discussion except in his native tongue. I believe that he understood English but would have considered it undignified to dispense with his interpreter on such occasions.

The opposition chief, Togbe Afede Asor, turned out to be young and agreeably expansive. Once again there was the business of waiting for the assembly of wing-chiefs before he could speak, but after this he brushed ceremony aside. We shook hands. I said, 'How do you do?' and the chiefs smiled widely and said, 'Okay.' After a brief discussion of local affairs the chief asked if I had any objection to his performing a libation. This pagan custom is in wide use all over the Gold Coast, despite the most vehement protests from the Christian clergy and in particular from the Bishop of Accra, and on national occasions it is carried out by Dr Nkrumah himself in exactly the same way as his counterpart in Europe might lay a wreath on a cenotaph. Dr Nkrumah when he makes a public libation uses the traditional Hollands Gin, but Chief Togbe Asor said that Black and White Whisky would in his opinion be just as acceptable to the ancestral spirits to whom the libation would be made, and he liked it better himself. We went into the chief's living-room, which was densely furnished in Victorian style, and there the chief poured about a teaspoonful of the whisky out on to the green linoleum, at the same time praying in a loud and matter-of-fact voice for the success of any mission I happened to be on, and – as at that time he still supposed me to be a Government servant – promotion in my particular department. After that we completed the ceremony in the approved fashion by drinking a stiff whisky apiece ourselves. Chief Asor told me that he was a Catholic, and that among the Catholic flock in Togoland only chiefs were allowed to pour libations and possess more than one wife. As another chiefly privilege he had 'medicine' buried in his back-yard to protect the household from malevolent spirits. When I left he invited me to come round next morning at six, when he would sacrifice a sheep in honour of the flag-raising ceremony of the new nation. He also presented me with a neatly written biographical note, reading as follows: 'Togbe Afede Asore II was born in June 1927 by Fia Afede XII of Ho Bankoe and Abla Dam of Taviefe. He was educated at the Catholic Mission School from 1936–46. He was Assistant Secretary to the Asogli State Council from 1947–52. He was installed on 22nd February, 1952, on the ancient Asogli Stool of Ho. Togbe Asor II was the descendant of the great grandfather Asor I of Ho who led the Ewe emancipation from Notse 360 years ago. Hobbies: Table-tennis, Walking, Gardening.' The stool referred to here is the ancient West African symbol of kingship: the counterpart of the crown in Europe. It is kept under close guard by a functionary known as the Stool Father, whose power may almost equal that of the chief. The stool is considered to be impregnated with a magical essence, which in the old days was 'fed' or revived, by the blood of human sacrifices, and although it is too small and too sacred to be sat upon, a chief may be held in contact with it in the seated position from time to time, to allow him to absorb some of its power.

After saying goodbye to Chief Togbe Asor II, I made up my mind to drive on to Kpandu, one of the principal centres of the resistance movement. In the preceding days, abandoned training camps had been found in the bush round Kpandu, and several caches of weapons and explosives had been unearthed. This was March 5th – eve of Independence Day – and it was feared that despite the precautions taken to send military units into the area, rebellion might break out at any moment. There were few signs of life in the villages we passed through. Houses and shops were shut up, and there were no decorations. The driver, who was understandably nervous at the possibility of running into a battle, took to stopping at every village to inquire about the situation along the road immediately ahead. This meant a de rigueur call on the chief and his council and a certain amount of punctilious time-wasting.

Dzolokpuita stands out in the memory. Dzolokpuita was a pretty little Italianate-looking cluster of neat stone houses built on rust-red earth and shaded by flame trees in full blossom. Here the opposing factions had withdrawn to opposite ends of the village and were waiting, so the chief told us, with their cudgels and knives, ready for the coming of night. This chief was a rare pro-Government one – that is to say, he was pro integration with Ghana, and he was in fear of his life because his party was in the minority. He was the poorest chief I had so far met. He received me on the veranda of his hut, seated in a deck-chair with a replica of his sacred stool at his side. A child's chamber-pot had been hurriedly pushed out of the way underneath the stool. The chief's linguist was literally dressed in sackcloth, although, when the council of wing-chiefs came scrambling in, I noted that some of them wore old French firemen's helmets – a suggestion that they had seen better times. The wing-chiefs were scared stiff – they expected to have their throats cut that night – and they fidgeted and peered nervously about while the interminable routine of formal questions and answers was being got through. It was clear to me that even in the shadow of bloody revolt the chief wasn't going to be balked of a prolonged exchange of the courtesies. After I had asked him how many children he had begotten, and he had gravely replied, 'They are numerous,' he was going on with a full recital of their names, together, so far as he could remember, with those of their mothers, until he was stopped by cries of protest from his thanes. An army truck with a soldier crouched purposefully behind a Bren gun rolled into the square, and a wing-chief went rushing out to demand its protection; but the driver hastily accelerated away again, leaving the wing-chief waving his helmet frustratedly after it. 'We shall all die, tonight,' the paramount chief said. He asked me to bring their desperate situation to the notice of Queen Elizabeth. After that a sackcloth-clad official poured a libation of locally-distilled bootleg gin, and I was allowed to get away.

I went up to Kpandu, and back through this brilliant and

menaced countryside. There were soldiers drilling in little groups of threes and fours in the open spaces of small towns, with the passion and dedication that West Africans bring to their military exercises. Where there were no soldiers there were lurking groups of cudgel-armed men. The market in Kpandu was nearly deserted and dreadfully malodorous. Here they sold millions of tiny sun-dried fish, and smoke-cured cane rats that filled the air with a fierce ammoniacal stench. You could also buy lovely ancient-looking beads copied from Phoenician models, spurious amber made in Japan, short-swords used in the north for protecting oneself from hyenas, pictures of Princess Margaret and Burt Lancaster, and a clearance line of portraits of Dorothy Lamour in her sarong. While I was mooching about, a small, spruce soldier arrived with a portable gramophone, wound it up and put on a tune called 'Ghana Land of Freedom', which, while serving as a kind of unofficial national anthem, has the unusual advantage of being a high-life, and is danced to as such (the other side of the record features Lord Kitchener in 'Don't Touch Me Nylon'). While the record was played through to the ostentatiously turned backs of the few traders about, the soldier stood to attention. A moment later, what was clearly a local man of substance came up. He was dressed in Accra style in toga and sandals, and after offering me his hand in the easy genial way of unspoilt Africa, he nodded at the back of the retreating soldier and we exchanged knowing smiles. 'I fear, sir, he is batting on a sticky wicket,' the new arrival said. I was inclined to agree with what was clearly an Achimota University man. And although that night, to most people's astonishment, passed off peaceably, and no one slit the throats of the chief and council of Dzolokpuita, it was a verdict that I was afraid might be applied to the nascent State of Ghana as a whole.

11

Fidel's Artist

In December 1959, shortly after the Castro victory in Cuba, I attended several of the trials of war criminals conducted in the Cabaña fortress of Havana, in the course of which I was subjected to an extraordinary encounter with Herman Marks, the American who had become the Cuban executioner. Marks spent some time justifying his activities and expounding his personal philosophy, in the hope that I might help to rectify his image 'in the world's eyes'. I suspected that his Cuban employers only saw him as a painful necessity. A year or so later a friend visited Cuba with the intention of writing a book, and I included Marks in a list of persons he might find interesting to see. When he returned I asked him how the meeting had gone. His reply was 'I was too late. They'd already put him up against the wall.'

'Well all right, all right, we know all about the stretches I may have done. I was waiting for that one. You may say I was a no good son of a bitch when I was a kid, and I might agree with you. But I suppose you've heard of such a thing as moral regeneration? I guess you'd say that any guy has the right to do what he can to put himself in the clear with society. Maybe that's why I'm doing what I'm doing – in other words a necessary job that nobody else wants to take on.

'I guess I feel this way I'm doing something to clean the slate, and I figure that's the way the people here see it too. They accept me. I'm regarded as a useful citizen. People like to be seen going round with me. If I happen to feel like taking an evening off and going to some place like the Riviera, for example, I get the best table that's going. Some guy I don't know is always picking up the tab for my drinks. Even Fidel gives me the big hello when he sees me. I do my job conscientiously, and I'm respected for it. That's the way it is.

'Listen, the way I figure it is, you have a job to do? OK, do it well. Maybe you know the Cadillac and Limousine Service on

Nott Street, Zenith? I was with that bunch as a senior servicing operator for five years, and believe me I was always noted for the pride I took in my work. Anyone there will tell you that. And if you think that anyone could do my present job – boy, you just can't imagine how wrong you are! Believe me, it calls for everything you've got. You're up against the human element all the time. The kids they send me to work with: you'd break your heart if you saw them. As a technician – that's how I see myself – I hate a bungled job.

'Listen, I'm only supposed to put the finishing touch – that and give the word of command. Not to have to check up on every detail with the dead-beats they send along for these parties. What I mean is they're supposed to be volunteers, but most of them turn out to be strictly chicken when it comes to the point. If I didn't watch them like a cat, you'd get half these characters only pretending to fire and then quietly unloading as soon as I turned my head. That kind of thing puts extra work on me. Believe me, I drive myself, I really do. Way back last year when we had our busy spell when I've been on special missions half the night, I've worked some nights from midnight until five or six in the morning. You can't rush this kind of thing. It takes time. And I might add, I don't touch a drop of liquor when I'm carrying out a mission. The most I have is a cup of coffee sent down every hour or so. With milk. Sleep well? Oh, sure I do.

'Another thing might surprise you, and that's the trouble I've put myself to make the whole thing go as smoothly as is possible in the circumstances. For example, whose idea do you think it was to fix up for these jobs to be done in the old moat under that big statue of Jesus Christ they light up at night? Why mine of course. I can't claim to be a religious man, but at least I understand the way other people feel about these things.

'When I put up that idea to the revolutionary committee at the Cabaña they said it was a masterpiece. You know the statue don't you? It stands up right over the wall. It must be 60 feet high. You can see it ten miles away at nights. It struck me as a kind of nice idea that that would be just about the last thing these poor guys would see. Now you see what I mean about giving all I've got on the job?

'The fact is, I suppose I feel somehow like a doctor does with

135

a patient. I go easy with them. Put it this way, I don't go in for rough talk, or wise-cracking, and I don't let any of the kids either. I'm ready to spend half an hour with a man kidding him along, just to see it goes smooth – you follow me? He wants to make a speech? OK, he makes a speech. He wants to give the orders himself? That's OK too. Anything within reason goes by me.

'This business about giving the orders themselves seems to be a sort of craze these days. They nearly all want to do it. I figure it's a kind of last minutes show off. Search me why anybody should want to show off at a time like that when there's only me and a bunch of stupid kids to see it. To tell you the truth, I wish they wouldn't do it. I warn them to space out the orders properly; to count up to six slowly between the take-aim and the fire. But they always make it too fast and what happens is the kids loose off before they get a chance to take proper aim. That way you get a really crummy result and it puts it all on me. Anyway, what I'm trying to get round to is this. I go out of my way to show consideration. These guys are in a highly nervous state.

'As I said, they can have half an hour to shoot the breeze. More if they want. Well of course, some of them try to drag things out. They're liable to beef on about their innocence. "Sure you're innocent," I say. "I know you're innocent. All right, fellow, all right. Now how about standing over here where we can get a look at you?" That's the way I kid them along. You have to be ready for anything in the way of propositioning. You get rich guys who want to give you a million dollars to fix it so that they go out of the Cabaña some other way but in that box. Some guys never give up hope. I mean that literally. I've known the time when a fellow's gone on trying to talk his way out right until I put the finishing touch – and that, by the way, throws a light on the quality of the workmanship I have to put up with. You'll get another customer who wants to shake hands.

'"I forgive you," he says.

'"Thank you, thank you," I tell him. "That sure makes me feel better." While I'm holding his hand I'm sort of strolling along with him, manoeuvring him into position, in a way like he doesn't realise what's going on. About one in three of them wants to pass you something they like to hang on to until the last moment, maybe it's a rabbit's paw or a locket with a picture of their mother, or something like that. Personally I make a strict rule not to touch anything of value. "Give it to one of the boys," I say. I don't object to the kids taking a locket or a ring or something like that if it's offered to them, but what I won't stand for is that racket they used to go in for of selling spent shells to those niggers who use them for some sort of voodoo stuff. The regular price used to be five bucks a shell till I stamped on it.

'I know what you're going to say now. You're going to bring up that story that I have cuff-links made out of them myself, and hand them out to my friends. Sure I do, and why shouldn't I? It's not a racket. I don't take payment for them, and nor do I see anything morbid about it.

'Listen, if you want to talk about people being morbid, maybe I should tell you about some of the characters who come and ask me about letting them come along to one of the performances, and I don't mean two-bit journalists either. I mean guys whose names you read every time you pick up a newspaper. If I could mention some of those names you'd certainly be surprised. Maybe you'd change your mind about who's morbid, or put it this way – who'd like to have the chance to be morbid.

'I had a case the other day. Two fellers came up to the Officers' Club and asked for me. I knew one of them quite a bit. He was a big wheel at one of the embassies. I don't want to say which one. He always wants to buy me a drink, whenever he sees me. "Good evening, Captain," he says, "I want you to meet a very distinguished friend of mine, and a very great creative artist. This is Mr Shiralee Shepherd".

'"Not *the* Shiralee Shepherd," I said. To tell you the truth, although I'd seen this guy on the films he looked somehow different. "I saw your last film," I said. "It sure was a gas."

'"Thank you. Thank you indeed," Mr Shiralee Shepherd says. "As from one artist to another I take that as a great compliment."

'I got a bang out of the artist stuff. "An artist," I said. "Well, I guess maybe you're right. I wouldn't say I was a creative one, though."

'We all had a laugh, and the diplomat fellow says. "Shiralee's been hearing a great deal about you, Captain, and I

was wondering if we couldn't get together. I guess you understand that a man engaged in his kind of imaginative work
requires a diversity of experience out of which to fashion his
material – experiences that others might wish to go out of their
way to avoid."

'I knew what was coming and I particularly liked that bit
about experiences that others might wish to go out of their way
to avoid. I could have given him the names of a hundred guys
who had their name down on my waiting list. "You mean Mr
Shepherd wants to come to a gala evening," I said.

'"If it can be arranged," Shepherd says. "Discreetly, of
course."

'I looked at the guy, and I can't say I was too crazy about
him. He looked kind of fat-lipped off the screen. I didn't go for
him in a great way, but his pal from the embassy was a good
enough guy, and I wanted to do what I could for him. "It
might be arranged," I said.

'"When?" says Shepherd, in a very anxious manner.

'"Ah, that I can't say," I told him. "Business has been
pretty slow lately. It's only just beginning to look up again. It
looks like we'll be getting a few candidates again before long,
but even then certain formalities have to be observed. As for
example the guys are supposed to be tried."

'"Yes, of course," Shepherd says, "but tell me, these trials,
and so forth – are they likely to take long? I mean do you think
it would be any use if I arranged to stay on another week?"

'For Christ's sake, what was I to say to the guy? Did he think
I could have someone knocked off specially for his benefit?
When I told him it might take a month you should have seen
the look on his face. I've never seen a man look so disappointed. I found out later he came all the way from New York
on the chance of seeing me slip somebody the pill.

'Now please do me a favour, will you? After that, don't talk
to me about a guy being morbid.'

12

Two Generals

General Enrique Loynaz took me to see General Garcia Velez, the other surviving hero of Cuba's War of Independence against Spain. General Velez sat in the cool, vaulted marble of his library, in his pyjamas surrounded by piles of magazines, mostly English. He had been ambassador to Great Britan for twelve years. A softly groaning symphony of distant car horns and loudspeakers came through the open window. There was a big military parade on in the city.

'I'm commonly stated in the press to be 94,' General Velez said. 'It's not true. I'm only 93.' General Loynaz was in his late eighties. Before leaving his house he had shown me a slightly bent Toledo sword. 'It's out of shape from whacking cowards on the backside,' he said. 'To keep their faces to the enemy.'

'The very opposite in fact, of my own methods,' Garcia Velez said. '*He* used to bully his men. I believed in kidding them along. In my opinion he was guilty of faulty psychology. How none of them ever had the guts to shoot him in the back I shall never understand.'

These two old men had sat quietly in the shadows for sixty years, watching with sardonic eyes the comings and goings of the politicians and the big business men who had gathered like vultures over their victories. They had sat through the revolutions and the *coups d'état*, had seen tyrants rise to power and fall, seen poor, honest men become rich and corrupt, seen young idealists transformed into bloody dictators, seen the vulgar image of Miami stamped over the soft, grey, baroque elegance of the Havana of their youth.

'Above all, my boy, don't get old,' Garcia Velez said. 'It imposes an excess of reflection. I do practically nothing these days but read and think. See that pile of *Edinburgh Journals*. I've every number since 1764, and I've read them all. Mostly I read history with the inner reservation that it's largely romance and lies. At least nearly everything that I can check on from my own personal experience is. Did you ever see the film *A Message to Garcia*, for example? The Garcia in the film was my father.'

'Calixto Garcia – the liberator of our country,' General Loynaz explained.

'I didn't see it myself,' General Velez said, 'As a matter of principle I've never been to the cinema. Nor have I even seen the television. I've always believed in living my life, not watching how other people are supposed to live theirs. But from what they tell me about this film, and the book it was based on, it was pure rubbish.'

'The actress was Barbara Stanwyck,' General Loynaz said. 'A very pretty girl. I much regret never having met her.'

'You cannot awaken the interest of Americans without a big fraud,' General Velez said. 'It was supposed to be some secret mission to my father, shown as carried through in the face of all kinds of nonsensical adventures. My father was depicted as a sort of romantic bandit hiding in the mountains. How they managed to bring Barbara Stanwyck into it, don't ask me. The real truth is there was no adventure. The American agent met my father in a hotel in the town of Bayamo. I don't think the message was particularly important either, whatever it was. My father certainly never bothered to mention it to me.'

'Our old friend's a sceptic,' Loynaz said, 'He's lost the power of passionate conviction.'

'A circumstance in which I rejoice,' Garcia Velez said. 'Our war was terrible enough, but when I say that it was conducted with the utmost brutality, I say this of both sides. Thousands of our people died of starvation and disease in the concentration camps the Spanish set up. Their *guerrilleros* didn't spare our women and children. But let's at least admit we weren't much better.'

He knocked the ash from the end of his cigar into a tin which had held herrings.

'Mind you, it wasn't particularly comfortable to be a general in those days. If you got into a mix-up in a battle they always went for the uniform. I can't remember how many times I was wounded. General Maceo collected 27 wounds. We seemed to be indestructible. When they took my father

140

prisoner, he shot himself in the head. The bullet came out of his mouth. He still lived for seventeen years. Tell us about that famous wound of yours, Enrique.'

General Loynaz said: 'Those were the days when generals died with their boots on. I was in 107 combats. The 107th was at Babinay in '98 – the last stages of the war, when our American deliverers had belatedly decided to come in. I was in command of an infantry brigade.'

'He was a real general, I might say,' Garcia Velez said. 'He was always at the head of his troops on a white horse. An admirable spectacle, but not for me. Not for my father, either.'

'On this occasion there was no white horse,' Loynaz said. 'I'd been on one earlier in the battle, but it had been shot under me. I can't remember the colour of the second horse, but it certainly wasn't white. Anyway, there I was on the horse, as usual, with a cavalry escort, and the Spanish *guerrilleros* were waiting for us behind a stockade. We were undergoing heavy rifle fire and a moderate artillery barrage. I gave the order to charge.'

'In true Cuban style,' Garcia Velez said. 'Light Brigade stuff. Into the Valley of Death. The kind of thing they love. I shudder at the thought of it.'

'When you run up against cannon fire at point blank range, it's the only way,' Loynaz said. 'Above all things, you want to get it over with. I was the first over the stockade. Unfortunately I was never much good at jumping, and this time I landed on the horse's neck. A Spanish *guerillero* brought his machete down on top of my head.'

'You should have led your charges from the rear,' Garcia Velez said.

General Loynaz took my hand and placed it on his scalp. I felt a shallow trough in the skull, about six inches long.

'Three American Presidents have asked to touch that wound,' Loynaz said; 'Teddy Roosevelt, Hoover, and I can't remember the name of the third. I managed to scramble back into the saddle holding in the few brains I possess with one hand, and I sat there not able to contribute much to the course of the battle, until it was over.

'They took me to a hut where a honeymoon couple had installed themselves, and I commandeered their bed. The effects of this wound by the way, after the initial pain quietened down, were wholly beneficial. Up till that time I was a martyr to headaches, but I've never had one since. It probably made more space for my brains. That was pretty well the end of the war so far as I was concerned. The Americans decided to come in after that. They were just about a year too late. We should have welcomed them in '97.'

'Friends are always welcome,' Garcia Velez said.

'We had won the war,' Loynaz said. 'The whole country was in our hands.'

'But not the towns,' Garcia Velez said. 'The Spanish still held the towns. You speak as a patriot, not a historian.'

'For six years the foreigners ran our country,' Loynaz said. 'They bought up the best land in the island. Do you know how much they paid? Ten cents a *caballeriá* of 33 acres. The price of two bottles of Coca Cola.'

Garcia Velez shook his head at him. When Loynaz had gone, he said: 'My old friend has always remained a Cuban, whereas the twelve years I spent in London has wrought a profound change in my character. I see things calmly now; almost I believe, through Anglo-Saxon eyes. Moreover, living abroad, I became wholly a pacifist. Had my twelve years in England come before the war, I don't believe I'd have fought in it. The things I was forced as a patriot to do, now seem to me to be hateful – against nature.'

It was within weeks of Fidel Castro's capture of the capital, and from where I sat I could see through the window a squad of feminine militia come marching down the road. Half of them were in uniform, the rest in pretty dresses. A sergeant marching beside them called out the time. With them came a blare of martial music from the speakers of an escorting van.

'Please close the window,' General Velez said. 'The noise oppresses me. What do their banners say?'

I read: 'Fatherland or Death. We will fight to the last drop of our blood against foreign aggressors.'

'And they will,' the general said. 'And they will if necessary. Alas, haven't I seen it all before.'

13

Genocide

If you happened to be one of those who felt affection for the gentle, backward civilisations – Nagas, Papuans, Mois of Vietnam, Polynesian and Melanesian remnants – the shy primitive peoples, daunted and overshadowed by the juggernaut advance of our ruthless age, then last year [1968] was a bad year for you.

By the descriptions of all who had seen them, there were no more inoffensive and charming human beings on the planet than the forest Indians of Brazil, and brusquely we were told they had been rushed to the verge of extinction. The tragedy of the Indian in the United States in the last century was being repeated, but it was being compressed into a shorter time. Where a decade ago there had been hundreds of Indians, there were now tens. An American magazine reported with nostalgia on a tribe of which only 135 members had survived ... too gentle almost to hunt. They lived as naked as Adam and Eve in the nightfall of an innocent history, catching a few fish, collecting groundnuts, playing their flutes, making love ... waiting for death. We learned that it was due only to the paternal solicitude of the Brazilian Government's Indian Protection Service that they had survived until this day.

In all such monitory accounts – and there had been many of them – there was a blind spot, a lack of candour, a defect in social responsibility, an evident aversion to pointing to the direction from which doom approached. It seemed that we were expected to suppose that the Indians were simply fading away, killed off by the harsh climate of the times, and we were invited to inquire no further. It was left to the Brazilian Government itself to resolve the mystery, and in March 1968 it did so, with brutal frankness, and with little attempt at self-defence. The tribes had been virtually exterminated, not *despite* all the efforts of the Indian Protection Service, but with its *connivance* – often its ardent co-operation.

The Service, admitted General Albuquerque Lima, the Brazilian Minister of the Interior, had been converted into an instrument for the Indians' oppression, and had therefore been dissolved. There was to be a judicial inquiry into the conduct of 134 functionaries. A full newspaper page in small print was required to list the crimes with which these men were charged. Speaking informally, the Attorney General, Senhor Jader Figueiredo, doubted whether 10 of the Service's employees out of a total of over 1,000 would be fully cleared of guilt.

The official report was calm – phlegmatic almost – all the more effective therefore in its exposure of the atrocity it contained. Pioneers leagued with corrupt politicians had continually usurped Indian lands, destroyed whole tribes in a cruel struggle in which bacteriological warfare had been employed, by issuing clothing impregnated with the virus of smallpox, and by poisoned food supplies. Children had been abducted and mass murder gone unpunished. The Government itself was blamed to some extent for the Service's increasing starvation of resources over a period of 30 years. The Service had also had to face 'the disastrous impact of missionary activity'.

Next day the Attorney General met the Press, and was prepared to supply all the details. A commission had spent 58 days visiting Indian Protection Service posts all over the country collecting evidence of abuses and atrocities.

The huge losses sustained by the Indian tribes in this tragic decade were catalogued in part. Of 19,000 Munducurus believed to have existed in the Thirties, only 1,200 were left. The strength of the Guaranis had been reduced from 5,000 to 300. There were 400 Carajas left out of 4,000. Of the Cintas Largas, who had been attacked from the air and driven into the mountains, possibly 500 had survived out of 10,000. The proud and noble nation of the Kadiweus – 'the Indian Cavaliers' – had shrunk to a pitiful scrounging band of about 200. A few hundred only remained of the formidable Chavantes who prowled in the background of Peter Fleming's Brazilian journey, but they had been reduced to mission fodder – the same melancholy fate that had overtaken the Bororos, who helped to change Lévi-Strauss's views on the nature of human evolution. Many tribes were now represented by a single family, a few by one or two individuals. Some, like the Tapaiunas – in this case from a gift of sugar laced with arsenic – had disappeared altogether. It is estimated that only between 50,000 and 100,000 Indians survive today.

Senhor Figueiredo estimated that property worth 62 million dollars had been stolen from the Indians in the past ten years.

He added, 'It is not only through the embezzlement of funds, but by the admission of sexual perversions, murders and all other crimes listed in the penal code against Indians and their property, that one can see that the Indian Protection Service was for years a den of corruption and indiscriminate killings.' The head of the service, Major Luis Neves, was accused of 42 crimes, including collusion in several murders, the illegal sale of lands, and the embezzlement of 300,000 dollars. The documents containing the evidence collected by the Attorney General weighed 103 kilograms, he informed the newspapermen, and amounted to a total of 5,115 pages.

In the following days there were more headlines and more statements by the Ministry:

'Rich landowners of the municipality of Pedro Alfonso attacked the tribe of Craos and killed about 100.'

'The worst slaughter took place in Aripuaná, where the Cintas Largas Indians were attacked from the air using sticks of dynamite.'

'The Maxacalis were given fire-water by the landowners who employed gunmen to shoot them down when they were drunk.'

'Landowners engaged a notorious pistoleiro *and his band to massacre the Canelas Indians.'*

'The Nhambiquera Indians were mown down by machine-gun fire.'

'Two tribes of the Patachós were exterminated by giving them small-pox injections.'

'In the Ministry of the Interior it was stated yesterday that crimes committed by certain ex-functionaries of the IPS amounted to more than 1000, ranging from tearing out Indians' finger-nails to allowing them to die without assistance.'

'To exterminate the tribe Beiços-de-Pau, Ramis Bucair, Chief of the 6th Inspectorate, explained, an expedition was formed which went up the River Arinos carrying presents and a great quantity of foodstuffs for the Indians. These were mixed with arsenic and formicides ... Next day a great number of the Indians died, and the whites spread the rumour that this was the result of an epidemic.'

As ever, the frontiers with Columbia and Peru (scene of the piratical adventures of the old British-registered Peruvian Amazon Company) gave trouble. A minor boom in wild rubber set off by the last war had filled this area with a new generation of men with hearts of flint. In the 1940's one rubber company punished those of their Indian slaves who fell short in their daily collection by the loss of an ear for the first offence, then the loss of the second ear, then death. When chased by Brazilian troops, they simply moved, with all their labour, across the Peruvian border. Today, most of the local land-owners are slightly less spectacular in their oppressions. One landowner is alleged to have chained lepers to posts, leaving them to relieve themselves where they stood, without food and water for a week. He was a bad example, but his method of keeping the Ticuna Indians in a state of slavery was the one commonly in use. They were paid 0.50 cruzeiros for a day's labour and then charged 3 cruzeiros for a piece of soap. Those who attempted to escape were arrested (by the landowner's private police force) as thieves.

Senhora Neves da Costa Vale, a delegate of the Federal Police who investigated this case, and the local conditions in general, found that little had changed since the bad old days. She noted that hundreds of Indians were being enslaved by landowners on both sides of the frontier, and that Colombians and Peruvians hunted for Ticuna Indians up the Brazilian rivers. Semi-civilised Indians, she said, were being carried off for enrolment as bandits in Colombia. The area is known as Solimões, from the local name of the Amazon, and Senhora Neves was shocked by the desperate physical condition of the Indians. Lepers were plentiful, and she confirmed the existence of an island called Armaça, where Indians who were old or sick were concentrated to await death. She said that they were without assistance of any kind.

From all sources it was a tale of disaster. No-one knew just how many Indians had survived, because there was no way of counting them in their last mountain and forest strongholds. The most optimistic estimate put the figure at 100,000, but others thought they might be as few as half this number. Nor could more than the roughest estimate be made of the speed of the processes of extermination. All the accounts suggest that when the Europeans first came on the scene four centuries back they found a dense and lively population. Fray Gaspar, the diarist of Orellana's expedition, claims that a force of 50,000 once attacked their ship. At that time the experts believe that the Indians may have numbered between three and six millions. By 1900, the same authorities calculate, there may have been a million left. But in reality, it is all a matter of guesswork.

The first Europeans to set eyes on the Indians of Brazil came ashore from the fleet of Pedro Alvares Cabral in the year 1500 to a reception that enchanted them, and when the ships set sail again they left with reluctance.

Pero Vaz de Caminha, official clerk to the expedition, sent off a letter to the King that crackled with enthusiasm. It was the fresh-eyed account of a man released from the monotony of the seas to miraculous new experiences, that might have been written to any crony back in his home town. Nude ladies had paraded on the beach splendidly indifferent to the stares of the Portuguese sailors – and Caminha took the King by the elbow to go into their charms at extraordinary length. The Indian girls were fresh from bathing in the river and devoid of body hair. Caminha describes their sexual attractions with minute and sympathetic detail adding that their genitalia would put any Portuguese lady to shame. In those days Europeans rarely washed (a treatise on the avoidance of lousiness was a best seller), so one supposes that the Portuguese were frequently verminous in these regions. Caminha cannot avoid coming back to the subject again before settling to prosaic details of the climate and produce of the newly-discovered land. 'Sweet girls,' he says ... 'Like wild birds and animals. Lustrous in a way that so far outshines those in captivity – they could not be cleaner, plumper and more vibrant than they are.'

The Europeans were overwhelmed, too, by the magnificence of the Indians' manners. If they admired any of their necklaces or personal adornments of feather or shells these were instantly pressed into their hands. In other encounters it was to be the same with golden trinkets, and temporary wives were always to be had for the taking. The bolder of the women came and rubbed themselves against the sailors' legs, showing their fascination at the instant and unmistakable sexual response of the white men.

Such openhandedness was dazzling to these representatives of an inhibited but fanatically acquisitive society. The official clerk filled page after page with a catalogue of Indian virtues. All that was necessary to complete this image of the perfect human society was a knowledge of the true God. And since these people were not circumcised, it followed that they were not Mohammedans or Jews, and that there was nothing to impede their conversion. When the first Mass was said the Indians, with characteristic politeness and tact, knelt beside the Portuguese and, in imitation of their guests, smilingly kissed the crucifixes that were handed to them. As discussion was limited to gestures the Portuguese suspected their missionary labours were incomplete, and when the fleet sailed, two convicts were left behind to attend to the natives' conversion.

It was Caminha's letter that encouraged Voltaire to formulate his theory of the Noble Savage. Here was innocence – here was apparent freedom, even, from the curse of original sin. The Indians, said the first reports, knew of no crimes or punishments. There were no hangmen or torturers among them; no poor. They treated each other, their children – even their animals – with constant affection. They were to be sacrificed to a process that was beyond the control of these admiring visitors. Spain and Portugal had become parasitic nations who could no longer feed themselves.

The fertile lands at home had been abandoned, the irrigation systems left by the Moors were fallen into decay, the peasants dragged away to fight in endless wars from which they never returned. Economic forces the newcomers could never have understood were about to transform them into slavers and assassins. The natives gave gracefully, and the invaders took what they offered with grasping hands, and when there was nothing left to give the enslavement and the murder began. The American continent was about to be overwhelmed by what Claude Lévi-Strauss described 400 years later as 'that monstrous and incomprehensible cataclysm which the development of Western civilisation was for so large and innocent a part of humanity.'

Caminha and his comrades landed at Porto Seguro, about 500 miles up the coast from the present Rio de Janeiro, and it is no more than a coincidence that a handful of Indians have somehow succeeded in surviving to this day at Itabuna, which is nearby. The continued presence of these Tapachós is something of a mystery, because for four centuries the area has been ravaged by slavers, belligerent pioneers and bandits of all descriptions. The survivors are found in a swarthy, austere landscape, tied together by ligaments of bare rock, in the crevices of which they have developed an aptitude for self-concealment; furtive creatures in tropical tatters, scuttling for cover as they are approached. One sees them in patches of wasteland by the roadside or railway track, which they fertilise by their own excrement to grow a few vegetables before moving on. Otherwise they eke out a sub-existence by selling herbal recipes and magic to neurotic whites who visit them in secret, also by a little prostitution and a little theft. They suffer from tuberculosis, venereal disease, ailments of the eye, and from epidemics of measles and influenza, the last two of which adopt particularly lethal forms.

Two of their tribes held on through thick and thin to a little of their original land until ten years ago when a doctor – now alleged to have been sent by the Indian Protection Service of those days – instead of vaccinating them, inoculated them with the virus of smallpox. This operation was totally successful in its aim, and the vacant land was immediately absorbed into the neighbouring white estates.

There are a dozen such dejected encampments along 3000 miles of coastline, and they are the last of the coastal Indians of the kind seen by Caminha, who once appeared from among the trees by their hundreds whenever a ship anchored offshore. The Patachós are officially classified as *integrados*. It is the worst label that can be attached to any Indian, as extinction follows closely on the heels of integration.

The atrocities of the Conquistadores described by Bishop Bartolomeo de Las Casas, who was an eye-witness of what must have been the greatest of all wars of extermination, resist the imagination. There is something remote and shadowy about horror on so vast a scale. Numbers begin to mean nothing, as one reads with a sort of detached, unfocused belief of the mass burnings, the flaying, the disembowellings, and the mutilations.

Twelve millions were killed, Las Casas says, most of them in frightful ways. 'The Almighty seems to have inspired these

149

people with a meekness and softness of humour like that of lambs; and the conquerors who have fallen upon them so fiercely resemble savage tigers, wolves and lions.... I have seen the Spaniards set their fierce and hungry dogs at the Indians to tear them in pieces and devour them.... They set fire to so many towns and villages it is impossible I should recall the number of them.... These things they did without any provocation, purely for the sake of doing mischief.' Wherever they could be reached, in the Caribbean islands, and on the coastal plains, the Indians were exterminated. Those of Brazil were saved from extinction by a tropical rain forest, as big as Europe, and to the south of it, the half million square miles of thicket and swampland – the Mato Grosso – that remained sufficiently mysterious until our days for explorers like Colonel Fawcett to lose their lives searching in it for golden cities.

For those who pursued the Indians into the forest there were worse dangers to face than poison-tipped arrows. Jiggers deposited their eggs under their skin; there was a species of fly that fed on the surface of the eye and could produce blindness; bees swarmed to fasten themselves to the traces of mucus in the nostrils and at the corners of the mouth; fire ants could cause temporary paralysis, and worst of all, a tiny beetle sometimes found in the roofs of abandoned huts might drop on the sleeper to administer a single fatal bite.

Apart from that there were the common hazards of poisonous snakes, spiders and scorpions in variety, and the rivers contained not only piranhá, electric eels and sting-rays, but also a tiny cat-fish with spiny fins which wriggled into the human orifices and could not be removed without a mutilating operation. Above all, the mosquitoes transmitted not only malaria, but the yellow fever endemic in the blood of many of the monkeys. The only non-Indians to penetrate the ultimate recesses of the forest were the Negroes of later invasions, who escaped in great numbers from the sugar estates and mines to form the *quilombas,* the fugitive slave settlements. But these, apart from helping themselves to Indian women, where they found them, followed the rule of live and let live, and they merged with the surrounding tribes, and lost their identity.

The processes of murder and enslavement slowed down during the next three centuries, but did so because there were fewer Indians left to murder and enslave. Great expeditions to provide labour for the plantations of Maranhão and Pará depopulated all the easily accessible villages near the main Amazonian waterways, and the loss of life is said to have been greater than that involved in the slave trade with Africa. Those who escaped the plantations often finished in the Jesuit reservations – religious concentration camps where conditions were hardly less severe, and trifling offences were punished with terrible floggings or imprisonment: 'The sword and iron rod are the best kind of preaching,' as the Jesuit missionary José de Anchieta put it.

By the 19th century some sort of melancholy stalemate had been reached. Indian slaves were harder to get, and with the increasing rationalisation of supply and the consequent fall in cost of Negroes from West Africa – who in any case stood up to the work better – the price of the local product was undercut. As the Indians became less valuable as a commodity, it became possible to see them through a misty Victorian eye, and at least one novel about them was written, swaddled in sentiment, and in the mood of *The Last of the Mohicans*. A more practical viewpoint reasserted itself at the time of the great rubber boom at the turn of the century, when it was discovered that the harmless and picturesque Indians were better equipped than Negroes to search the forests for rubber trees. While the eyes of the world were averted, all the familiar tortures and excesses were renewed, until with the collapse of the boom and the revival of conscience, the Indian Protection Service was formed.

In the raw, abrasive vulgarity it displayed in its consumption of easy wealth, the Brazilian rubber boom surpassed anything that had been seen before in the Western world since the days of the Klondyke. It was centred on Manaus which had been built where it was at the confluence of two great, navigable rivers, the Amazon and the Rio Negro, for its convenience in launching slaving expeditions, a city that had fallen into a decline that matched the wane in interest for its principal commodity.

With the invention of the motor car and the rubber tyre, and the recognition that the *hevea* tree of the Amazon produced incomparably the best rubber, Manaus was back in business, converted instantly to a tropical Gomorrah. Caruso refused a staggering fee to appear at the opera house, but Madame Patti accepted. There were Babylonian orgies of the period, in which courtesans took semi-public baths in champagne, which was also awarded by the bucketful to winning horses at the races. Men of fashion sent their soiled linen to Europe to be laundered. Ladies had their false teeth set with diamonds, and among exotic importations was a regular shipment of virgins from Poland. These, averaging 13 years of age, might cost up to £100 (about £500, modern equivalent) for the first night, because intercourse with a virgin was regarded as a certain cure for venereal disease. After that the price would drop to one twentieth of this figure.

The most dynamic of the great rubber corporations of those days was the British-registered Peruvian Amazon Company, operating in the ill-defined north-western frontier of Brazil, where it could play off the governments of Colombia, Peru and Brazil against each other, all the better to establish its vast, nightmarish empire of exploitation and death.

A young American engineer, Walter Hardenburg, carried accidentally in a fit of wanderlust over the company's frontier, was immediately seized and imprisoned for a few days during which time he was given a chance to see the kind of thing that went on. Several thousand Huitoto Indians had been enslaved and at the post where Hardenburg was held, El Encanto (Enchantment), he saw the rubber tappers bringing back their collection of latex at the end of the day. Their bodies were covered with great raised weals from the overseers' tapir-hide whips, and Hardenburg noticed that the Indians who had managed to collect their quota of rubber danced with joy, whereas those who had failed to do so seemed terror-stricken, although he was not present to witness their punishment. Later he learned that repeated deficiencies in collection could mean a sentence of 100 lashes, from which it took six months to recover.

An element of competition was present when it came to killing Indians. On one occasion 150 hopelessly inefficient workers were rounded up and slashes to pieces by macheteiros employing a grisly local expertise, which included the *corte do bananeiro*, a backward and forward swing of the blade which removed two heads at one blow, and the *corte maior*, which sliced a body into two or more parts before it could fall to the ground.

High feast days, too, were celebrated by sporting events when a few of the more active – and therefore more valuable – tappers might be sacrificed to make an occasion. They were blindfolded and encouraged to do their best to escape while the overseers and their guests potted at them with their rifles.

Barbadian British subjects were recruited by the Peruvian Amazon Company as wild Indian-hunters, being sent on numerous expeditions into areas where the company proposed to establish new rubber trails. These were paid on a basis of piecework, and were obliged to collect the heads of their victims, and return with them as proof of their claims to payment. Stud farms existed in the area where selected Indian girls would breed the slave-labour of the future, when the wild Indian had been wiped out. Some rubber companies have been suspected, too, of not stopping short of cannibalism, and there were strong rumours of camps in which ailing and unsatisfactory workers were used to supply the tappers' meat.

The world-wide scandal of the Peruvian Amazon Company, exposed by Sir Roger Casement, coincided with the collapse of the rubber boom caused by the competition of the new Malayan plantations, and a crisis of conscience was sharpened by the threat of economic disaster. The instant bankruptcy of Manaus was attended by spectacular happenings. Sources of cash suddenly dried up, and the surplus population of card-sharpers, adventurers and whores pouring into the river steamers in the rush to escape to the coast paid for their passages with such possessions as diamond cuff-links and solitaire rings. Merchant princes with their fortunes tied up in unsaleable rubber committed suicide. The celebrated electric street cars – first of their kind in Latin America – came suddenly to a halt as the power was cut off, and were set on fire by their enraged passengers. A few racehorses found themselves between the shafts of converted bullock carts. The opera house closed, never to open again.

When Brazilians had got used to the idea that their rubber income was substantially at an end, they began to examine the matter of its cost in human lives in the light of the fact, now generally known, that the Peruvian Amazon Company alone had murdered nearly 30,000 Indians. Brazil was now Indian-conscious again and its legislators reminded each other of the principles so nobly enunciated by José Bonifacio in 1823, and

embodied in the constitution: 'We must never forget,' Bonifacio said, 'that we are usurpers, in this land, but also that we are
Christians.'

It was a mood responsible for the determination that nothing of this kind should ever happen again, and an Indian Protection Service – unique and extraordinary in its altruism in
America – was founded in 1910 under the leadership of Marshall Rondon, himself an Indian, and therefore, it was supposed, exceptionally qualified to be able to interpret the
Indian's needs.

Rondon's solution was to integrate the Indian into the main-
stream of Brazilian life – to educate him, to change his faith, to
break his habit of nomadism, to change the colour of his skin
by inter-marriage, to draw him away from the forests and into
the cities, to turn him into a wage-earner and a voter. He spent
the last years of his life trying to do this, but just before his
death came a great change of heart. He no longer believed that
integration was to be desired. It had all been, he said now, a
tragic mistake.

The conclusion of all those who have lived among and studied
the Indian beyond the reach of civilisation is that he is the perfect human product of his environment – from which it should
follow that he cannot be removed without calamitous results.
Ensconced in the forest in which his ancestors have lived for
thousands of years, he is as much a component of it as the tapir
and the jaguar: self-sufficient, the artificer of all his requirements, at terms with his surroundings, deeply conscious of his
place in the living patterns of the visible and invisible universe.

It is admitted now that the average Indian Protection Service official recruited to deal with this complicated but satisfactory human being was all too often venal, ignorant and
witless, and it was natural that he should call to his aid the
missionaries who were in Brazil by the thousand, and were
backed by resources that he himself lacked. But the missionary
record was not an imposing one, and even those incomparable
colonisers of the faith, the Jesuits, had little to show but failure.

In the early days they had put their luckless converts into
long white robes, segregated the sexes, and set them to 'godly
labours', lightened by the chanting of psalms in Latin, mind-
developing exercises in mnemonics, and speculative dis-

cussions on such topics as the number of angels able to perch on the point of a pin. It was offered as a foretaste of the delights of the Christian heaven, complete with its absence of marrying or giving in marriage, and many of the converts died of melancholy. After a while demoralisation spread to the fathers themselves and some of them went off the rails to the extent of dabbling in the slave trade. When these settlements were finally overrun by the bloodthirsty pioneers and frontiersmen from São Paolo, death can hardly have been more than a happy release for the listless and bewildered Indian flock.

When the Indian Protection Service was formed the missionaries of the various Catholic orders were rapidly being outnumbered by non-conformists, mostly from the United States. These were a very different order of man, no longer armed only with hellfire and damnation, but with up-to-date techniques of salesmanship in their approach to the problems of conversion. By 1968 the *Jornal de Brasil* could state: *'In reality, those in command of these Indian Protection posts are North American missionaries – they are in all the posts – and they disfigure the original Indian culture and enforce the acceptance of Protestantism.'*

Whereas the Catholics for all their disastrous mistakes, had on the whole led simple, often austere lives, the non-conformists seemed to see themselves as the representatives of a more ebullient and materialistic brand of the faith. They made a point of installing themselves, wherever they went, in large, well-built stone houses, inevitably equipped with an electric generator and every modern labour-saving device. Some of them even had their own planes. If there were roads they had a car or two, and when they travelled by river they preferred a launch with an outboard engine to the native canoe habitually used by the Catholic fathers.

As soon as Indians were attracted to the neighbourhood a mission store might be opened, and the first short step towards the ultimate goal of conversion be taken by the explanation of the value and uses of money, and how with it the Indian could obtain all those goods which it was hoped would become necessary to him. The missionaries are absolutely candid and even self-congratulatory about their methods. To hold the Indian, wants must be created and then continually expanded – wants that in such remote parts only the missionary can supply. A greed for unessential trifles must be inculcated and fostered.

The Portuguese verb employed to describe this process is *conquistar* and it is applied without differentiation to subjection by force or guile. What normally happens is that presents – usually of food – are left where the uncivilised Indians can find them. Great patience is called for. It may be years before the tribesmen are won over by repeated overtures, but when it happens the end is in sight. All that remains is to encourage them to move their village into the mission area, and let things take their natural course.

In nine cases out of ten the local landowner has been waiting for the Indians to make such a move – he may have been alerted by the missionary himself – and as soon as it happens he is ready to occupy the tribal land. The Indians are now trapped. They cannot go back, but at the time it seems unimportant, because for a little longer the missionary continues to feed them, although now the matter of conversion will be broached. This usually presents slight difficulty and natural Indian politeness – and in this case gratitude – accomplishes the rest. Whether the Indian understands what it is all about is another matter. He will be asked to go through what he may regard with great sympathy as a rain-making ceremony, as water is splashed about, and formulae repeated in an unknown language. Beyond that it is likely to be a case of let well alone. Any missionary will tell you that an Indian has no capacity for abstract thought. How can he comprehend the mystery and universality of God when the nearest to a deity his own traditions have to offer may be a common tribal ancestor seen as a jaguar or an alligator?

From now on the orders and the prohibitions will flow thick and fast. The innocence of nudity is first to be destroyed, and the Indian who has never worn anything but a beautifully made and decorated penis-sheath to suppress unexpected erections, must now clothe himself from the mission's store of cast-offs, to the instant detriment of his health. He becomes subject to skin diseases, and since in practice clothes once put on are never taken off again, pneumonia is the frequent outcome of allowing clothing to dry on the body after a rainstorm.

The man who has hitherto lived by practising the skills of the hunter and horticulturist – the Indians are devoted and

156

incomparable gardeners of their kind – now finds himself, broom or shovel in hand as an odd-job man about the mission compound. He shrinks visibly within his miserable, dirty clothing, his face becomes puckered and wizened, his body more disease-ridden, his mind more apathetic. There is a terrible testimony to the process in the Brazilian Ministry of Agriculture's handbook on Indians, in which one is photographed genial and smiling on the first day of his arrival from the jungle, and then the same man who by this time appears to be crazy with grief is shown again, ten years later. 'His expression makes comment unnecessary,' the caption says. 'Ninety per cent. of his people have died of influenza and measles. Little did he imagine the fate that awaited them when they sought their first contact with the whites.'

There is a ring about these stories of enticement down the path to extinction, of the cruel fairy-tale of children trapped by the witch in the house made of ginger bread and barley sugar. But even the slow decay, the living death of the missionaries' compound was not the worst that could happen. What could be far more terrible would be the decision of the fazendeiro – as so often happened – to recruit the labour of the Indians whose lands he had invaded, and who were left to starve.

Extract from the atrocity commission's report: *'In his evidence Senhor Jordao Aires said that eight years before the (600) Ticuna Indians were brought by Fray Jeremias to his estate. The missionary succeeded in convincing them that the end of the world was about to take place, and Belem was the only place where they would be safe ... Senhor Aires confirmed that when the Indians disobeyed his orders his private police chained them hand and foot. Federal Police Delegate Neves said that some of the Indians thus chained were lepers, and had lost their fingers.'*

Officially it is the Indian Protection Service and 134 of its agents that are on trial, but from all these reports the features of a more sinister personality soon emerge, the fazendeiro – the great landowner – and in his shadow the IPS agent shrinks to a subservient figure, too often corrupted by bribes.

One would have wished to find an English equivalent for this Portuguese word *fazendeiro*, but there is none. Titles such as landowner or estate owner which call to mind nothing harsher than the mild despotism of the English class system will not do. The fazendeiro by European standards is huge in anachronistic power, often the lord of a tropical fief as large as an English county, protected from central authority's interference by vast distances, the traditions of submission, and the absolute silence of his vassals. All the lands he holds – much of which may not even have been explored – have been taken by him or by his ancestors from the Indians, or has been bought from others who have obtained it in this way. In most cases his great fortress-like house, the fazenda, has been built by the labour of the Indian slaves, who have been imprisoned when necessary in its dungeons. In the past a fazendeiro could only survive by his domination of a ferocious environment, and although in these days he will probably have had a university education, he may still sleep with a loaded rifle beside his bed. Lonely fazendas are still occasionally attacked by wild Indians (i.e. Indians with a grievance against the whites), by gold prospectors turned bandit, by down-right professional bandits themselves, or by their own mutinous slaves. The fazendeiro defends himself by a bodyguard enrolled from the toughest of his workers – many of them, in the backwoods, fugitives from justice.

It has often been hard by ordinary Christian standards for the fazendeiro to be a good man, only too easy for him to degenerate into a Gilles de Raïs, or some murderous and unpredictable Ivan the Terrible of the Amazon forests. It can be Eisenstein's *Thunder Over Mexico* complete with the horses galloping over men buried up to their necks – or worse. Some of the stories told about the great houses of Brazil of the last century in their days of respectable slavery and Roman licence bring the imagination to a halt: a male slave accused of some petty crime castrated and burned alive ... a pretty young girl's teeth ordered by her jealous mistress to be drawn, and her breasts amputated, to be on the safe side ... another, found pregnant, thrown alive into the kitchen furnace.

An extract from the report by the President of last year's inquiry commission into atrocities against the Indians corrects the complacent viewpoint that we live in milder days.

'In the 7th Inspectorate, Paraná, Indians were tortured by grinding the bones of their feet in the angle of two wooden stakes, driven into the ground. Wives took turns with their husbands in applying this torture.'

It is alleged, as well, in this investigation, that there were

158

cases of an Indian's naked body being smeared with honey
before leaving him to be bitten to death by ants.

Why all this pointless cruelty? What is it that causes men
and women probably of extreme respectability in their everyday lives to torture for the sake of torturing? Montaigne
believed that cruelty is the revenge of the weak man for
his weakness; a sort of sickly parody of valour. 'The killing
after a victory is usually done by the rabble and baggage
officials.'

It is the beginning of the rainy reason, and from an altitude of
2,000 feet the forest smokes here and there as if under sporadic
bombardment, while the sun sucks up the vapour from a local
downpour.

The Mato Grosso seen from the air is supposed to offer
a scene of montonous green, but this is not always so. At this
moment, for example, a pitch-black swamp lapped by ivory
sands presents itself. It is obscured by shifting feathers of
cloud, which part again to show a Cheddar Gorge in lugubri-
ous reds. The forest returns, pitted with lakes which appear to
contain not water but brilliant chemical solutions; copper
sulphate, gentian violet. The air taxi settles wobbling to a
scrubbed patch of earth and vultures go by like black rags.

All these small towns in this meagre earth are the same. An
unpronounceable Guaraní name for a street of clapboard,
tapering off to mud and palm thatch at each end; a general
store, a hotel, Laramie-style with men asleep on the verandah;
a scarecrow horse, bones about to burst through the hide, tied
up in a square yard of shade; hairy pigs; aromatic dust blown
up by the hot breeze.

Life is in slow motion and on a small scale. The store sells
cigarettes, meticulously bisected if necessary with a razor
blade, ladlefuls of mandioca flour, little piles of entrails for
soup, purgative pills a half-inch in diameter, and handsomely-
tooled gun holsters. The customers come in not to buy but to
be there, wandering through the paper-chains of dusty dried
fish hanging from the ceiling. They are Indians, but so de-
racialised by the climate of boredom and their grubby cotton
clothing, that they could be Eskimos or Vietnamese. They
have the expression of men gazing, narrow-eyed, into crystal
balls, and they speak in childish voices of great sweetness. Like

Indians everywhere, the smallest intake of alcohol produces an instant deadly change.

The only entertainment the town offers is a cartomancer, operating largely on a barter basis. He tells fortunes in a negative but realistic way, concerned not so much with good luck, but the avoidance of bad. All the children's eyes are rimmed with torpid, hardly moving flies. The fazenda, some miles away, has absorbed everything; owns the whole town, even the main street itself.

This is a place where cruelty is supposed to have happened, but the surface of things has been patched and renovated and the aroma of atrocity has dispersed. Everything can be explained away now in terms of extreme exaggeration, or the malice of political enemies, and all the witnesses for the defence have been mustered. Finally, the everyday violences of a violent country are quoted to remind one that this is not Europe.

Senhor Fulano lives with his family in three rooms in one of the few brick-built houses. His position is ambiguous. An ex-Indian Protection Service agent, he has been cleared of financial malpractices, and hopes shortly for employment in the new Foundation. He has an Abyssinian face with melancholy, faintly disdainful eyes, a high Nilotic forehead, and a delicate Semite nose. He is proud of the fact that his father was half Negro, half Jewish; a trader who captured in marriage a robust girl from one of the Indian tribes.

'Not all fazendeiros are bad,' Fulano says. 'Far from it. On the contrary, the majority are good men. People are jealous of their success, and they are on the look-out for a way to damage them.

'In the case you mention the man was a thief and a trouble maker. As a punishment he was locked in a shed, nothing more. He was drunk, you understand, and he set fire to the shed himself. He died in the fire, yes, but the doctor certified accidental death. There was no case for a police inquiry. In thirty years' service I have only seen one instance of violence – if you wish to call it violence. The Indians were drunk with *cachaça* again, and they attacked the post. They were given a chance by firing over their heads, but it didn't stop them. They were mad with liquor. What could we do? There's no blood on my hands.' He holds them up as if for confirmation. They are small and well cared for with pale, pinkish palms. His wife rattles about out of sight in the scullery of their tiny flat. There is a picture of the President on the wall, and another of his little girl dressed for her first communion, and no evidence in the cheap, ugly furniture that Senhor Fulano has been able to feather his nest to any useful extent.

He joined the service out of a sense of vocation, he says. 'We were all young and idealistic. They paid us less than they paid a postman, but nobody gave any thought to that. We were going to dedicate our lives to the service of our less fortunate fellow men. If anyone happened to live in Rio de Janeiro, the Minister himself would see him when he was posted, and shake hands with him and wish him good luck. I happened to be a country boy, but my friends hired a band to see me off to the station. Everybody insisted in giving me a present. I had so many lace handkerchiefs I could have opened a shop. There was a lot of prestige in being in the service in those days.'

There are three whitish, glossy pock-marks in the slope of each cheek under the sad, Amharic eyes, and it is difficult not to watch them. He shakes his head. 'No-one would believe the conditions some of us lived under. They used to show you photographs of the kind of place where you'd be working; a house with a verandah, the school and the dispensary. When I went to my first post I wept like a child when I saw it. The journey took a month and in the meanwhile the man I was supposed to be assisting had died of the smallpox. I remember the first thing I saw was a dead Indian in the water where they tied up the boat. I'd hit a measles epidemic. Half the roof of the house had caved in. There never had been a school, and there wasn't a bottle of aspirin in the place. When the sun went down the mosquitoes were so thick, they were on your skin like fur.'

He finds a book of press-cuttings in which are recorded the meagre occasions of his life. A picture shows him in dark suit and stiff collar receiving a certificate and the congratulations of a politician for his work as a civiliser. In another he is shown posing at the side of Miss Pernambuco 1952, and in another he is a paternal presence at a ceremony when a newly pacified tribe are to put on their first clothing. There are 'before' and 'after' pictures of the tribal women, first naked and then in jumpers and skirts, not only changed but facially unrecognis-

161

able from one minute to the next, as if some malignant spell had been laid upon them as they wriggled into the shapeless garments. The few cuttings scanned through out of politeness speak of Senhor Fulano as the pattern of self abnegation, and the words *servicio* and *devoçao* constantly reappear. 'My pay was 100 new cruzeiros (£12) a month,' he says, 'and it was sometimes up to six months overdue. In the first year only, I had measles, jaundice and malaria three times. If it hadn't have been for the fazendeiro I'd have died. He looked after me like a father. He was a man of the greatest possible principles, and among many other benefactions he gave 100,000 cruzeiros to a church in Salvador. I see now that his son's been formally charged with invading Indian lands. All I can say to that is, what the Indians would do without him, I don't know.'

Fulano is nothing if not loyal. 'Fazendeiros are no different from anyone else,' he says. 'They try to make out they're monsters these days. You mustn't believe all you read.'

It was certain that no-one would be found now in this town to contradict him.

For a half-century rubber had been the great destroyer of the Indian, and then suddenly it changed to speculation in land. Rumour spread of huge mineral resources awaiting exploitation in the million square miles that were inaccessible until recently – and the great speculative rush was on. Nowhere, however remote, however sketchily mapped, was secure from the surveyors sent by the fazendeiros, the politicians and the real-estate companies to measure out their claims. Back in São Paolo, the headquarters of the land boom, the *grileiro* – specialist in shady land deals – went into secret partnerships with his friend in the Government, who was in a position to see that the deals went through. A great deal of this apparently empty land was only empty to the extent that it contained no white settlements, and the map-makers had not yet put in the rivers and the mountains. There might well be Indians there – nobody knew until it had been explored – but this possibility introduced only a slight inconvenience. In theory the undisturbed possession of all land occupied by Indians is guaranteed to them by the Brazilian constitution, but if it can be shown that Indian land has been abandoned it reverts to the Government, after which it can be sold in the ordinary way. The grileiro's task is to discover or manufacture evidence that such land is no longer in occupation – a problem, if sincerely confronted, complicated by the fact that most Indians are semi-nomadic, cultivating crops in one area during the period of the summer rains, then moving elsewhere to hunt and fish during the dry winter season.

A short cut to the solution of the problem is simply to drive the Indians out. Other grileiros quite simply ignore its existence, offering land to the gullible by map reference, sight unseen, and hoping to be able to settle the legal difficulties by political manipulations at some later date.

The grileiro with his manoeuvrings behind the scenes was kept under some control while President João Goulart was in power, and it finally became clear to the big-scale land speculators that they were going to get nowhere until they got a new President. Goulart, although a rich landowner himself, held the opinion that Brazil would never occupy the place in the Western Hemisphere to which its colossal size and resources entitled it, while it limped along in its feudalistic way with an 86 per cent. illiteracy figure and the land in the hands of an infinitesimally small minority, many of which made no effort to develop it in any way. The remedy he proposed was to redistribute 3 per cent. of privately-owned land, but also – what was far more serious – he announced the resuscitation of an old law permitting the Government to nationalise land up to six miles in depth on each side of the national means of communication – roads, railways and canals.

This would have been a death blow to the speculators, who hoped to resell their land at many times the price they had paid, as soon as it was made accessible by the building of roads. One such firm had advertised 100,000 acres of land for sale in the English Press. The land was offered in 100-acre minimum lots of £5 an acre. An initial purchase of land had already been sold, the company announced, 'mainly to investment houses and trusts, insurance companies and a number of syndicates.' A charter flight would be arranged for buyers from Manchester, Birmingham, Glasgow, Edinburgh and Liverpool, and representatives of Kenya farmers who had already bought 50,000 acres. 'There is little hope,' said the promotion literature, 'of any return from the purchase of the land for a few years yet.'

But in 1964 the speculative prospects brightened enormously when a *coup d'état* was staged to depose the troublesome Goulart, and the land rush could go ahead. A promotional assault was launched on the United States market with lavishly produced and cunningly-worded brochures offering glamour as well as profit, and phrased in the poetic style of American car advertisements. Amazon Adventure Estates were offered, and there were allusions to monkeys and macaws and the occult glitter of gems in the banks of mighty rivers sailed by the ships of Orellana. They had some success. A number of film stars took a gamble in the Mato Grosso. In April, 1968, in fact, a Brazilian deputy, Haroldo Veloso, revealed that most of the area of the mouth of the Amazon had passed into the hands of foreigners. He mentioned that Prince Rainier of Monaco had bought land in the Mato Grosso twelve times larger than the principality, whereas someone, stabbing presumably with a pencil point at a map, had picked up the highest mountain in Brazil – the Pico de Nieblina – for an old song, although it would have taken a properly equipped expedition a matter of weeks to reach it.

This was doomsday for the tribes who had been pacified and settled in areas where they could be conveniently dealt with. Down in the plains on the frontiers with Paraguay it was the end of the road for the Kadiweus. In 1865 in the war against Paraguay they had taken their spears and ridden naked, bare-backed, but impeccably painted – a fantastic Charge of the Light Brigade, at the head of the Brazilian army – to rout the cavalry of the psychopathic Paraguayan dictator Solano Lopez. For their aid in the war the Emperor Pedro II had received their principal chief, clad for the occasion in a loin-cloth sewn with precious stones, and granted the Kadiweu nation in perpetuity two million acres of the borderland. Here these Spartans of the West – poets and artists who practised infanticide, adopting the children of other tribes when they were old enough to ride horses – were reduced now to 200 survivors, working as the cowhands of fazendeiros who had taken all their lands.

It was doomsday too for Lévi-Strauss's Bororos. The great anthropologist had lived for several years among them in the 1930s, and they had led him to the conclusions of 'structural anthropology', including the proposition that 'a primitive people is not a backward or retarded people, indeed it may possess a genius for invention or action that leaves the achievements of civilised people far behind'. He had said of the Bororos, 'few people are so profoundly religious ... few possess a metaphysical system of such complexity. Their spiritual beliefs and everyday activities are inextricably mixed'. They had been living for some years now far from the complicated villages where Lévi-Strauss studied them, in the Teresa Cristina reserve in the South Mato Grosso, given them 'in perpetuity', as ever, in tribute to the memory of the great Marshall Rondon, who had been part-Bororo himself.

Life in the reserve was far from happy for the Bororos. They were hunters, and fishermen, and in their way excellent agriculturists, but the reserve was small, and there was no game left and the rivers in the area had been illegally fished-out by commercial firms operating on a big scale, and there was no room to practise cultivation in the old-fashioned semi-nomadic way. The Government had tried to turn them into cattle-raisers, but they knew nothing of cattle. Many of their cows were quietly sold off by agents of the Indian Protection Service, who pocketed the money. Others – as the Bororos had no idea of building corrals – wandered out of the reservation, and were impounded by neighbouring fazendeiros. The Indians ate the few cows that remained before they could die of disease or starvation, after which they were reduced to the normal diet of hard times – lizards, locusts and snakes – plus an occasional handout of food from one of the missions.

They suffered, too, from the great emptiness and aimlessness of the Indian whose traditional culture has been destroyed. The missionaries, upon whom they were wretchedly dependent, forbade dancing, singing or smoking, and while they accepted with inbred stoicism this attack on the principle of pleasure, there was a fourth prohibition against which they continually rebelled, but in vain.

The Indians are obsessed by their relationship with the dead, and by the condition of the souls of the dead in the afterlife – a concern reflected in the manner of the ancient Egyptians by the most elaborate funerary rites – orgies of grief and intoxication, sometimes lasting for days. The Bororos, seemingly unable to part with their dead, bury them twice, and the custom is at the emotional basis of their lives. In the first instance – as if in hope of some miraculous revival – the body is placed in a temporary grave, in the centre of the village, and covered with branches. When decomposition is advanced, the flesh is removed from the bones, which are painted and lovingly adorned with feathers, after which final burial takes place in the depths of the forest. The outlawing of this custom by an American missionary reduced the Bororos to despair, but the missionary was able to persuade the local police to enforce the ban, and the party of half-starved tribesmen who dragged themselves 200 miles on foot to the State capital and presented themselves, weeping, to the *comissario* were turned away.

Final catastrophe followed the devolution by the Federal Government of certain of its powers – particularly those relating to the ownership and sale of land – to the Legislative Assembly of the Mato Grosso State. This at once invoked a law by which land that, after a certain time limit, had not been legally measured and demarcated, reverted to the Government. It was a legal device which saddled Indians, many of whom did not even realise that they were living in Brazil, with the responsibility of employing lawyers to look after their interests. It had been employed once before, and with additional refinements of trickery, in an attempt to snatch away the last of the land of the unfortunate Kadiweus. On this occasion it seems that only two copies of the official publication recording the enactment were available, one of which had been lodged in the State archives, and the other taken the same day to the reserve by the persons proposing to share the land between them.

Hardly less haste was shown in the occupation of the Teresa Cristina reserve. It was a muddled, untidy operation, and it turned out in the end that considerably more land had been sold on paper than the actual area of the reserve. This was before the final demoralisation and collapse of the Indian Protection Service, and local officials not only challenged the legality of the sale but called in vain for State troops to be sent to repel an invason of fazendeiros supported by their private armies carrying sub-machine guns.

The state of affairs that had come to pass at Teresa Cristina only five years later, in 1968, is depicted in the testimony of a Bororo Indian girl. 'There were two fazendas, one called Teresa, where the Indians worked as slaves. They took me from my mother when I was a child. Afterwards I heard that they hung my mother up all night ... She was very ill and I wanted to see her before she died ... When I got back they thrashed me with a raw-hide whip ... They prostituted the Indian girls ... One day the IPS agent called an old carpenter and told him to make an oven for the farmhouse. When the carpenter had finished the agent asked him what he wanted for doing the job. The carpenter said he wanted an Indian girl, and the agent took him to the school and told him to choose one. No-one saw or heard any more of her ... Not even the children escaped. From two years of age they worked under the whip ... There was a mill for crushing the cane, and to save the horses they used four children to turn the mill ... They forced the Indian Otaviano to beat his own mother ... The Indians were used for target practice.'

Thus were the Indians disarmed, betrayed, and hustled down the path towards final extinction. Yet in the heart of the Mato Grosso and the Amazon forests, there were tribes that still held out. Classified by the Government manual on Indians as *isolados*, they are described as those that possess the greatest physical vigour. Nobody knows how many such tribes there are. There may be 300 or more with a total population of 50,000, including tiny, self-contained and apparently indestructible nations having their own completely separate language, organisation and customs. Some of these people are giants with herculean limbs, armed with immense longbows of the kind an archer at Crécy might have used. A few groups are ethnically mysterious with blue eyes and fairish hair, provokers of wild theories among Amazonian travellers, that there is one tribe supposed by some to have migrated to these forests some 2,000 years ago from the island of Hokkaido in Japan. One common factor unites them all; a brilliant fitness for survival – until now. For 400 years they have avoided the slavers and lived through the epidemics. They have armed themselves with constant alertness. They have been ready to embrace a new tactical nomadism. They have made distrust the greatest of their virtues. Above all, their chieftains have had the intelligence and the strength to reject those deadly offerings left outside their villages by which the whites seek first to buy their friendship, then take away their freedom.

The Cintas Largas were one such tribe living in magnificent if precarious isolation in the upper reaches of the Aripuaná River. There were about 500 of them, occupying several villages.

They used stone axes, tipped their arrows with curare, caught small fish by poisoning the water, played four-feet long flutes made from gigantic bamboos, and celebrated two great annual feasts: one of the initiation of young girls at puberty, and the other of the dead. At both of these they were said to use some unknown herbal concoction to produce ritual drunkenness. They were in a region still dependent for its meagre revenues on wild rubber, and this exposed them to routine attacks by rubber tappers, against whom they had learned to defend themselves. Their tragedy was that deposits of rare metals were being found in the area. What these metals were, it was not clear. Some sort of a security blackout had been imposed, only fitfully penetrated by vague news reports of the activities of American and European companies, and of the smuggling of plane-loads of the said rare metals back to the USA.

David St Clair in his book *The Mighty Mighty Amazon* (Souvenir Press, 1968) mentions the existence of companies who specialised in dealing with tribes when their presence came to be considered a nuisance, attacking their villages with famished dogs, and shooting down everyone who tried to escape. Such expeditions depended for their success on the assistance of a navigable river which would carry the attacking party to within striking distance of the village or villages to be destroyed. The Beiços de Pau had been reached in this way and dealt with by the gifts of foodstuffs mixed with poisons, but the two inches on the small-scale map of Brazil separating these two neighbouring tribes contained unexplored mountain ranges, and the single river ran in the wrong direction. The Cintas Largas, then, remained for the time being out of reach. In 1962, a missionary, John Dornstander, had reached and made an attempt to pacify them but he had given them up as a bad job.

The plans for disposing of the Cintas Largas were laid in Aripuaná. This small festering tropical version of Dodge City 1860 has the face and physique of all such Latin-American hell-holes, populated by hopeless men who remain there simply because for one reason or other, they cannot leave. A row of wooden huts on stilts stand in the hard sunshine down by the river. Swollen-bellied children squat to delouse each other; dogs eat excrement; vultures limp and balance on the edge of a ditch full of black sewage; the driver of an ox-cart urges on the animal wreckage of hide and bones by jabbing with a stick under its tail. Everyone carries a gun. Cachaça offers oblivion at a shilling a pint, but boredom rots the mind. There are two classes: those who impose suffering, and the utterly servile. In this case nine-tenths of the working population are rubber tappers, and most of them fugitives from justice.

It is cheap and sometimes effective – besides being the quite normal procedure where a tribe's villages are beyond reach – to bribe other Indians to attack them; and this was tried in the first instance with the Cintas Largas. The Kayabis, neighbours both of the Cintas Largas and the Beiços de Pau, had been dispersed when the State of Mato Grosso sold their land to various commercial enterprises, part of the tribe migrating to a distant range of mountains, while a small group that had split off remained in this Aripuaná area, where it lived in destitution. This group took the food and guns that they were offered in down-payment, and then decamped in the opposite direction and no more was seen of them.

Later a *garimpa* – an organised body of diamond prospectors – appeared in the neighbourhood. They were all in very bad shape through malnutritional disorders. They had attacked an Indian village and had been beaten off and then ambushed, and several of them were wounded. The intention had been to capture at least one woman, not only for sexual uses, but as a source of supply of the fresh female urine believed to be a certain cure for the infected sores from which garimpeiros habitually suffer, and which are caused by the stingrays abounding in the rivers in which they work. Garimpeiros are organised under a captain who supplies their food and equipment, and to whom they are bound – under pain of being abandoned in the forest to die of starvation – to sell their diamonds. Like the rubber tappers – who are their traditional enemies – they are mostly wanted by the police. The feud existing between these two types of desperado is based on the rubber tappers' habit of stalking and shooting the lonely garimpeiro, in the hope that

he may be found with a diamond or two. In this case emiss-
aries arranged a truce, and the garimpeiros were brought into
town, and given food; a company doctor patched up the
wounded men. Common action against the Cintas Largas was
then proposed, and the captain fell in with the suggestion and
agreed to detach six men for this purpose as soon as everyone
was fully rested. In the condition in which he found himself, he
may have been ready to agree to anything, but by the time the
garimpeiros had put on a little flesh and their wounds had
cleared up, there was an abrupt cooling in the climate of
amity. Aripuaná was not a big enough town to contain two
such trigger-happy personalities as the garimpa captain and
the overseer of the rubber tappers. For a while the poverty-
stricken rubber tappers put up with it, while the affluent
garimpeiros swaggered in the bars, and monopolised the
town's prostitutes. Then, inevitably, the *entente cordiale* foundered in gunplay.

In 1963 a series of expeditions were now organised under the
leadership of Francisco de Brito, general overseer of the rubber
extraction firm of Arruda Junqueira of Juina-Mirim near Aripuaná, on the river Juruana.

De Brito was a legendary monster who kept order among
the ruffians he commanded by a .45 automatic and a five-foot
tapir-hide whip. He was a joker with Indians, and when one
was captured he was taken on what was known as 'the visit to
the dentist', being ordered to 'open wide' whereupon De Brito
drew a pistol and shot him through his mouth. There was a
lively competition among the rubber men for the title of cham-
pion Indian killer, and although this was claimed by De Brito,
local opinion was that his score was bettered by one of his
underlings who specialised in casual sniping from the river
banks.

The expeditions mounted by De Brito were successful in
clearing the Cintas Largas from an area, insignificant by Brazilian standards, although about half as big as England south
of the Thames; but there remained a large village considered
inaccessible on foot or by canoe, and it was decided to attack
this by plane. At this stage it is evident that a better type of
brain began to interest itself in these operations, and whoever
planned the air-attack was clearly at some pains to find out all
he could about the customs of the Cintas Largas.

It was seen as essential to produce the maximum number of casualties in one single, devastating attack, at a time when as many Indians as possible would be present in the village, and an expert was found to advise that this could best be done at the annual feast of the *Quarup*. This great ceremony lasts for a day and a night, and under one name or another it is conducted by almost all the Indian tribes whose culture has not been destroyed. The *Quarup* is a theatrical representation of the legends of creation interwoven with those of the tribe itself, both a mystery play and a family reunion attended not only by the living but the ancestral spirits. These appear as dancers in masquerade, to be consulted on immediate problems, to comfort the mourners, to testify that not even death can disrupt the unity of the tribe.

A Cessna light plane used for ordinary commercial services was hired for the attack, and its normal pilot replaced by an adventurer of mixed Italian-Japanese birth. It was loaded with sticks of dynamite – 'bananas' they are called in Brazil – and took off from a jungle airstrip near Aripuaná. The Cessna arrived over the village at about midday. The Indians had been preparing themselves all night by prayer and singing, and now they were all gathered in the open space in the village's centre. On the first run, packets of sugar were dropped to calm the fears of those who had scattered and run for shelter at the sight of the plane. They had opened the packets and were tasting the sugar ten minutes later when it returned to carry out the attack. No-one has ever been able to find out how many Indians were killed, because the bodies were buried in the bank of the river and the village deserted.

But even this solution proved not to be final. Survivors had been spotted from the air and were reported to be building fresh settlements in the upper reaches of the Aripuaná, and once again De Brito got together an overland force.

They were to be led, in canoes, by one Chico, a De Brito underling. The full story of what happened was described by a member of the force, Ataide Pereira, who, troubled by his conscience and also by the fact that he had never been paid the fifteen dollars promised him for his bloody deeds, went to confess them to a Padre Edgar Smith, a Jesuit priest, who took his statement on a tape recorder and then handed the tape to the Indian Protection Service.

'We went by launch up the Juruana,' Ataide says. 'There were six of us, men of experience, commanded by Chico, who used to shove his tommy-gun in your direction whenever he gave you an order!' (Chico, it was to turn out, was no mere average sadist of the Brazilian badlands. For this kind of Latin American – and they have been the executioners of so many revolutions – the ultimate excitement lies in the maniac use of the machete on their victims, and it was to use this machete that Chico had gone on this expedition.) 'It took a good many days upstream to the Serra do Norte. After that we lost ourselves in the woods, although Chico had brought a Japanese compass with us. In the end the plane found us. It was the same plane they used to massacre the Indians, and they threw us down some provisions and ammunition. After that we went on for five days. Then we ran out of food again. We came across an Indian village that had been wiped out by a gang led by a gunman called Tenente, and we dug up some of the Indians' mandioca for food and caught a few small fish. By this time we were fed up and some of us wanted to go back, but Chico said he'd kill anybody who tried to desert. It was another five days after that before we saw any smoke. Even then the Cintas Largas were days away. We were all pretty scared of each other. In this kind of place people shoot each other and get shot, you might say without knowing why.

When they drill a hole in you, they have this habit of sticking an Indian arrow in the wound, to put the blame on the Indians.'

This expedition breathed in the air of fear. Ataide reports that there were diamonds and gold in all the rivers, and the shadow of the garimpeiro stalked them from behind every rock and tree. A violent death would claim most of these men sooner or later. Premature middle-age brought on by endless fever, malnutrition, exhaustion, hopelessness and drink overtook the rubber-tappers in their late twenties, and few lived to see their thirtieth birthday. An infection turning to gangrene or blood-poisoning would carry them off; or they would die in an ugly fashion, paralysed, blind and mad from some obscure tropical disease; or they would simply kill each other in a sudden neurotic outburst of hate provoked by nothing in particular – for a bet, or in a brawl over some sickly prostitute picked up at a village dance.

Hacking their way through this sunless forest a month or more's march from the dreadful barracks that was their home, they were dependent for survival on the psychopathic Chico and his Japanese compass. It was the beginning of the rainy season when, after a morning of choking heat, sudden storms would drench them every afternoon. They were plagued with freshly-hatched insects, worst of all the myriads of almost invisible *piums* that burrow into the skin to gorge themselves with blood, and against which the only defence is a coating of grime on every exposed part of the body. Some of the men were blistered from the burning sap squirted on them from the lianas they cut into.

'We were hand-picked for the job,' Ataide says, with a lack-lustre attempt at *esprit de corps*, 'as quiet as any Indian party when it came to slipping in and out of trees. When we got to Cintas Largas country there were no more fires and no talking. As soon as we spotted their village we made a stop for the night. We got up before dawn, then we dragged ourselves yard by yard through the underbrush till we were in range, and after that we waited for the sun to come up.

As soon as it was light the Indians all came out and started to work on some huts they were building. Chico had given me the job of seeking out the chief and killing him. I noticed there was one of these Indians who wasn't doing any work. All he did was to lean on a rock and boss the others about, and this gave me the idea he must be the man we were after. I told Chico and he said, 'Take care of him, and leave the rest to me,' and I got him in the chest with the first shot. I was supposed to be the marksman of the team, and although I only have an ancient carbine, I can safely say I never miss. Chico gave the chief a burst with his tommy gun to make sure, and after that he let the rest of them have it ... all the other fellows had to do was to finish off anyone who showed signs of life.

'What I'm coming to now is brutal, and I was all against it. There was a young Indian girl they didn't shoot, with a kid of about five in one hand, yelling his head off. Chico started after her and I told him to hold it, and he said, 'All these bastards have to be knocked off.' I said, 'Look, you can't do that—what are the padres going to say about it when you get back?' He just wouldn't listen. He shot the kid through the head with his

45, and then he grabbed hold of the woman – who by the way was very pretty. 'Be reasonable,' I said. 'Why do you have to kill her?' In my view, apart from anything else, it was a waste. 'What's wrong with giving her to the boys?' I said. 'They haven't set eyes on a woman for six weeks. Or failing that we could take her back with us and make a present of her to De Brito. There's no harm in keeping in with him.' All he said was, 'If any man wants a woman he can go and look for her in the forest.'

'We all thought he'd gone off his head, and we were pretty scared of him. He tied the Indian girl up and hung her head downwards from a tree, legs apart, and chopped her in half right down the middle with his machete. Almost with a single stroke I'd say. The village was like a slaughter-house. He calmed down after he'd cut the woman up, and told us to burn down all the huts and throw the bodies into the river. After that we grabbed our things and started back. We kept going until nightfall and we took care to cover our tracks. If the Indians had found us it wouldn't have been much use trying to kid them we were just ordinary backwoodsmen. It took us six weeks to find the Cintas Largas, and about a week to get back. I want to say now that personally I've nothing against Indians. Chico found some minerals and took them back to keep the company pleased. The fact is the Indians are sitting on valuable land and doing nothing with it. They've got a way of finding the best plantation land and there's all these valuable minerals about too. They have to be persuaded to go, and if all else fails, well then, it has to be force.'

De Brito, the man who organised this expedition, was to die within a year of it in the most horrific circumstances. When he found cause for complaint in one of his men he would normally tie him up and thrash him until the blood ran down and squelched in the man's boots, but in a aggravated case he would have one of his henchmen use the whip while he raped the culprit's wife as the punishment was being inflicted. An Italian called Cavalcanti, who tried to attack the overseer after receiving the more serious punishment, was promptly shot dead and his body burned. A revolt of the rubber tappers followed in which nine men were killed. De Brito when cornered was like Rasputin, very difficult to disable, and absorbed several bullets and a thrust in the stomach with a machete before he went down. After this he was stripped, the bowels plugged back with a tampon of straw, then dragged still alive into the open and left 'for the ants'.

How many Indian hunts of the kind mounted against the Cintras Largas must have gone unnoticed in the past, condemned at worst as a necessary evil? Ataide speaks of them as if they were commonplace, and the likelihood is confirmed by a statement, made to the police inspector of the 3rd Divisional Area of Cuiabá Salgado who investigated the case, by a Padre Valdemar Veber. The Padre said, 'It is not the first time that the firm of Arruda Junqueira has committed crimes against the Indians. A number of expeditions have been organised in the past. This firm acts as a cover for other undertakings who are interested in acquiring land, or who plan to exploit the rich mineral deposits existing in this area.'

When one considers the miasmic climate of subjection in which these remote rubber baronies operate, in which the voice raised in protest can be instantly suffocated, and as many false witnesses as required created at the lifting of a finger, it seems extraordinary that police action could ever have been contemplated against Arruda Junqueira. It appears even more so when one surveys the sparse judicial resources of the area.

Denunciations of the kind made by Ataide lie forgotten in police files by the hundred, simply because the police have learned not to waste their strength in attempting the impossible. Nine major crimes out of ten probably never come to light. The problem of the disposal of the body – so powerful a deterrent to murder – does not exist where it can be thrown into the nearest stream, where – if a cayman does not dispose of it – the piranhás can reduce it to a clean skeleton in a matter of minutes.

In the case of the brazen and contemptuous tenth, where a man murders his victim in public view, and makes not the slightest attempt to hide the crime, he knows he is under the powerful protection of distance and inaccessibility. Aripuaná is 600 miles from Cuiabá, the capital and seat of justice of Mato Grosso, and it can be reached only by irregular planes. Moreover at the time Inspector Salgado began his investigation, about 1,000 criminal cases were awaiting trial in

Cuiabá, where, since the tiny local lock-up can accommodate some 50 persons (all ages and sexes are kept together), most criminals manage to remain at liberty awaiting their trial, which may be long delayed.

Salgado's task was immediately complicated by factors unrelated to the normal frustrations of geography and communications. Ataide, principal witness and self-confessed murderer, was now the owner of a sweet stall on the streets of Cuiabá, and could be picked up at any time, but other essential witnesses were beginning to disappear. Two of the members of Chico's expedition had managed to drown themselves 'while on fishing trips'. The pilot of the plane used in the attack on the Cintas Largas was reported to have been killed in a plane crash. De Brito had of course been murdered in the rubber tappers' revolt, and even Padre Smith, who had taped Ataide's confession, could not be found.

Despite the series of contretemps, Salgado completed the police's case against Antonio Junqueira and Sebastião Arruda exactly three years after his investigations had begun, and the documents were sent to the judge. Under Brazilian law, however, the next procedure is the formal charge, the *denuncia*, which must be made by the public prosecutor, and it now became evident that the case might never surmount this hurdle. In all such countries as Brazil where a middle class is only just emerging, the landed aristocracy and the heads of great commercial firms are almost impregnably protected from the consequences of misdemeanour by dynastic marriages, interlocking interests and the mutual security pacts of men with powerful political friends. This is by no means an exclusively Latin American phenomenon, even, and is equally prevalent in Mediterranean Europe.

In this case the public prosecutor, Sr Luis Vidal da Fonseca, promptly objected that the case could not be tried in Cuiabá because Aripuaná came under the jurisdiction, he said, of Diamantino. The papers were therefore sent to Diamantino where the judge immediately sent them back to Cuiabá. The question being referred to the supreme judiciary, it was ruled that the trial should take place in Cuiabá. So far only a month had been lost.

Fonseca now claimed exemption from officiating on the grounds that he was lawyer to the firm of Arruda and Junqueira. A second public prosecutor refused to be saddled with this embarrassing obligation, and the judge of the Cuiabá assize agreed with him and turned down Fonseca's application. Fonseca then applied to the supreme court again for an annulment of the local decision. The application was refused. By now nine months had been used up in manoeuvres of this kind, and it was April 1967.

At this point an attempt was made to settle these difficulties, to the satisfaction of all concerned, by the appointment of a substitute public prosecutor – who immediately claimed exemption on the grounds of his wife's somewhat remote relationship with Sebastião Arruda. The plea was accepted and another public prosecutor found, who declined to officiate, basing his refusal on the legal invalidity of Fonseca's objection. All papers were therefore returned to Fonseca.

In September 1967 a fourth substitute public prosecutor was appointed who, instead of taking action, sent the papers to the Attorney General who confirmed the original decision that Fonseca, who had moved away, was competent to act. This was followed by an endless bandying of legal quibbles and the appearance and departure of a succession of substitute prosecutors until March 1968 when the Attorney General was goaded to a protest: 'Since August 1966 the papers relating to this case have been shuffled about in an endless game of farcical excuses and pretexts, to the grave detriment of the prestige of justice.' Thus encouraged, the eighth or ninth substitute public prosecutor took action, and made a formal charge against the murderers of the Cintas Largas nearly all of whom were by now, after five years, either dead or not to be found. The names of Antonio Junqueira and Sebastião Arruda were omitted from the *denuncia* 'as their assent to the massacre of the Indians has never been established'. At this, the police attempted to take the law into their own hands by ordering the two men's preventive arrest. This could not be carried out, because they had gone into hiding.

One reads the history of the four years' legal battle against the firm of Arruda and Junqueira, and the imagination reels at the thought of what lies in store for the champions of justice for the Indians – the practised and methodical wasting of time, the pleas for exemption, the demands for re-trials, the appeals and the counter-appeals, while the months run into years, and the years into decades, and the Indian slowly vanishes from the earth.

And when, if ever, after all the lawsuits are settled, a little land is wrested back from the great banks, the corporations, the fazendeiros, the timber and mining concessionaires that now hold it – still what is to be done? Can the mission hanger-on, miraculously refurbished in body and spirit, return once again to the free life of the *isolado*? Does any remedy exist for the Indian, who, when the great day comes for the repossession of his land, finds the forest gone, and in its place a ruined plain, choked with scrub? Can a happy, viable, self-sufficient people be reassembled from those few broken human parts?

The new protective body, the National Foundation for the Indian finds some cause for hope in the Xingu National Park. This is the magnificent and almost single-handed creation of two dedicated Indian fundamentalists, the Vilas Boas brothers, who believe that it will remain for all eternity an unchanging redoubt of the old Indian way of life – a view it is hard to discover anyone who shares. It was founded a generation ago when the ranches and fazendas were still busily digesting frontier territories hundreds of miles away, but now their appetites have sharpened again.

The park shelters perhaps a dozen tribes, and there they live cheerfully obsessed with their Stone Age rituals, absorbed in perfectionist handicrafts, body-painting, keeping precious fires alight. The Vilas Boas brothers believe that even aspirin is detrimental to the Indian's self-sufficiency, they exclude missionaries, and do not particularly welcome visitors of any kind. There are dotted lines on the map of the park in the Foundation's office, showing the extensions they propose to make, which will allegedly double its present area; and, remembering the fate of President Goulart when idealism and commercial interests were in collision, one can only wonder.

At best, and should this growth in the park's area ever take place, a total of 4000 *isolados* will have been salvaged, plus a few hundred in a new reserve just created in the Tumucumac mountains in the far north, and these will be guarded like rare birds of prey in the Highlands of Scotland. The future of the 50,000 or 100,000 Indians – whatever the figure is – left outside these reserves seems obscure indeed. At the moment they are to some slight extent protected by a national mood of self-recrimination, which is almost certain to calm once again to indifference. There are only 100,000 pure Indians at most out of a total population of 80 millions and it is unrealistic to believe that their welfare can ever become an obsession in a country in which such multitudes are thrown together in the pit of destitution.

14

Surviving with Spirit

Of all the great cities Naples has suffered least at the hands of
that destroyer of human monuments, the dark angel of Development. Pliny himself, who once stood on a headland there to
watch the great eruption of Vesuvius 'shaped like a many-
branching tree' in the moment of the obliteration of Pompeii,
would have little difficulty in picking out the landmarks of our
times. Nor would Nelson and his Emma, who chose roughly
the same viewpoint to watch the eruption of their day – nor,
certainly, Casanova looking down from his gambling house
over the layered roofs and the soft-yellow walls of volcanic *tufa*
which hoard and dispense the special Naples sunshine. Hardly
a stone of Santa Lucia has been disturbed (except by air-
bombardment) since its celebration in the ballad of the Nineties. When the traveller of the last century was adjured to 'See
Naples and Die', it was notwithstanding the competition
offered by so many glittering rivals. How much more valid and
enticing is the invitation now that so many of them have withdrawn into their shells of concrete.

Naples is a once-capital city, glutted with the palaces and
churches of the Kingdom of the Two Sicilies. Seen from the
heights above it, it is a golden honeycomb of buildings curved
into a sea which, beyond a bordering of intense pollution, is as
brilliant and translucent as any in the world. It is built on
ancient lava fields, and has been threatened by numerous
eruptions – only one of which, in 1855, came near to engulfing
it: it was saved by the miraculous intervention of a statue of its
patron saint, San Gennaro, on the Maddaloni Bridge, spreading its marble arms to halt the passage of the lava. Its history
abounds with similar marvels, all of them attested to and recorded by responsible citizens of the day: a plague of mer-
maids, figures in Giotto's frescoes in the Castel dell'Ovo, so
marvellously drawn that they were actually seen to move and,

more recently, the prodigies performed by Padre Pio, the flying monk, who flew from an outer suburb to the rescue of Italian pilots shot down in combat with Allied planes, bearing them safely to earth in his arms. Dependably in March of every year the dried blood of San Gennaro liquefies in its ampoule in the Cathedral – the most hallucinatory of spectacles surviving from the Middle Ages.

It is characteristic of Naples, described by Scarfoglio as 'the only oriental city having no resident European quarter', that one of its kings, Ferdinand I, should not only have delighted to play the hurdy-gurdy but have commissioned Haydn to compose six nocturnes for performance on the instrument. He was the ruler of a people infatuated with music, and there is music still, everywhere in the Neapolitan air. There can be few more poetic experiences in the local manner than to visit the Parco della Rimembranza, where the young of the city go to make love in their cars, and to clamber down the cliff to a point where, the passing fishing boats still out of sight, they can be tracked by the trail of their mandolin music on their way out to sea.

Naples has been taken by a long succession of foreign conquerors, the cruellest of them being Lord Nelson, who collaborated in the fearsome slaughter of the city's liberals; and possibly the most corrupt being the Allies in the last war, who virtually handed over civic control to the American gangster Vito Genovese, in the guise of adviser to the Allied Military Government – an experience from which the city has never wholly recovered. A continuing resistance to so many alien conquerors has sharpened the native capacity for self-defence, and, since few of the laws Neapolitans are subjected to are of their own making, they have a tendency to mistrust law in general. They are gregarious and gay with a frank devotion to the pleasures of the table and bed. In the last war, Naples was almost certainly the only city in a theatre of warlike operations where civilian employees of our armed forces could apply for transport facilities to their homes at *noon*, to enable them to fulfil their marital obligations.

Those cities, such as Naples, which remain wonderfully unchanged, have usually survived not because developers have recognised their charms, but because, for one reason or another, the developers see no hope of a return on their money.

The economy of Naples is chronically ailing and slides from one crisis to another. It is generally accepted that an expanded tourist industry could be its salvation, but the tourists do not come. Some of the reasons why it fails to entice foreigners to break their journey on their way to Sorrento or Amalfi and spend a night or two in its half-empty hotels were listed in *Il Mattino* last year.

Sorrowfully the newspaper admitted that Naples had become the home-town of petty criminality. In the past 12 months, 77,290 minor crimes had been reported, but in only 1,300 cases had arrest been made or the criminals even been identified. During this period 29,000 cars had been stolen in the city – possibly a world record taking into account the number of vehicles registered. The Vespa-mounted *scippatori*, the Black Knights of the alleyways, buzzing in and out of the crowds in search of camera or handbag to snatch, had become so commonplace a sight as hardly to evoke interest or comment.

From a glance at the newspaper's statistics it seemed, too, that an evening meal out was to be recommended neither to the native citizen nor the visitor to Naples, since fourteen leading restaurants had been raided by bandits in the past twelve months. It was the kind of experience most of us would want to avoid, but a Neapolitan friend involved in a hold-up had been stimulated rather than alarmed. He had been invited to Da Pina's for a christening celebration. A nice party, he said. The best of everything, with the wine flowing like water. But about half-way through the proceedings three hooded men carrying sawn-off shotguns had walked in and ordered the guest to lie face down on the floor. He was impressed with their courtesy, their correct use of the language, and by the way they addressed their victims using the polite *lei* rather than the familiar *tu*. All in all, it was a bit of an adventure, he said, and well worth the trifling £4 or so he had been obliged to part with. His only fear had been that by some incredible mischance the police might show up and start a battle, as they had done at Lombardi's Pizzeria last June, when fifteen customers were wounded.

But most of the coups pulled off by the organised gangs, the Camorra, which imitate the Mafia of Sicily, are theatrical rather than violent. Three robbers who succeeded in sealing off Parker's Hotel from the outside world, and who took two hours to ransack it from top to bottom, prepared and consumed a leisurely meal before departing.

The recent capture of the Ischia ferry-boat was another episode that might have been modelled on a film; having despoiled the passengers with the now familiar show of civility and regret, the bandits leaped to the deck of a following motor-launch waving farewells and blowing kisses to the girls before vanishing into the night.

If one has an affection for such movies as *The French Connection* this is an environment not wholly without its own brand of attraction. What in its way can be more pleasant than to draw a chair out on to the balcony of a room in the Hotel Excelsior overlooking the exquisite small harbour of Santa Lucia, and there, glass in hand and without the slightest risk to one's safety and comfort, play the part of an extra in such a film? The view is of the majestic fortress of the Castel dell'Ovo, dominating a port scene by a naïve painter: simple fishermen's houses that have become restaurants, painted boats, tiny, foreshortened maritime figures, going nowhere in particular, a quayside stacked with the pleasant litter of the sea.

There is less innocence in the prospect than at first meets the eye, because a corner of the port has been taken over by a fleet of some forty large motor launchs, painted the darkest of marine blues, devoid of all trappings, and having about them an air of sinister functionalism. From time to time one starts up with a tremendous chuckle of twin 230 Mercury engines, is manoeuvred in swaggering fashion round the other boats and out of the port before, a moment later, trailing a wake like a destroyer, it heads for the horizon.

This is the fleet of the best-organised and most successful *contrabandisti* in southern Italy, and in these launches (which give the impression of having been specially designed for the trade) are smuggled in the cigarettes and who knows what else picked up in incessant rendezvous with the ships steaming out from the ports of Tunisia. Smuggling is hardly the word to describe these operations, all stages of which, taking place in Italian waters, are on open display. The boats come and go throughout the day, unload their cargoes without concealment and cut a few jubilant capers in the harbour before tying up. There are no signs of the law in the harbour area, and motorcycle policemen passing through Santa Lucia do so hurriedly with eyes averted. Understandings have clearly been reached at high levels. Customs launches lack the speed to catch the *contrabandisti* at sea, and rarely dare to enter the port. Occasional disagreements among the smugglers themselves can, however, be explosive: hotel guests a week or so before our arrival had a ringside seat at a brief battle, followed by a spectacular incineration of boats.

It is a situation viewed by Neapolitans with tacit approval, if not with enthusiasm, and the benefits of the direct trade with north Africa to the man in the street are immediately visible. There is hardly a street without a small boy seated at a table to offer Marlboro cigarettes, made in Tunis (only the government health-warning is missing), at less than 500 lire as opposed to the 800 lire charged in the shops. The authorities seem to regard the traffic as hardly more than an inevitable evil. 'I refuse to admit that this is a crime,' said Maurizio Valenzi the Communist Mayor of Naples. 'For me it is an illegal solution.' The Mayor shared the frequently voiced Neapolitan view that his city is the victim of a calumnious outside world. 'If you are looking for crime on a big scale, go to Rome or Milan,' he said. 'The worst things that can happen to you here is to have your pocket picked. Nobody gets violently robbed in Naples and we treat women with respect. Whoever heard of a Neapolitan being pulled in for knocking a child about? Even the Red Brigade don't operate here.'

Valenzi is as Neapolitan as Brezhnev is Muscovite; he is lively of expression and gesture, a distinguished painter, and a first-rate oratorical performer in a country in which no politician can survive without the knack of rhetoric and a powerful voice. His appearance recalls the views on matters of dress held by Togliatti, party-leader for so many years: 'What pleases me is to see a comrade dressed in a good double-breasted suit – if possible, dark-blue.' Valenzi is wholly congruous in the rococo furnishings, the marble and the glitter of the Naples Town Hall. He is fired by local patriotism, impatient of criticisms of his city, and particularly saddened by those contained in a book by a Communist author, Maria Antoinetta Macciocchi, who had been a parliamentary candidate for one of the poor quarters of the city. 'She wasn't much liked here,' the Mayor said.

Macciocchi had mentioned that the rat population of central Naples was 7 million. Many of these, she said, were shared out in the *bassi*, those claustrophobic dwellings consisting of a single room that line the streets of the old town, in which as many as 15 members of a family may live as best they can with no windows, the street doors shut at night, no running water and a closet behind a curtain. The Mayor, who showed a partiality for euphemism, shied away from the word *bassi*, but agreed that 69,000 families lived in 'unhygienic houses'. 'The municipality,' he said, 'has plans to do something.'

'Our submerged economy' was Valenzi's description for the child-labour which exists in Naples to an extent found nowhere else in the Western world. There is no way of calculating the number of children from the age of eight upwards employed in cafés, bars, or the innumerable sweat-shops tucked away in the narrow streets; but there are certainly tens of thousands of them. It would appear to be another 'illegal solution'. Naples has the highest birth-rate in Italy – twice the national average – and it is an everyday accomplishment for a woman to have born ten children by the age of thirty-five and to have completed a brood of fifteen or sixteen by the time she ceases to reproduce. Such families are a source of complacency rather than despair. One is assured that they testify to a woman's sexual attraction and her husband's virility. More importantly, perhaps, they represent an insurance policy against economic disaster. When up to five or six children contribute small regular sums to the budget a family is not only more affluent but also securer than a less numerous one in the trap of chronic unemployment.

These are the facts of Neapolitan life against which Mayor Valenzi struggles like Canute against the waves. If the child in proletarian Naples is an economic weapon in the family armoury, it follows as a consequence that such central areas of the city as the Vicaria district have the highest population density in Europe – possibly in the world – with up to three people occupying every two square metres. But if over-crowding, and its damaging effect on public health, are the most pressing problems that face the Mayor and his council, it is the terrific anachronism of child labour with its whiff of early Victorian

England that gives the city a bad name. Therefore gestures have to be made, and from time to time the police are ordered into action to close down all establishments employing child labour, and to punish their owners with exemplary fines. What follows is economic disaster for all involved – sometimes desperate impoverishment for the families thrown back on the providing power of the father who, statistically speaking, can expect to spend a third of his life unemployed. At this point, the exploiters and the exploited only too often join forces in protest, and their votes are lost to whatever party is held responsible for their plight.

How is this situaton to be tackled? How can any political party hope to put an end to the Neapolitan tradition of the large family which engenders the poverty which is to be fought by even larger families? Schooling in Italy is compulsory up to 14 years of age, but the school inspectors are as helpless as the politicians. The little courtyards tucked away everywhere in Naples are full of small boys aged upwards of eight years who work 10 or 12 hours a day, for as little as £2 a week, stitching and glueing shoes. A happier-looking, more intelligent collection of children it would be hard to find in the family atmosphere that pervades even the workshop. None of them will ever read or write.

Naples sharpens the stranger's wits and teaches him to look after himself. The lesson is not a difficult one to learn, and in a matter of hours, days at most, amusement is apt to take over from indignation. One exchanges laughter with the agreeable young man who offers a perfect imitation of a Seiko watch that only ticks for a minute or two when it is wound up; or points without severity, on taking a taxi, to the meter inevitably still registering the fare clocked up by the last passenger. There are basic precautions to be taken: passports and valuables are automatically committed to the hotel's safe, and only enough money carried to meet immediate requirements. When parking a car it is not a bad idea to secure the steering wheel with a chain and padlock. These things attended to, one can relax and join in the local games.

Our own arrival in Naples was on the second day of the ancient and popular feast of Santa Maria del Carmine, held in the streets adjacent to the old church at the far end of the port. Del Carmine is the parish church of one of a number of districts, once virtually separate villages. Each has its history, traditions, customs – and often the enfeebled remnant of a once-powerful ruling family. And such was the spirit of rivalry between one district and another that fifty years ago inter-marriage between districts was rare.

The church possesses a picture of a 'black' Virgin, held responsible for many cures, in particular of epileptics and lepers and of those afflicted with all kinds of pox. The most unusual and attractive feature of the *festa* is the 'burning' of the church tower, by the setting alight of bales of straw fastened to its walls with the intention of cleansing it, and thus the district itself, of evil spirits during the forthcoming year. It was a disappointment to learn that the tower was not to be 'burned' on this occasion: repairs to its structure had been found necessary, and the scaffolding was already in place. The cancellation of the ceremony had cast a certain gloom in the neighbourhood, which depends largely on fishing and feared that catches might be affected.

The Corso Garibaldi, a wide if dishevelled street running past the church, was filled by early evening with a holiday crowd. Here all the familiar ingredients of a Neapolitan *festa* were assembled: the stalls with tooth-cracking nougat, solid cakes, and cheroots; the shooting booths; the intimidating display of strange shellfish; balloons and holy pictures – and black-market cigarettes.

In Naples the cult of the enormous Japanese motorcycle has arrived and they were here in fearsome concentration, roaring through whatever space they found among the press of human bodies. We saw one elfin girl mounted on a Kawasaki 'King Kong' hyper-bike. Children are not over-protected in Naples. The minimum age for a Vespa rider seemed to be 12 or 13; and crash helmets were absolutely out.

These are the occasions when, in holiday mood, Neapolitans resolutely suspend belief. A professional 'uncle from Rome' was there, aloof and immaculate in his dark suit, ready to hire himself to any family wishing to impress its guests on an occasion such as a christening, wedding or funeral. *Magliari* – confidence tricksters who flock to all such *festas* – were there in numbers, instantly recognisable, even to an outsider, by the apparatus of their trade.

The grade-A hoax operator presents himself as rejected

suitor offering the 'silver' service bought for the wedding that will no longer take place. *Magliari* in truck-drivers' overalls and with oil on their fingers flog trashy radios and defective tape-recorders 'off the back of the van'. A local boy in burnous and headcloths, skin yellowed by several layers of instant-tan, hawks vile carpets which, he claims, have been brought over from Tunisia with the cigarettes. How do Neapolitans – those masters of guile – allow themselves to be taken in?

Until two years ago the seller of Acqua Ferrata would have been here. This most esteemed and expensive of curative waters, nauseatingly flavoured with iron, was drawn from a hole in the ground somewhere in Santa Lucia and offered – exactly as illustrated in the Pompeii frescoes – in containers shaped like a woman's breast. Since then, following a typhoid scare, the health department has stepped in and Acqua Ferrata is at an end – temporarily, perhaps – to be replaced with a poorish substitute: fresh lemonade animated with bicarbonate of soda.

One figure alone from the remote past had survived at del Carmine: the *pazzariello*, the joker of antiquity, also shown in the Pompeii frescoes. Once he drove out devils, and as recently as the time of the last war no new business could be opened before a *pazzariello* had been called in to lash out with his stick at every corner of a building where a devil might have concealed himself. The office was an honoured one, hereditary and indispensable, too, in a city where even now people cross the road in the Via Carducci to avoid passing too close to a building notoriously under the influence of the evil eye. But now the magic power of the *pazzariello* has drained away; the one we saw, doing his best to dodge the motorcyclists as he capered about in the Corso Garibaldi, was there to advertise a fish restaurant.

Our visit to del Carmine provided a mild adventure. Among the exhibition of holy pictures, most of them crude versions of the celebrated ikon on display in the church, we noted one of a strikingly different kind; a portrait of a somewhat stolid looking middle-aged man, stiff in a formal suit: *Il Santo Dottore Moscati*. It turned out that the holy doctor was a GP of the district, recently deceased and newly canonised by popular acclamation (without reference to Vatican or Church) as a result of a number of miraculous cures he had effected.

The display with its new, popular saint seemed to call for a photograph, but the elderly lady in charge fought shy of the camera and retreated in haste, shielding her face with one of the ikons and leaving her husband to conduct any further negotiations. The old man made no objection to being photographed when we agreed to buy a picture of Dr Moscati. Since the light was already failing, the camera was set up on a tripod and the preparations put in hand. Immediately a crowd began to collect, drawn away from the competing attractions of a shooting booth and a nearby church. A Neapolitan friend who had guided us to the *festa* became concerned, feeling that we were attracting too much attention and were too vulnerable, surrounded by photographic gear, to a passing *scippatore*. But the crowd was co-operative and affable; working Neapolitans, as gregarious as pigeons, love nothing better than a new face and an excuse to exchange a smile with a foreigner. People were actually jostling each other and manoeuvring to be included in the photograph, so that, realising that we were among friends, all warnings were ignored and the photography went ahead.

A moment later there was a sudden chill in the atmosphere and the smiles faded. A grim-faced, gesturing man had pushed himself to the front to demand payment of 50,000 lire – about £30. His story was that he was acting for the owner of the pictures; but it was to be supposed that he was an enforcer of one of the protection gangs said to levy a toll on most Neapolitan business enterprises. We decided to resist the extortion: there were four of us, and we were certain that we had the crowd on our side. The situation was saved when the old man had the courage to admit that he had never seen the presumed gangster before in his life. With this, the unwelcome stranger went off, and the emergency was at an end.

In 1943–44 I spent a year in Naples, arriving a day or so after its capture from the Germans in October 1943, when the city lay devastated by the hurricane of war. The scene was apocalyptic. Ruins were piled high in every street, and in these people camped out like bedouins in a wilderness of brick, on the verge of starvation and close to dying of thirst. There had been no water supply since the great Allied air-bombardment a month before. Families experimented with sea-water to cook herbs and edible roots grubbed up in gardens and parks. Some squatted by the shore with weird contraptions with which they hoped to distil sea-water to drink. At the same time an absurd and disastrous ban on fishing kept the boats from going out, and children by the hundred were to be seen scrambling about the rocks, prising off limpets to sell at a few lire a pint, supplies of winkles and sea-snails having been long exhausted. All the rare and extraordinary fish from all parts of the world in the famous aquarium had been eaten by the populace, and a manatee, the aquarium's most prized possession, preserved for a while only by its ugliness, had finally been slaughtered and disguised in the cooking to be served at a banquet in honour of General Mark Clark.

Men and women who had lost all their possessions in the bombardments went about dressed in sacking or in garments confected from curtains and bed-covers. But at the many funerals, professional mourners still tore at their clothes as well as their cheeks. A problem had arisen over the shortage of funeral horses, many of which had gone into the stewpot; and the most extraordinary sight of all was of two old men harnessed up with a pair of enfeebled donkeys in the shafts of a hearse. It was at a time when Naples was threatened with outbreaks of smallpox and typhoid; armed deserters from the Allied forces were attacking and looting private houses; and Moorish troops committed atrocities against men, women and children on the outskirts of the city.

The printing of occupation money, plus the devaluation of the lire from 100 to 400 to £1, spelt instant ruin to those dependent upon fixed salaries. An American corporal then received about ten times the pay of an Italian major, and the Questore, the Chief of Police of Naples, the highest paid civil servant, with a salary of 5,496 lire a month, was earning the equivalent of £14. This man was incorruptible, and I was present in his office when he fainted from hunger.

Men of lesser calibre turned to the black market, organised and presided over by Vito Genovese – and nourished by one-third of all the supplies shipped through the Port of Naples for the provisioning of the Allied forces in Italy.

In families deprived of their menfolk, the women frequently supported themselves and their children by prostitution. A bulletin issued by the Bureau of Psychological Warfare gave a figure for women in Naples who had become regular or occasional prostitutes of no fewer than 42,000. That this could have happened when there were possibly 150,000 girls of marriageable age in Naples seems incredible: there is no more convincing illustration of the extremity of their agony.

It was Naples's calvary of fire and destitution; the days of reproach through which it came at long last so astonishingly unmarred. The Neapolitans' salvation was their fortitude; their incapacity for despair. Perhaps too, there was a kind of austerity in their make-up which was unsuspected in southerners – a readiness to make do with little and a lack of affinity with the acquisitiveness already beginning to dominate Western European society.

Revisiting Naples, I saw it as a city that has achieved its own kind of emotional stability, is content to drift with no eye to the future, has rejected change and is unchangeable. In this way, as Scarfoglio had observed, it is oriental rather than European. Economically it has stagnated where the industrial North with its separate identity and ideals has pushed further and further ahead. Nearly half the Neapolitan workforce is unemployed or under-employed, but Neapolitans help each other. The income per capita is only a third of that in Milan; but, for me, Naples will always be the better place to live in.

The sensation of continuity – that here in Naples one was recapturing the vanished past – was reinforced by a visit to a famous shore-side restaurant, unaltered in any way in its furnishings and atmosphere from the days in 1944 when it had been full of Allied officers and the barons of the black market. The house troubadours, facsimiles of their fathers, attended the guests as ever to strum the everlasting *Torn' a Sorrento* on their mandolins. The same algae-spotted showcase with its display of octopus and crabs was there still and so, too, was the old man hunched behind the antique cash register with its bell chiming like the cathedral's angelus.

All the rituals had been preserved. Fish were still presented with hooks hanging from the mouths to suggest that they had been cut in that very instant from the line; and what used to be known as the 'show-fish', a majestic bass or *merou*, passed on a lordly salver from table to table to cries of admiration from diners who should have known that, whatever they ordered, it would not be this that they would eat. At the proper moment the visitors' book was produced – but here, at least, there had been changes. All the great, blustering Fascist names had been weeded out 35 years before, but now the pages dealing with the years 1944–45 had gone too, and with them Mark Clark, and the rest of the Allied generals. Enduring fame now belonged only to such as Axel Munthe and Sophia Loren, the local girl (surely well on her way to popular canonisation) from Pozzuoli, just round the corner of the bay. Neapolitans had thrust the politicians and the soldiers out of memory.

Close to us a number of tables had been pushed together to accommodate a family, later identified as a man of fifty, his wife, two teenaged children, a son in his twenties and the daughter-in-law, their three children, the host's elder brother, his widowed sister, and the grandfather, who was placed out of respect at the top of the table and to whom the show-fish was first presented for his nod of approval. In Naples there are no baby-sitters: the family takes its pleasures and suffers its tribulations as a unit, and the aged are excluded from none of its experiences.

With the exception of the eldest son, in his *moda inglese* pin-striped suit, and his stylish wife, the general impression the group gave was one of less than affluence; yet it was clear that a small fortune was being spent on this meal. By the time coffee came I found myself chatting to the head of the house. He had just been released from hospital – hence the celebration. The family went out on the town two or three times a year, he said, 'whenever an excuse can be found'. So the money went.

It was the kind of household based on a three-roomed flat – the young couple and their children would live separately – with nothing on hire-purchase, the minimum of furniture and a kitchen of the old-fashioned kind with nothing electrical in it apart from the toaster.

The father went on to say that he had been employed as a mechanic in the Alfasud factory, then laid off. He added that while drawing what benefits he could, he had managed to get his hands on a list of Alfasud buyers in the area and, by servicing their cars at cut price, had been able 'to keep the soup flowing'. His daughter went to school, but took time off before Christmas to make figurines for Nativity cribs, which at that season were in great demand. If necessary his wife could always turn her hand to sewing umbrellas for sale in the London stores. Should a financial emergency arise, the eldest son, who 'worked on the boats' – he nodded in the direction of the piratical launches in the harbour – could be counted on to pitch in. '*Si arrangia*,' he said: 'We get by somehow.' It had always been the true motto of Naples.

15

The White Promised Land

Dr Guido Strauss, Bolivian Under Secretary for Immigration, caused a stir throughout Latin America last year [1977] when he announced his government's intention to encourage the entry into Bolivia 'of large and important numbers of white immigrants ... especially from Namibia, Rhodesia and South Africa.'

His statement was published by Bolivia's leading newspaper, *Presencia*, which later revealed that 150,000 whites would be accommodated and that the scheme had been financed by a 150-million-dollar credit to Bolivia offered by the Federal German Republic.

Censorship in Bolivia fosters eagerness on the part of the Press to study and reflect the governmental viewpoint, but in this instance *Presencia* seems to have been in a quandary as to the official line. A vigorous denial by one department of the plan's very existence, coincided with a wealth of confirmatory detail poured forth by another. 'At the very time,' wailed the newspaper, 'when the Institute of Colonisation affirmed that they had no knowledge of such a project ... Under Secretary Guido Strauss said that the immigration plan was a matter of top priority.'

Confusion was worse confounded by publication of extracts from a confidential letter written by Strauss to his minister, General Juan Lechín Suarez. The letter was full of precise figures and facts. The white settlers would be admitted in stages, taking possibly as long as six years, although 30,000 families could be admitted in the first year if the financial arrangements were settled by then. The exact areas to be taken over by the newcomers were listed and the amount of land they would receive (800,000 hectares). Strauss noted that the cost of purchasing this land – which was to be given to settlers – and of building roads was 250 million dollars, and that this sum had been funded.

The letter breathed the sentiments of humanity, and warned of the holocaust that awaited South African whites once black majority rule became a fact. Mr Sean McBride, High Commissioner for Namibia at the UN, was quoted as having said that Namibian whites would have to abandon the country. 'There is no doubt that the factors of a catastrophe are imminent,' Dr Strauss wrote. Motives of national self-interest were also touched upon. Bolivia's economically under-developed, under-populated areas cried out for the drive and the technical skills of the energetic South Africans. He also made the claim that Britain, the US and France between them were ready to put up 2,000 million dollars to indemnify white Rhodesians, 'who would be unable to resist the process of Africanisation.'

Adverse reaction to this colonisation was to be expected, and was led by the Catholic Church, the only body in Bolivia prepared to stand up to the dictatorship. A conference of religious leaders was held last July and a declaration followed listing numerous objections to the plan. What clearly disturbed the Church was the prospect of apartheid in Bolivia. *Presencia* was permitted to publish the criticisms. I quote from two paragraphs only:

'The South African immigrants, with their violently racial mentality, condemned even in their own countries, could import the principles of apartheid into those under-populated areas where they would form compact groups. Bolivia, as the South Africans write so often in their newspapers, is the richest of the Latin American countries, requiring only an advanced technology for the exploitation of its raw materials ... "three-quarters of its population are illiterate natives". This is a point of view echoed by the contemptuous remarks of some of our own authorities who say, "The Indians cost more to keep than animals. They have to be fed, and work less."'

The well-meaning objections of the Church, and of so many liberal Bolivians, are as naive as they are creditable, since in some ways apartheid already exists in a purer and more extreme form in Bolivia than the version professed by the racists of South Africa. This, a visitor to the country quickly discovers.

La Paz, at 12,400 feet is, the highest capital in the world. The plane lands on the edge of a plateau high above it, engines screaming in reverse and wing-flaps clawing at the thin air. A few hundred yards from the runway's end, the abyss awaits. The city lying below is crammed into a monstrous crater. Here, in this hole in the earth, its original Spanish builders, who went there to mine gold, huddled out of reach of the terrible wind that whines like a persistent beggar at every turn. From the almost infernal vision beneath, one turns back to that of the flat world of the Altiplano, almost all of it over 13,000 feet.

This is the homeland of the Aymara Indians, whose grandiose civilisation preceded that of the Incas. They have been forcibly Christianised, and enslaved over four centuries, and they are still tremendously exploited. But somehow they have survived. Now, with the Church turned benign, they are no longer compelled to carry priests in chairs on their backs, or scourged for persisting in their ancient worship of *Pachamama*, the mother-goddess, and *Tío*, the Devil, who is also, appropriately, god of the tin mines. In their honour the Aymara sacrifice innumerable llama foetuses and get drunk whenever they can. Their distrust of all whites has become instinctive, and can be belligerent. At best one is ignored, and at worst hustled away. Whites who insist on fraternising with Aymaras in their state of holy drunkenness may even find themselves attacked.

Bolivia is a poor country; its per capita income of about £200 a year putting it at the bottom of the league of South American nations. Its adult literacy is about 30 per cent. Oil revenues have brought about some increase in prosperity in recent years, but this has been diverted to a small sector of the population and largely spent on non-essential consumer goods. Far from bringing comfort to the peasant majority, the new prosperity has in fact done the reverse, for while the prices of agricultural produce has been rigorously held down, almost everything else is imported and subject to the inflationary process.

National poverty and under-development formed the theme of Under Secretary Guido Strauss's argument in favour of mass immigration of whites from South African countries when I interviewed him in La Paz. He was communicative and direct, a man with a reputation for not mincing words. Occasionally he is indiscreet, and is widely quoted as having said in public,

'They (the white immigrants) will certainly find our Indians no more stupid or lazy than their own blacks.' He confirmed to me with enthusiasm all the details of the project so far published, whether or not they had been denied elsewhere, and added to these a little fresh data.

Bolivia, Dr Strauss explained, a country twice the size of Spain, had a population of five millions. Such people as it had were crowded into the semi-barren Altiplano and a number of upland valleys, leaving the vast and rich territory of the eastern provinces virtually unpopulated. Through lack of development of its agricultural wealth, the country was even obliged to import food. When, therefore, discreet international moves had been set afoot to discover possible areas of resettlement for whites whom it was believed would sooner or later be forced out of Rhodesia, Namibia and South Africa, Bolivia had recognised that its acceptance of such refugees might provide a partial solution to this problem.

Dr Strauss said that approaches had been made (through the German Federal Government) not only to Bolivia, but to Argentina, Brazil, Uruguay and Venezuela. Brazil and Venezuela had agreed to accept a limited number of technicians.

Only Bolivia had been ready to take on immigrants of all classes en bloc. Dr Strauss said that any white settler would be given, free, a minimum of 50 hectares of first class agricultural land, and would also receive social, technical and economic assistance. Those who wished to engage in ranching would receive 'very much more', together with ample low-cost labour.

Dr Strauss handed me a copy of the Bolivian immigration laws, which also stressed Bolivia's demographic predicament, and the inducements offered to immigrants who could contribute to its solution. Settlers from all countries would be welcomed with open arms, but, he said, a special and natural sympathy pre-disposed Bolivians in favour of persons of European origin, who shared with them a common heritage of culture and religion.

Asked how many immigrants from the South African countries had already arrived, Dr Strauss said that some 'spontaneous' immigration had taken place. He believed that this trickle would soon become a flood, an inundation which could be expected as soon as black majority rule becomes a fact. The infrastructure, including the building of roads in areas where the colonialists were to be settled, was complete. Bolivia for them, Dr Strauss said, is a promised land.

One question remained. Forty-one Indian tribes, with a total population of about 120,000, are recorded as living in the nominal emptiness of Eastern Bolivia. Some of them occupy precisely those areas shown on Dr Strauss's map as designated for development. What was to become of them?

This was a question which Dr Strauss did not feel competent to reply to. If I wanted to know anything about Indians, and the nation's plans for them, he suggested that I should go and talk to the Summer Institute of Linguistics, the largest of the group of North American evangelical missionaries working in Bolivia. This I did.

The mildness of Mr Victor Halterman's personality came as surprise after learning something of his formidable reputation as head of the Summer Institute of Linguistics. With the exception of Under Secretary Strauss, who was naturally obliged to keep his thoughts to himself, I never met a Bolivian who did not regard the Summer Institute of Linguistics as the base for operations of the CIA in Bolivia; possibly in South America itself.

Mr Halterman's reticence and modesty were reflected in his bare office in a ramshackle building. Shoved into a corner at the back of the cheap furniture stood a splendid object of carved wood and macaw's feathers, an Indian god, said the missionary, that had been joyously surrendered to him by some of his converts. The other decoration was a coloured photograph of a Chácobo Indian wearing handsome nose-tusks, and a long gown of bark.

The presence of these reminders of the Indians' uncivilised past came as a surprise, because, in the mood of the Pilgrim Fathers, most missionaries frown on all such things, banning personal adornments of all kinds (unless produced in a modern factory) as well as outlawing musical instruments, and jollifications of any kind in missionary compounds. Mr Halterman was more liberal in his outlook. Indians might dress up as they pleased, and even sing and dance, but only in a 'folkloric' spirit, in other words as long as such activities were stripped of any possibility of a hidden 'superstitious significance'.

Among the innumerable North American religious bodies devoted to the spiritual advancement of South America are three main missionary groups: the New Tribes Mission, the South American Mission, and the Summer Institute of Linguistics, all of whom concern themselves with the capture of Indian souls. Of these the SIL is possibly the richest and most powerful, with 13 active posts throughout the country. Not only does it have the government's support, but one learns with surprise that it comes under the Ministry of Culture and Education, of which Mr Halterman is an official.

It may be in acknowledgement of this official co-operation that the biblical text that features most prominently in the SIL's well-produced promotional literature is Romans 13:1, offered in Spanish and eight Indian translations. The Institute's text is at variance both with that of the English Revised Version of the Bible, and its Spanish equivalent. '*Let every soul be subject unto the higher powers*' becomes '*Obey your legal superiors, because God has given them command*', while the SIL quite remarkably re-translates '*the powers that be are ordained by God*' as '*There is no government on earth that God has not permitted to come to power.*' (Could General Banzer, who seized control of the country in 1971, have had a hand in this linguistic exercise?)

Mr Halterman agreed that the SIL, as well as the two other evangelical missions, were religious fundamentalists, and therefore ready with a tooth and nail defence of every line of the Holy Writ, including the world's literal creation in six days, and Eve's origin as a rib from Adam's side.

Fundamentalists also believe that all the non-Christians of this world, including those who have never heard of the existence of the Christian faith, are doomed to spend eternity in hell. As the printed doctrinal statement of the New Tribes Mission – with whose theology Mr Halterman said he was in complete agreement – puts it: 'We believe in the unending punishment of the unsaved.' It is this belief that inspires so many missionaries to save souls at all costs, often with disregard for the converts' welfare in this world.

'We have a very limited medical programme,' Mr Halterman said, and one could be sure he meant what he said. It is this indifference to anything but the act of conversion that explains the almost incredible experience reported by the German anthropologist Jürgen Riester in an encounter with a missionary who in 1962 had been entrusted by the Bolivian government with the pacification of the Ayoreo Indians.

'The missionary allowed more than 150 Ayoreos to die in cold blood, after establishing contact with them. The Indians were dying of a respiratory disease accompanied by high fever, and the missionary held back medicine, using the following argument: "In any case they won't allow themselves to be converted. If I baptise them just before they die, they'll go straight to heaven."'

Mr Halterman agreed that a certain number of Indians remained at large in the forest areas designated for future occupation by the white immigrants. It was a matter for regret, he thought, and he seemed to blame himself and his brother missionaries for incompetence in this matter. The Indians could be dangerous, he said, mentioning that only two days before, a member of an oil exploration team had been shot to death by arrows. However, there were still souls to be harvested, and he described with quiet relish the methods used to entice the occasional surviving Indian group from its natural environment so that this could be accomplished.

'When we learn of the presence of an uncontacted group,' said the missionary, 'we move into the area, build a strong shelter – say of logs – and cut paths radiating from it into the forest. We leave gifts along these paths – knives, axes, mirrors, the kind of things that Indians can't resist – and sometimes they leave gifts in exchange. After a while the relationship develops. Maybe they are mistrustful at first, but in the end they stop running away when we show, and we all get together and make friends.'

But the trail of gifts leads inevitably to the mission compound, and here, often at the end of a long journey, far from the Indian's sources of food, his fish, his game, it comes abruptly to an end.

'We have to break their dependency on us next,' Mr Halterman said. 'Naturally they want to go on receiving all those desirable things we've been giving them, and sometimes it comes as a surprise when we explain that from now on if they want to possess them they must work for money. We don't employ them, but we can usually fix them up with something to do on the local farms. They settle down to it when they realise that there's no going back.'

'Something to do' on a local farm is only too often indistinguishable from slavery. Mr Halterman, whether he knows it or not, is the first human link in the chain of a process that eventually reduces the Indians to the lamentable condition of all those we saw in Bolivia, and there are many hundreds of missionaries like Mr Halterman all over South America, striving with zeal and with devotion to save souls whose bodies are condemned to grinding labour in an alien culture.

While the North American missionaries have become – often officially – the servants of such right-wing military dictatorships as that of Bolivia, opposition in the name of Human Rights is frequently organised by Catholic priests and members of the religious orders. Their efforts, although at best hardly more than an attempt to alleviate harshness and cultivate compassion, involve them in some risk, and shortly before we arrived in La Paz gunmen murdered two assistants of a priest who had been troublesome. We were told that such gunmen could be hired to assassinate someone of small importance for as low a fee as 100 pesos (rather less than £3).

A number of our informants were churchmen of a staunchly liberal kind, but it is not possible to mention them by name, or even identify the organisations to which they belong. One of them described the current Banzer regime as a confident and therefore fairly mild form of Fascism. Unlike Chile, which had lost all self-respect, it valued its good name. When, in January 1974, the peasants in Cochabamba showed too spirited a resistance to its authority, it had not been above sending in planes and tanks and killing a hundred or so, but for the moment it had fallen like a digesting crocodile into a kind of watchful inactivity.

In the meanwhile, the Church had cautiously involved itself in the formation of peasant groups that could by-pass the fraudulent government-rigged trades unions. He expected that eventually the crocodile would show that it was far from asleep. Future repression, he thought, was certain.

It was a priest who introduced us to some of the facts about the abundant labour promised by Dr Strauss to the new white immigrants, and he took us to see cane-cutters at work on an estate near Santa Cruz. Some 40–50,000 migrant workers are brought in to deal with the cotton harvesting and the cane-cutting. These are all Indians, the majority from the Altiplano. Of the two groups, the cotton pickers seem marginally the worse off, being housed in dreadful barracoons in which they sleep packed in rows, sexes mixed, thirty or forty to a hut.

The working day is from just before dawn until dark. Altiplano Indians, accustomed to the cold, clear air of the high plateau, suffered dreadfully, the priest said, in the heat of the tropics, and also from the incessant attacks of insects, unknown in the highlands, but which made life unbearable to them here. It was difficult to estimate how much a worker earned, but, allowing for loss of working time through bad weather, the priest estimated that this might average out at 50p a day. But this was far from being the take-home wage. Various deductions had to be made, including the contractor's cut.

All the estates employed agents who scoured the country in their search for suitable labour. The plantation owners paid them 50p to £2.50 for every man, plus a percentage deducted from the worker's pay.

There were other drawbacks. The migrant worker would be forced to buy his supplies from the estate's stores, where prices could be three or four times those normally charged. Jürgen Riester noted in his work on the Indians of Eastern Bolivia that a kilo of salt might be charged up in this way at ten times its market price, and a bottle of rum at twenty times normal cost. Thus the average daily wage could be reduced from 50p to 20p, or less. Worst of all, said the priest, almost all migrant workers were debt-slaves, and the debts they had been induced to incur went on mounting up every year, so that they were bound for life to a particular employer; their children, who would inherit the debt, would be bound to him, too.

The cane-cutters we visited were on a sugar estate about twenty miles from the city. They were Chiriguano Indians, from Abapó Izozóg – one of the two principal areas designated for the new white settlements. These men worked a 15-hour day, starting at 3 am, by moonlight or the light of kerosene flares, except on Sunday, when 13 hours were worked. The two free hours on Sunday were dedicated to a visit by lorry to buy supplies at the estate owner's shop in

Montero, the nearest village. They were paid about 50p a day.

Although their contracts stipulated that water, firewood and medicines would be provided free, there was no wood, two inches of a muddy brown liquid in the bottom of one only of the two wells, and the only medicine given was aspirin, used impartially in the treatment of enteritis, tuberculosis (from which many of them suffer), and snake-bite. Every woman over the age of 18 had lost her front teeth as a result of poor nutrition, leaving the gums blue and hideously swollen.

A contractor hung about, keeping his eye on us; a sleek and smirking young man in a big sombrero, a digital watch strapped on his wrist and a transistor to his ear. Part of his duties would be to keep a look out for cane-cutters who were obviously not long for this world and ship them off back to their villages where they could die out of sight. All these cane-cutters were debt-slaves. It should be stressed that the estate was not specially singled out for this investigation, but was chosen at random, largely because it was easily reached from the main road. It was almost certainly no better nor any worse than the rest.

The current fight championed by the Church on such estates is for the elimination of the contractor and the abolition of a system by which 20 per cent of wages are withheld until the end of the harvest to prevent desertion. Even when, despite this precaution, workers do cut and run, they may be brought back by the police as absconding debtors. Little objection is seen from above to controlling labour by brute force: a mentality inherited from the days before 1962, when estates were bought and sold *with* their workers.

In 1972, at the time of the cotton boom and the trebling of cotton prices on the world market, workers were forcibly prevented from leaving the cotton fields, and troops sent to the Altiplano to recruit labour, while in Santa Cruz schools were closed so that the children might be free to help out.

The following news-clipping from *Excelsior*, dated 23 June 1977, gives some idea of labour conditions that can still exist in odd corners.

Slave Camp Denounced in Bolivia

La Paz, 22nd June. The unusual case of a slave camp's existence was denounced here today. The denunciation was received in the labour

office of the town of Oruro against the owners of the Sacacasa estate
alleging this to be a slave camp. Apart from harsh treatment received
by both adults and children, they are forced to work from 6 am to 6 pm
for a daily wage of 10 pesos (25p). The slaves are threatened with
firearms and brutal floggings to compel them to submit to this exploi-
tation.

The migrant workers I have described are classified as Indians
integrated into the national society. They have, in some cases,
been in painful contact with white people for several centuries.
They dress as whites, are nominally Catholics, and often no
longer speak an Indian language. The Chiriguano cane-
cutters were descendants of those who survived the wholesale
exterminations of the great rubber boom of the 19th century,
when Indians who were dragged from their villages to become
rubber tappers had no more than a two-year expectation of life,
and could expect punishment, which might include the ampu-
tation of a limb for failure to produce the expected quota of rubber.

There exists a class of even cheaper and more defenceless
labour. These are 'non-integrated' Indians, who have only recently been driven or enticed from the jungle. They are at the
bottom of the pyramid of enslavement.

On 16 October 1977, two days before our arrival in Santa
Cruz, *Presencia* published an account of the kind of misadven-
ture that can befall a forest Indian – in this case one of a band
of refugees who escaped from a mission compound – who happens to follow a road and arrive at the end of it, dazzled, bewildered, and quite unable to make himself understood, in the
streets of a boom city.

This Indian, an Ayoreo named Cañe, was washing his
clothes in the River Piraí, a few yards from the Santa Cruz
main railway station, when he heard screams coming from a
parked car in which two men were attacking a girl. Cañe ran to
the girl's aid, and the two men drove off, but they soon
returned with a police car. In this, after a thorough beating,
Cañe was taken to the police station, where, being unable to
give any account of himself in Spanish, and in the absence of
an interpreter, one of the policemen simply drew his gun and
shot him through the head. The bullet entered the right side of
the head, low down, behind the ear, and exited, astonishingly,
without damage to the brain.

What is unusual about this story, besides Cañe's miraculous escape that got him into the newspapers, was that he was then taken to hospital. In Latin America it is unusual for an ambulance ever to be sent for an Indian.

This happened on 9 October, and on 20 October, learning that Cañe and the rest of his fugitive groups were still to be seen on a piece of waste-ground outside the Brazil Station, we found an interpreter and went in a taxi to talk to him. The taxi-driver had some reason to know just where the Ayoreos were to be found, because he mentioned that the Ayoreo women had been driven by starvation to prostitute themselves for 5 pesos (13p) per visit. He himself had had intercourse with one of them several days before, copulation having taken place at dusk, in the open, by the side of the well-illuminated and busy road. He now awaited with anxiety the possible appearance of dread symptoms.

We found approximately twenty Ayoreos on waste land by the side of the new dual carriageway. Cañe was among them, and we examined the still raw wound in the back of his head. He told us that a number of ribs had been broken in the beating he had been given, and that an attempt had been made to break both his wrists, using a device kept at the police station for that purpose.

Cañe, a magnificently strong young man, had put up such resistance to this that the policeman had had to give up his efforts, and then in frustration had drawn his gun and shot him instead.

The Ayoreos are the proudest of the tribes of Bolivia, making a fetish of manly strength and courage, particularly as demonstrated in their hunting of the jaguar. To acquire status in the tribe and marry well, an Ayoreo must be prepared to tackle a jaguar at close quarters, in such a way that the maximum amount of scarring is left by the encounter on his limbs and his torso.

For these Ayoreos the days of hunting the jaguar in the Gran Chaco were at an end. They had gone through the mission, been deprived of their skills and been taught the power of money. As a last resort, since food had to be bought, they sold their women. Cañe remembered being taken by a missionary as a boy from the Chaco. Since then he had slaved for farmers, being paid with an occasional cast-off garment or a little rice.

In the end, he and his companions could stand the life no longer, and had just wandered away following the road through the jungle, and then a railway track until they reached Santa Cruz.

We learned that the mission from which the Ayoreos had decamped was a South American mission station in the jungle some 20 kilometres from the village of Pailón. Deciding to see for ourselves what were the conditions that could have caused this apparently hopeless headlong flight into nowhere, we visited the mission on 22 October, in the company of three Germans, one of whom spoke Ayoreo.

The scene, when we arrived in the camp, was a depressingly familiar one: the swollen bellies, pulpy, inflated flesh, toothless gums and chronic sores of malnutrition, the slow, listless movements, the eyes emptied by apathy. Here, 275 Ayoreos, a substantial proportion of the survivors of the tribe, had been rounded up with their jaguar-scarred chief, who presented himself, grotesque in his dignity, wearing a motorcycle crash-helmet. We inspected a deep cleft in his forehead where he had attempted to commit suicide, using an axe.

The only signs of food we saw was a bone completely covered by a black furry layer of putrefaction, being passed round to be gnawed, and a cooked tortoise being shared among a group. With our arrival a commotion began, led by some weeping women, and we soon learned the reason. Here in the tropics, at the height of the dry season, the water supply had been cut off by the missionary in punishment for some offence. The Indians, several of them ill, and with sick children in the camp, had been without water for two days.

We saw the missionary, Mr Depue, a lean shaven-headed North American of somewhat austere presence, who confirmed that he had ordered a collective punishment he believed most likely to be effective to deal with a case in which two or three children had broken into a store and stolen petrol. There was to be no more water until the culprits were found, and brought into his compound, there to be publicly thrashed.

The situation was a difficult one because, as Mr Depue explained, in all the years he had spent as a missionary, he had never heard of a single instance of an Indian punishing a child, which was to say that the conception of corrective chastisement seemed to be beyond their grasp. Mr Depue spoke of this aversion to punishment as of some genetic defect inherited by the whole race. It had now come to be a trial of strength, and he could only hope that the deadlock would soon be resolved. He took up an 'it-hurts-me-as-much-as-it-hurts-them' attitude, assuring us that he had decided to share the general discomfort by ordering the water supply to the mission house to be cut off as well. It occurred to us that he might have prudently arranged for a reserve, because we happened to arrive when the missionary and his family were at lunch, and both water and soft drinks appeared to be in reasonable supply.

Mr Depue happened to have read the newspaper's account of Cañe's misfortunes, and remembered that he himself had 'brought him in', during a pacification drive in the Chaco. Three or four youngsters, including Cañe, had become separated in the panic from their tribe. 'I kept out of sight and sent Ayoreo-speaking Indians to offer them a better life, and to persuade them to come in, and they did.'

It was by chance on our way back from this expedition that we saw our first *criada* – a Chiquitano Indian girl who had been 'adopted' by a white family, and happened to serve us in her foster-parents' bar. The *criada* system is far from being exclusively Bolivian, and exists under different names in backward rural areas in most Latin American countries where there are groups of depressed and exploited Indians.

In the hope that they will receive some education, and an economically brighter future, Indians give their children away to white families. The little Indian – usually a girl – becomes a Cinderella no prince will ever discover. She will be put to unpaid drudgery from the age of four or five, be traditionally available for the sexual needs of the sons of the family, and will not be able to marry, although she will be allowed to have children, who in their turn will become *criadas*.

Our German friends knew this girl well, but having lived for some years in Bolivia, and become accustomed to its institutions, they were not horrified, as we were, that such barely disguised forms of slavery could exist.

A *criada*, they informed us, could be lent or given away. They had no rights of any kind: rural untouchables of Latin America, whose existence went unnoticed. There was no saying how many there were in Bolivia, they said. In some parts of the eastern provinces almost every farm kept one.

Santa Cruz is a boom town, a little dizzy with quick profits, and displaying its wealth as best it can. It has a new Holiday Inn, full of American oilmen in baseball caps, and possesses no fewer than four ring-roads. Among its leading citizens are Germans, the most successful and affluent of the foreigners in Bolivia. There are about 300,000 of them, and it is said that President Banzer, who is a descendant of one of the older German families, came to power through a military coup financed by the German colony.

The powerful Dr Strauss, in control of immigration, comes of German forebears, and Teutonic surnames are scattered liberally through the lists of directors of the country's leading enterprises. Near Abapó Izozóg, immediately adjoining the nominally empty area (save for a few thousand Indians) that Dr Strauss proposes to people with Rhodesians, South-West-Afrian whites of German descent and refugees from South Africa, the Germans occupy a colony about the size of Holland. They have founded other vast colonies at Asención de Guarayos in the centre of the country, and at Rurrenaháque, in the north, and they have sunk fortunes into building roads and costly irrigation schemes.

A high percentage of German immigrants arriving since the war had remained loyal to Nazi political philosophy, and recently neo-Nazi groups had also emerged. The Bolivian government appears indifferent to this phenomenon, and has pushed its neutrality to the lengths of resisting the extradition of at least one war criminal. Neo-Nazi journals imported from Germany, and such militaristic publications as *Soldaten-Zeitung*, find avid readers.

Our own brief experience of martial nostalgia was to be warned at our hotel of an impending dinner for some 300 Germans, to raise funds for the German school (the best in Eastern Bolivia). With some embarrassment it was hinted that many of the guests were ex, or actual, Nazis and that we might find some of their old wartime drinking songs offensive. We listened to the clamour but kept out of the way. Most extraordinary of all, to us, was to be assured that German Jews in Bolivia had sunk their differences with their old Aryan persecutors, and now

208

fraternised at such gatherings, joining to chorus the 'Horst Wessel' along with the rest.

Our final conclusion was that Dr Strauss's justification for the plan to bring in whites from the South African countries – i.e. economic necessity – was not quite the whole story. Bolivia is potentially one of the richest of South American countries, since apart from other largely untapped timber resources in the east, aerial surveys have indicated that the Amazon Basin it shares with Brazil contains one of the most valuable and diverse mineral profiles in the world. It is also among the weakest of these countries, with a population of five millions, many of whom are illiterate and subjugated Indians, contributing little to the country's muscle. With these human resources it must be ready to defend the thousand miles of frontier it also shares with Brazil, which has 110 millions.

At the moment, Brazil is fully engaged in gobbling up its own resources, but it can be imagined that sooner or later it might turn its eyes westwards with renewed appetite and in a mood for expansion. Brazilian roads have either been built or resurfaced by Army engineers to take the heaviest tanks. One such road points to the heart of Bolivia through Corumbá, after which, crossing the frontier, it dwindles to dirt. Also, through foreclosures, Brazilian banks already own much land along Bolivia's eastern borders.

Almost imperceptibly, Bolivia has been a country bleeding to death. In a series of wars fought and lost over the past century it has seen its territory whittled away by victorious neighbours: first the nitrate-rich Atacama Desert and the port of Antofagasta to Chile; then the Acre Territory to Brazil; then three-quarters of the Chaco to Paraguay. Always these losses have been the result of its failure to fill 'empty' spaces occupied by the Indians, who do not count.

Seeing into the future with Dr Strauss's eyes one might be tempted to agree with him that, from his viewpoint, and that of the Bolivian government, the problem of filling this territorial vacuum is urgent. Strauss has to have his immigrants, and sooner or later he will probably get them, as the intransigence of the South African whites stokes up fuel for the fire tomorrow.

Together with the powerful German-Dutch minority already in place, these newcomers could transform Bolivia into a strong, white-dominated, ultra-right, anti-Communist state in the heart of Latin America. This vigorous transformation would discourage the future covetousness of neighbouring states, and it would delight the United States by laying forever the ghost of Che Guevara – himself once attracted to empty spaces in Bolivia.

16

Seville

There are few hotel beds to be had in Seville when it acclaims the Spring in its inimitable fashion. I found a place to stay out of town dumped my baggage, and travelled in by taxi. At the San Telmo bridge over the Guadalquivir we ran into snarled-up traffic dominated by a woman policeman with a dark, ecstatic face. She ran, leaped and cavorted, unmeshing and directing the crawl of cars with competence and with artistry, and the drivers wound down their windows to shout their applause. 'That's a gypsy,' the taxi driver said. 'She used to dance at the Arenal. If we pull over and wait till the traffic clears, she'll do a seguidilla for us.' But the policewoman snapped her fingers at us and threw back her head, and we joined the queue on the bridge. There was another jam on the further side and the driver had a suggestion. We turned left into the wide and relatively quiet Avenida Colon that follows the river, then stopped and he pointed to a narrow street entrance across the road. 'Why don't you do the rest on foot?' he asked. 'The centre's only a couple of hundred yards up there.'

I walked up the Call Dos de Mayo, as directed, a calm and almost countryfied street of white walls, and windows draped in sumptuous folds of baroque plaster, picked out in sober yellow. Orange blossom bespattered the cobbles, and there was a champagne sparkle of May in the air. A victoria of the most fragile elegance – a 'milord' of the kind introduced by Edward VII – passed with a clip-clop of hooves and a soft rumble of wheels. Blind white cubist shapes were piled round a Moorish battlement at the end of the street, and above and beyond, the Giralda Tower, once the greatest of all the minarets of Islam, possessed the sky. A wall panel in ceramic tiles showed the Calle Dos de Mayo as it was nearly a century ago, and there has been little change. The panel was put up by a soap-maker and it is one of the many magnificent advertisements for such things as the first Kodaks, for gramophones with horns, cough mixtures, mustard plasters, and forgotten motor cars that decorate the city's walls. All the products promoted in this charming fashion have one thing in common: they no longer exist.

At the end of this short cut to the centre, I was confronted with the grey, fortress shape of the Cathedral. 'Let us build a church so big that we shall be held to be insane,' a member of the Chapter urged as soon as the great mosque had been levelled and the building of the Cathedral began. The Emperor Charles V, most human of the Spanish monarchs, who gardened and kept parrots in his modest quarters in the Alcazar nearby, would not have approved; but he was too late upon the scene, although in time to abort a similar operation on the Mosque at Cordoba. 'You have built here what you or anyone might have built anywhere,' he said, 'but you have destroyed what was unique in the World.'

The Cathedral of Seville is vast high and very dark, with visitors wandering a little apprehensively in the gothic twilight, like travellers lost in a foreign railway station. Light invests the gloom from a side-chapel in which a Madonna with the tear-streaked face of an unhappy fourteen-year-old girl broods over piled up church treasure. A thousand candles flicker and the great organ crashes and booms.

I had hoped to see the tomb of Pedro the Cruel, but it turned out that this, which is in the crypt could be visited only on one day in the year. Of the doings of this monarch, identifiable to his trembling subjects, as he stalked the streets at night, by his creaking knee joints, a single episode illustrates the utter foreignness of the medieval mind. When rejected by a celebrated beauty, Señora Urraca Osorio, the King had her burned to death. Having studied his record, this does not surprise us. What does – what remains beyond the compass of our mentality – is that the one thing that seems to have been of importance on this occasion was that Señora's modesty should not have been placed in jeopardy, and that to prevent this possibility her maid leaped into the flames so as to screen her mistress from any such exposure.

Pedro is supremely the 'bad' king of Spanish history. St Ferdinand, conqueror of Seville from the Moors, whose 'incorruptible' body lies in a silver casket in the Cathedral's Capilla-Real, the one who meant well. The saint, a rigorous pietist who died eventually through excessive fasting, was the scourge of heretics, setting his people an example of righteous severity in one instance by lighting in person the pyre on which an assortment of dissenters of one kind or another were to be incinerated. 'His Majesty wore a rough gown tied by a rope, and carried a large cross. He ordered all those who had come to the place to kneel and pray, and imposed upon them a penance. Before taking the torch from the hand of the executioner he kissed the cheek of each of those who were about to suffer.'

The Cathedral expresses conquest and domination in architectural terms of sheer mass, and it comes as a surprise to learn that it is not the largest building in Seville, being second to the nearby tobacco factory, now the University, in itself only exceeded in size by the Escorial. It was here that Don Jose had his first encounter with Carmen. Five thousand girls were employed to make cigars, and the Victorian British visitor found sexual release at the sight of a girl rolling a cigar on her thigh, which she could be persuaded to do for a payment of ten centavos, equivalent of a penny. Murray, of the celebrated guidebook, viewed the scene with both unction and disapproval, although he clearly found it hard to tear himself away. He found the girls handsome but smelly, and 'reputed to be more impertinent than chaste.'

My visit to Seville in the Spring of this year [1984] had followed one in the autumn of 1981, and I was delighted and relieved to discover the town transformed by change and renewal. In 1981 it had seemed dirty, depressed and anarchistic, a prey still to moral confusion and lack of guidance following the disappearance of the dictatorship. Sevillians had shown themselves at a loss to know what to do with civil liberty, and some excesses had stirred up a sullen reaction. The walls were covered with resentful graffiti. 'Democracy is a lie, democracy kills', they said. Franco's face had been stencilled everywhere, accompanied sometimes by the supplication, 'Come back to us. We can't carry on without you. All is forgiven'.

Municipal workers – like so many Spaniards at that time – had been on strike for months, and the streets were piled high

213

with rubbish, visited by innumerable rats. Pornography had arrived – a stunning experience for a strait-laced people – with blue cinemas everywhere, horror video cassettes, and window displays of the Karma Sutra in booksellers previously specializing in devotional manuals and the lives of the saints. For nearly forty years prior to Franco's death in 1975, Spanish lovers had been forbidden to kiss in public, and in small-town cinemas a priest stationed himself at the projectionist's side ready with a square of cardboard to be held over the lens where a romantic episode might be held to weaken public morality. With the return of democracy there was time to be made up. In 1981 public courtship had become a ritual, and in Seville couples fell into each other's embrace in any square that provided suitable benches, and lay locked together while the hours passed and the rats scuttled through the rubbish under their feet.

Package-deal trips to London were advertised to deal with unwanted pregnancies, at the all-in charge including two nights in the British Capital, of £250. The restraining influence of the Catholic Church seemed to have collapsed along with that of the State, and the city filled up with mystic carpet-baggers eager to fill the vacuum, with mediums, sun-worshippers, 'cosmobiologists', whirling dervishes, American fundamentalists howling for Armageddon, and sects dating from the pre-Christian era, including one, as the newspapers reported, that sacrificed chickens and drew omens from a study of their entrails.

All the symptoms of a society in advanced decay were present, yet suddenly, in the twinkling of an eye, Sevillians had managed to work the poison out of their systems, and the phase was at an end. Now all appeared sweetness and light. The streets had been swept and garnished, flowers were in bloom in all the parks, Pied Pipers had lured all the rats away, and the walls had been cleansed of their nostalgia and their hate. Some Sevillians were of the opinion that the Virgin known as La Hiniesta had come to their aid in response to the conferment to her image – despite the steadfast opposition of Communist councillors – of the City Medal of Honour. Now she was junior only to the Macarena Virgin, who not only held the medal but had been promoted in 1937 by General Queipo de Llano to Captain General of the Nationalist Armed forces.

I looked up an old Sevillian friend. 'What finally happened about Cristina?' (Three years ago he had been in despair after his only daughter, aged 20, had gone off to live with a married man aged 44.) He seemed surprised that the matter should have been brought up. 'Oh, that's a thing of the past. She's settled down now with a nice chap who works in the Banco de Espana. Daughter aged two and expecting their second.'

The talk turned to the condition of Seville, and some mention was made of the fact there had been four bank robberies on the previous day, May 10th.

'It's nothing,' he said. 'Something they picked up from Butch Cassidy and the Sundance Kid. A boy walks into a bank, pulls out a gun, tries to speak Spanish with an American accent, and say *esto es un robo* just like they do in the film. The customers line up with their hands up against the wall, the cashier pushes a few thousand pesetas through his window, and the kid picks it up and gets out. It's a phase. Not a thing to take seriously. Nobody gets hurt.'

This relaxed view was in part shared by Charles Formby, H.M. Consul in Seville. 'In this town they snatch hand-bags and break into cars,' he said. 'We have specialists called *semaforazos* who break the windows of cars held up at traffic lights and grab what they can. This is not a dangerous city. No-one gets violently robbed. You're safer walking the streets of Seville at night than you are in London.'

Charles Formby supplied the statistic that at 38% Seville's unemployment (it is the centre of a depressed agricultural area) is the highest in Spain, and that 12% of the unemployed are university graduates. He did not agree that petty criminality was a product of this economic situation, but believed it was a matter of obtaining money to buy drugs.

Don Rafael Manzano, Director of the Alcazar of Seville, agreed with him, adding his conviction that Spanish society was now the most permissive in Europe. Since the departure of Franco, the police were no longer feared, persons found to be in possession of small amounts of drugs were not charged, and gaol sentences were light except for serious crime. He mentioned that on May 10th – the day of the four bank robberies – a young man only released from prison a few hours previously had been arrested in the act of throwing packets of cannabis and heroin over the prison wall.

One of Seville's problems seems to lie in its nearness to the point of entry of drugs from North Africa. 'I happened to be down at Algeciras, the other day,' said a reporter on El Correo de Andalucia, 'and watching all these pregnant women getting off the ferry from Tangier, I wondered how many were really great with child, and how many with bundles of hashish.'

So the drug problem remained, but otherwise Sevillians seemed to be ridding themselves of the social sickness mild or grave, largely transmitted through the movies. The likely lads of Spain were no more immune than the youth of any other country from the cultural revolution inspired by such films as *The Wild Ones*, and the first bikers had appeared ten years ago. But they were a dwindling cult, and the Sevillian Hell's Angels Chapter were down to a fraction of its former membership. I found a group tinkering with their Yamahas in a square on the edge of town. The majority were gypsies with sensitive Asiatic faces and melancholy eyes, and one was quite frank about their problems. 'It never really took off here. In my view to be a real *Angel del infierno* you have to wear the right leather gear, and how can you expect anybody to do that when the temperature never drops below ninety in the shade?'

In 1981 there had been a few poorish imitations of punks and skinheads about, but now they were out of fashion, and were no more to be seen. On the other hand, youngsters in plenty thronged the well-lit squares and avenues far into the night. It was something new in Spain, a phenomenon the beginnings of which I had observed on the earlier visit, bands of well-dressed and well-behaved children ranging in age between 12 and 16, who turned the nocturnal streets into a playground.

Back to Don Rafael in his cell of an office, tucked away behind the scenes in the magnificence of the Alcazar. 'We are suffering,' he said, 'from the side effects of the levelling process. Until recently, only rich people who didn't have any work to do, could stay up enjoying themselves all night. Now everyone tries to. At the time of Holy Week it's understandable. The processions are going on all night, and it's something you have to see. No sooner is Holy Week over and we're into the Spring Fair.' The upper class rent chalets in the fairground and give parties that finish at six in the morning. Nowadays, however bad the unemployment crisis people were determined to defend their democratic rights, one of them being to stay up as late as the rich. If the parents stay up all night, said Don Rafael, so do the children, their argument being that democracy knows no age limits. As a result they fell asleep over their books at school. 'We as a nation,' he said, 'have lost the ability to say no.'

All the old Spanish things were staging a come-back, including bullfighting. In the Autumn of 1981 so gloomy was the outlook for the national spectacle that the concluding *corrida* of that year had to be put forward a day because *Sevilla F.C.* would be playing at home on the Sunday originally planned. Of this overshadowed occasion, the Correo de Andalucia's sportswriter said, 'So the present decadent season draws to its end. It has offered little but boredom for the public, and bad business for the promoters, with about half the seats unsold. In this last *novillada* we saw underweight bulls, the fourth with a marked tendency to slip away, and the last two virtually calves, tottering about on shaky legs. There was great protest from the crowd that the fifth was lame. It wasn't. It was numb from being shut up in a pen for so many weeks. As for the fighters, what can we say? Carlos Aragon was sad and insipid. He spread boredom like a disease. When they trundled the sixth bull in I said to my neighbour, "wake me up if anything happens". He didn't because he, too, fell asleep.'

The aficionados blamed it on the quality of the bullfighters themselves. The spirit had ceased to breathe upon them, leaving them cold and cautious, and their performance a tawdry commercial transaction in which a minimum is returned for money received. Fighters of old such as Joselito, drew more crowds to Seville than a visit by the King. Half his personal fortune went into the purchase of four emeralds for the Macarena Virgin, protectress of bullfighters (and, unofficially, smugglers), and when, at the age of 25, he died in the ring in exemplary fashion, the image was dressed by her attendants in widow's weeds in which she remained for a month.

Could there ever be a return to those days? Even that seemed possible. The bullfights accompanying the Spring Fair this year suggested a long hoped-for renaissance, and at a time when the enthusiasm for football was on the wane, all seats in the Seville rings were sold out. At last, we were assured, the bullfighters had put their house in order, and meek bulls with shaved horns were a thing of the past.

It was too soon to hope for another Joselito, but there were plenty of newcomers of promise, including Manuel Ruiz Manili, a rising star of the old order, already nicknamed *El Jabato* (the young wild boar), who put on a near-suicidal display. 'This man,' said one critic, 'really hurls himself into the fray ... If only he lasts!' He made another sportswriter shiver. 'I could *feel* those horns scrape his cuticles. Number two was as wicked a beast as I've ever seen. "Watch me cut him down," Manili said. "They'll either carry me out on their shoulders, or I'm going to hospital." They carried him out. Delirium.'

Manili, accorded the title *El Triunfador* (the triumphant) at the fair, was a gypsy, and he could have been the brother of the stylish policewoman I had seen directing the traffic at the Puente San Telmo. In 1984, as ever, the gypsies remain a little mysterious, uncharted human territory on the fringes of Spanish society. There was not a gypsy bank manager in the whole of Spain, but the best bull-fighters, the best musicians and the best dancers were, and always had been, gypsies. For many foreigners, and quite a few natives, too, the mental image called to mind that typified the attraction of Spain was that of the arrogant dancing gypsy.

The capital of gypsy Spain had been the Sevillian suburb of Triana, birthplace of the Emperor Trajan, but the developers laid seige to it, and it fell. In Triana of old, fountain-head of the popular music of Spain, the gypsies lived in extended families in tiny, immaculate communal houses around a courtyard glutted with flowers. These were called corrals, and now of the hundreds of such nuclei of which Triana had been composed, one only remained. It was occupied by twenty three perplexed families lost among the upsurge of modern buildings, their main problem seeming to be how to pay for the water for the 400 pot plants which turned their courtyard into a tiny Amazonian jungle.

For all the changes, stout-hearted pockets of resistance remained. In Triana, the secluded patios where dances dating in all likelihood from before the days of Trajan had been taught and practised, had all been swept away, but the dance went on. Anita Domingo's Academy of Spanish Art, where little girls go to stamp their heels and click their castanets, while Anita thumps out a *Sevilliana* on the stiff piano has a longer waiting list than ever. Half the pupils are gypsies, neat and small-boned, with flashing black eyes and the classic profiles stamped on ancient coins. Ancient customs refused to die. Newspapers reported the case of a gypsy working in a Triana department store, who was involved in a dispute over the granting of three days leave of absence to allow her ritual abduction, the essential preliminary to a gypsy marriage.

Holy Week was at an end and, graced by the Royal Family's participation, it was spoken of as the greatest success since the days before the Civil War. The Spring Fair had been – to use a fashionable adjective – a marathon one, but here there was an undertow of caution in the deluge of praise. It was noted that only fifty years back three days had been considered ample for civic festivities, originally based on the conviction that they were essential to the production of Spring rains. Now it was commented upon that not only had the fair been increased to seven official days, but that further prolongation was threatened by tacking two more days onto the front 'to test the illuminations'.

With these excitements at an end, we had slipped into the calm aftermath of the 'Easter of Flowers' when the city turns back with reluctance to the routines of normal existence. There was nothing at this time, I was assured, likely to be of interest to the visitor, except relatively unimportant processions when local Madonnas were carried on tours of their zones of influence, as if to be allowed to see for themselves that all was well. Arrangements were informal. Sometimes the little cortege might stop at the door of a particularly devout household to allow its head to be summoned into the presence, bowing a little anxiously to report on the doings of the family. Such outings were collectively known as 'Her Majesty in Public'.

In the Easter of Flowers a light diet and early to bed were the orders of the day. 'Good fun while it lasted,' was the general view of the fiesta. 'Now let's catch up on some sleep.' Released from the treadmill of pleasure, people escaped out from the bustle of the centre to take a quiet stroll by the river or settle for a nightcap and a chat in one of the cafés on the Avenida de las Constitucion, among night-scented flowering trees and within sight of the great and ancient places of their history.

Sitting with them, I noticed the pull exercised by these grandiose surroundings; how, as if moved by the tug of a magnet, they would shift their chairs for a better view of the floodlit palaces, the spires, the domes and the impeccable profile of the Giralda, the contemplation of which by night is claimed by some Sevillians to foster a lucid tranquility conducive to untroubled sleep.

The last of the milords passed homeward-bound, ghostly against the sash of mist marking the course of the Guadalquivir. An exceedingly polite waiter who always said 'at your service' whenever he took or served an order, caught in a moment of inactivity swayed a little, eyes half-closed. Somebody at the next table said, 'Early night tonight, then,' but nobody moved.

At this moment a tremendous din started in the side-street to my rear, and within seconds an excited crowd came into view. In their midst, though towering over their heads, stalked a dozen outlandish figures, on 6 foot-high stilts to which their legs were bound. They were patched and masked in medieval style, some of them disfigured with beaks and flapping wings like nightmarish birds. There was something compulsive and a little sinister about their vitality as they came on with a pounding of drums and a clash of cymbals, sometimes breaking into a grotesque, stiff-legged dance.

One by one my neighbours straightened in their chairs, rose to their feet as if at the command of a powerful hypnotist, allowed themselves to be drawn away into the street and into the crowd, began to clap and fell into step. The café emptied, and the tired waiter, roused by the rhythm to the point of tapping it out on his tray, caught my eye and came over. 'At your service,' he said, and I asked him what it was all about.

'Clowns,' he said. 'They're limbering up for *Cita en Sevilla* (Appointment in Seville). Starts tomorrow and finishes on June 21st.'

'Don't tell me another fiesta,' I said.

'Not quite that,' the waiter said. 'The Municipality's trying out something new. They didn't want us to be bored, so they're importing six jazz bands, two Czech-Slovak orchestras, visual poetry from Italy (whatever they mean by that), Son et Lumiere, an ice-show with a real ice-breaker, musicians from Morroco, and clowns from all over. Half a dozen famous opera singers have been invited; there'll be poetry readings, cante-flamenco, art and photographic shows, and the biggest antiques fair ever, or so they say. That's about the lot.'

'What happens after the 21st June?' I asked.

'We haven't been told yet. Be sure they'll think of something.'

'It's a lively town,' I said.

'You're right,' the waiter agreed. 'There's always something to look forward to.'

He dropped into a chair at the next table, and put his head in his hands for a moment. 'Sometimes I think they overdo it,' he said.

17

The Cossacks Go Home

The bad news when I came in on the pellucid evening of October 22nd 1944, from a day in the apple-scented criminal villages encircling Naples, was that I would be leaving for Taranto next morning to take 3,000 Soviet prisoners back to the Soviet Union.

Our senior sergeant and I stood together under the vast, dusty chandeliers of the Palace of the Dukes of Satriano, where 312 F.S. Section had its headquarters, and the doleful cries of Naples reached us through its open windows. The sergeant said that this was something that couldn't be handled by an N.C.O. Arrangements would have to be made for an emergency commission, but the Field Security Officer was away and it was too late to do anything that day. 'We'll try and fix it up in Taranto for you as soon as you get there,' he said.

Next morning I took the train to Taranto, a pleasant trip in the almost icy perfection of the South's most splendid month, after the air is washed and cooled by the first autumnal rains. At Taranto there was no talk of emergency commissions. A major was waiting for me at Movement Control. He wore no Intelligence green flash, but the faint aroma of lunacy, and the fierce but vague eyes identified him almost certainly as a member of the Intelligence Corps.

'You're taking over 3,000 shits,' the major said. 'My orders are these. If any man so much as attempts to escape, you personally will shoot him. Is that clear?'

At this point the correct reply should have been, 'With all due respect sir, this is an improper order,' but I said nothing, assuming the man to be mad.

'Show me your gun,' the major said.

I took the .38 Webley out of its holster and handed it to him.

'Is this the only weapon you have?'

'Yes, sir.'

'I see. Well I suppose there are plenty of guns to be had. Are you a good shot?'

'No, sir. I'm a bad one.'

'Oh. Well, you must do your best. Where do you come from? Naples, is it? Do they have any foxes up there?'

'Not as far as I know, sir.'

'Pity. They do in Rome. That may surprise you. In the woods.'

Mention had been made a few weeks before by a Taranto section member on visit to Naples of a concentration camp for Russians having been put up outside the town. The news had surprised us because it was the first intimation we had received of the presence of any quantity of Russians in Italy. I was too late to visit the camp, for just before my arrival they had been moved out – with some difficulty, as it appeared – and put aboard the Reina del Pacifico, a regular troopship providing stark accommodation for troops and '3rd class families'. Here they were confined in remarkably cramped conditions below deck, guarded by the infantry company that would travel with them, via Khorramshahr in Iran, whence they would entrain for the last stage of their journey to the Soviet Union.

I went aboard, and went below immediately to inspect the prisoners, finding a dispirited rabble of men in rumpled German uniforms, lying about wherever they could, and covering every inch of deck space. An army that has suffered defeat and captivity is like a man overtaken by a sudden illness. The change is dramatic and instantaneous. Men seem to have shrunk in their uniforms which now no longer fit; movements behind the wire had slowed down, and discussions become spiritless and desultory. To this familiar climate of demoralisation, the prisoners had added a depressing ingredient of their own, for a number were singing an endless and mournful song. This was explained by a young Jewish interpreter, supplied by the army, as a tribal death chant. Nearly all the prisoners were from Soviet Central Asia.

According to Benjamin, the interpreter, the 'Russians' had not been told that they were to be repatriated to the Soviet Union, until Red Army officers had arrived in the camp to inspect them, like looking over cattle that would soon go to the slaughterhouse. The result had been panic, and some attempts at suicide. These mens' grievance lay in the fact that, although compelled – as they claimed – to serve in the German army in Italy, they had deserted as soon as possible to the partisans, and when rounded up by advancing British forces they had been promised Allied status, which was to include re-fitting them out in British uniforms.

A young Russian – the only obvious European in sight – presented himself. His name was Ivan Golik, a Muscovite with the rank of senior lieutenant, who had assumed command. Golik was miraculously spruce and untouched by the demoralisation which surrounded him, but the message he had for us contained no comfort. Golik said violence had been used, and a number of men injured before they could be driven aboard, and that if our promise of Allied status was not kept we could expect mass suicides. I passed this information to the Officer Commanding Troops who promised to contact GHQ for further instructions. On the strength of this, I told Golik that I believed that any promise made to the prisoners would be honoured, but that as the ship was leaving forthwith, nothing could be done about relieving them of the detested German uniforms until we reached Port Said. The assurance seemed to cool the atmosphere, and the Kalmuck death chant ceased, but it was still thought prudent to search the prisoners for combustible materials that might be used to set fire to the ship, and to keep them below hatches until Egypt was reached.

In the meanwhile, there were urgent problems to be dealt with, one being the production of a nominal roll required by the O.C. Troops – all original documentation relating to the prisoners having been lost. This task was complicated by the fact that many men possessed the same name, and there were accusations among the Russians that some men had given false names in an attempt to conceal their identities. The inference was that certain of the prisoners had committed crimes while serving in the Wehrmacht.

In the course of these routine enquiries the facts soon proved to be less simple than we had supposed. Practically all these Asiatics had been members of the 162 Turkoman Infantry Division, composed of Uzbecks, Khirgiz, Kazakhis and other Muslim racial groups, who had fought in Northern Italy under the command of Lt General Von Heygendorff. The mere fact that they had served in the Turkoman Division was significant, because that meant that they were 'volunteers', and not mere *freiwillige*, who normally served in non-combatant labour battalions.

The division had begun life in 1942 in German-occupied Poland under the command of an eccentric Wehrmacht officer General Von Niedermeyer, who thought of himself as the German Lawrence of Arabia, spoke Turkic even in his home, embraced Islam, and dressed as a native. In 1943 the division operated in the Ukraine, and after the defeat at Stalingrad it returned to Germany for re-organisation, before being sent to Northern Italy.

Here it fought well under the German officers, but committed to battle in July 1944 against American armour it began to disintegrate. It took a bad mauling near Orbetello-Grosetto and Massa Maritima, and this provided the opportunity for many of the Asiatics to change sides. They were terrified, they said, of falling into the hands of the Americans who, as they thought, believed them to be Japanese auxilliaries under German command, and who – as the rumour went – ran over such prisoners with their tanks. For this reason they took care to surrender only to the Partisans, and it was to the Partisans that they gave themselves up in large numbers on September 13th during heavy defensive fighting near Rimini.

Starvation and the most atrocious treatment in German POW camps, and the realisation that they were faced with the alternative of certain death had induced these men to serve in the German armed forces. These ultimate survivors spoke in the most matter-of-fact way of their experiences, some of which had been macabre indeed, and I soon came to know that for every Soviet who had come through the fiery furnace of the POW camps, a hundred had found a miserable death.

It was a fire of a magnitude that Russia and Central Asia could never have known in all history, for there were vast human surpluses to be cleared as rapidly and as economically as possible. Every prisoner was ready with his own personal recital of horror, but a typical account providing a hundred variations on the same theme was provided by a young Tadjik herdsman. This boy who had hardly ever seen a real Russian, and never heard of Germany, had been snatched suddenly out of the steppes, put into uniform and given the first train ride of his life, in the great westward scramble of an unprepared and ill-equipped army to face the Nazi tanks. The train stopped and the soldiers began to march towards a distant canonading, but a few hours later were ordered to turn back. Marching thereafter in the direction from which they had come they were halted by soldiers in unfamiliar uniforms who disarmed them, put them in lorries and drove them a short distance to an enormous barbed-wire enclosure. It was only at this point that they realised that they were prisoners of the Germans. They remained here for three days without food and water, before a body of Germans arrived accompanied by one who addressed them in Russian through a loud-hailer. The Tadjik remembered him as short, bespectacled and mild in his manner. 'There are far more of you than we expected,' he explained. 'We have food for a thousand, and there are ten thousand here, so you must draw your own conclusions.'

The prisoners were then lined up and the order was given for Officers, Communists and Jews to step out of rank, but no-one moved. All the prisoners had by now torn off their badges of rank. The bespectacled German then invited any prisoner who wished to do so to denounce any of his comrades belonging to these catagories. He promised that those who co-operated in this way would receive favoured treatment, including all the food they could eat, and after some urging and more promises and threats on the German's part a number of men stepped out of the ranks and the betrayal began. Those selected in this way were marched off to a separate enclosure, and at this point the bespectacled German said that a further problem had arisen through the shortage of ammunition. The men who had betrayed their comrades were given cudgels, and ordered on pain of instant death to use these to carry out the execution.

The Germans, on the whole, contrived to have prisoners kill prisoners. There were not enough SS 'special squads' to go round, and it was found that regular army soldiers were reluctant to engage in mass murder. It was true, too, that ammunition for such secondary uses was running low. Later in the war an SS squad leader provided me with the official statistic that unless a man was shot in such a way that the muzzle of the weapon virtually touched a vital area of the body, it took on average three shots to kill him, and inexperienced squads armed with automatic weapons and firing at a range of 12–15 feet, used up double that number of rounds. At that time there were countless thousands to be destroyed.

In the disorder of those early days of the German push to the East, I learned from my SS informants that the method of selecting Jews for elimination was both rapid and unscientific. Prisoners, as soon as taken, were ordered to drop their trousers, and those found to be circumcised, shot on the spot. As all the Muslims composing the Asian units were also circumcised, these, too were butchered en masse.

Later, when the Germans came to realise that many of the Asiatics were fiercely anti-Russian, and therefore employable as required in the German armed forces, the selection became more careful, but mistakes were still made. At one camp, in which several of the men I questioned had been held, the shibboleth of old was still in use. Every captive in turn was made to repeat in the presence of a Muscovite collaborator the sentence 'Na garye araratye rostut krupniye vinogradi' (On the Mountain of Ararat grow great vineyards), and those who had difficulty with their Ps were assumed to be Jews, although in fact many Asian tribesmen found this as difficult to cope with as the Jews.

Between four and five million soldiers died in these camps, most of them of starvation, but for those men of iron resistance determined to survive, come what might, the first hurdle to be cleared was an aversion to cannibalism; and I was convinced that all the men on this ship had eaten human flesh. The majority admitted to this without hesitation, often – as if the confession provided psychological release – with a kind of eagerness. Squatting in the fetid twilight below deck they would describe, as if relating some grim old Asian fable, the screaming, clawing scrambles that sometimes happened when a man died, when the prisoners fought like ravenous dogs to gorge themselves on the corpse before the Germans could drag it away. It was commonplace for a man too weak from starvation to defend himself, to be smuggled away to a quiet corner, knocked on the head and then eaten. One of the Asiatic Russians I interviewed displayed the cavity in the back of his leg where half his calf had been gnawed away while in a coma. In these episodes there were certain privileges that fell to the strong, who like lions over a kill, were left to take their share of the meat before the hyenas were permitted to approach. Cruel-

lest of the camps from which my informants had sought any
way of escape, seemed to have been at Salsk in the Kalmuck
steppes, on the railroad between Stalingrad and Krasnodar.
Here, seven days of total starvation prepared the prisoners for
what was to come. When bread finally arrived they were
forced to crawl on their hands and knees to reach it under the
fire of German soldiers, who were being trained as marksmen.
Nearly all killings were carried out by prisoners. Jews were
buried alive by their non-Jewish comrades, force-fed with
excrement, and very commonly drowned in the latrines. There
were spectacles here from the dementia of the Roman Empire
in its death throes, when naked prisoners were compelled to
fight each other to death with their bare hands, while their
captors stood by urging them on and taking photographs with
their Leicas. An innocent-faced Uzbek hardly out of his teens
described these combats. A killer could earn a little favour,
gather a little following among the Germans by developing his
own murderous speciality. One man used to kill a defeated op-
ponent by biting his throat out. Another would bring a man
down by twisting his testicles, before breaking his neck by a
kick to the head. The Uzbek claimed to have despatched one of
the guards' favourites by braining him with a femur he had
wrenched from a corpse and kept hidden until the moment
came. For this he was much applauded, given a crust of bread
and the chance to volunteer for service in one of the Muslim
auxillary units being formed at that time.

Deep divisions and animosities had developed among the
prisoners as a result of their sufferings in the camps, where it
had been every man for himself; and I soon came to the
conclusion that only Ivan Golik could keep them in order,
and that our dependence upon him was total. Two days out
from Taranto the interpreter, Benjamin, told me that
Golik had asked to see me alone and I had him brought to my
cabin.

A discussion was conducted with some difficulty in a mix-
ture of Russian and German, and Golik told me that a mutiny
was being planned by a mullah, who was held in great awe by
the Asiatics. This mullah's official name on the nominal roll
was Sultanov, but he was known to the prisoners as Haj el Haq
(the Pilgrim of Truth). Although enlisted as a mere private in
the Red Army, he had been a member of the royal family of the

Emirs of Bokhara, who had been such a thorn in the side of the Kremlin, until the Russians had entered the city in the early twenties and had this man's murderous old great-uncle thrown from the tower of his own palace.

The mullah, a detester of all Russians, and enthusiastically pro-German, managed to convince most of the Muslim soldiers that Adolf Hitler was working secretly for their cause and had made the pilgrimage to Mecca. Golik explained that a leadership struggle had developed between him and the holy man, with both pulling in opposite directions. 'I am determined,' Golik said, 'to take these men home. I am their guardian angel. Haj el Haq believes in paradise. He wants us all to die.' Golik's view was that the mullah would be shot as soon as he set foot on Russian soil, and therefore the mullah had nothing to lose by instigating a revolt. Golik believed that as soon as he gained enough following, the mullah would order the men to force their way past the guards up on to the deck, and there commit suicide by throwing themselves into the sea.

As part of his strategy, he said, the mullah had ordered the men to resist the reintroduction of army discipline and to reject all orders given them either by Golik himself, or by the two junior lieutenants, or by men who had previously held non-commissioned rank in the Red Army. He believed that the mullah's influence could only be combatted by the transformation of this rabble into something like the semblance of a fighting force. The argument came back to the British uniforms. If the prisoners got them all would be well, because the mere wearing of them would proclaim to the Soviets when they arrived at the end of their journey, that the British had recognised them as their allies. The new uniforms, worn with Red Army badges of rank would transform sluggards into soldiers and banish day-dreaming and despair. Golik wanted to be able to hold inspections, arrange parades, award punishments, do a little ceremonial drilling on deck if that could be sanctioned, as soon as the uniforms came. If they did not, the mullah would have won, and the men would fall in behind him.

I asked for the mullah to be pointed out to me, and we went below together. Despite the late season, the weather remained hot. The ventilation had failed and the prisoners, crammed into the holds, and stripped to their underpants, lay in rows, as

African slaves must have done, their limbs shining with sweat. The wooden partitions dividing up the holds released an ingrained sourness adding to the sharp odour of so many bodies in close confinement. There was a great shortage of water, because all the Muslims were obliged to wash ritually six times daily. One or two spaces had been cleared for the men to squat in circles to listen to their story-tellers, and Golik called my attention to the mullah seated cross-legged in one of these circles, a small man with a polished ivory head and a face full of scepticism and malice. It was the mullah who led the audience's formal outcry of astonishment or alarm whenever the story-teller reached a dramatic crisis in his narrative; and whenever a man had to pass behind him he went over to kiss the prayer beads the mullah dangled from his hand. We noted men at prayer, taking care, Golik said, to make their prostrations well within the mullah's view. This in itself was a bad sign, he said, for public prayer was discouraged in the Red Army, and could cost a man promotion. If no uniforms came, they would all fall back in prayer.

The journey from Taranto was slow and tedious with the ever present threat of trouble brewing in the holds. A hot wind from Africa breathed on the ship night and day. The Mongul Buryat tribesmen chanted interminably about death and paradise, and the water dripped ever more slowly from the latrine pipes. Golik felt his authority draining away. The two junior lieutenants, Pashaev and Genghis Khan (there was also a private with this distinguished name) pretended no longer to hear his orders, while the mullah terrified the men by his trances during which he prophesied doom for all of them.

On 28th October we reached Port Said, where we were told that there would be a delay of some days during which we would trans-ship to the Devonshire. Here we were joined by two more interpreters, Private Shor from Aleppo, and a Bulgarian Jew, Sergeant Manahem, who had led the 12-man demolition team in Colonel Keyes' unsuccessful commando raid on Rommel's headquarters.

With the arrival of these fluent Russian speakers I saw my presence on the Devonshire as unnecessary. I had never been given any indication, except by the mad major at Taranto, as to what I was expected to do, and I had had virtually no contact with the O.C. Troops, who was in all probability himself

230

completely mystified as to what I was doing there, and had at no time sought to make use of my services.

I therefore visited Movement Control at Port Said to request permission to return to Naples, hoping to be favoured by the technicality that the movement order issued in Taranto instructed me to accompany the Reina del Pacifico to its destination, and made no mention of a further voyage on the Devonshire. My reception by the Movement Control Officer was a bleak one.

Seeing that my arguments were without effect, I produced for the first and last time an extraordinary identity document issued to members of my previous North African section when sent on the more absurd kind of missions. This authorised the bearer to wear any uniform and called upon all persons subject to military law to assist him in any way, etc. The effect on the officer was less than electrifying. He took the paper, glanced at it, and threw it down. 'This may have worked for you in North Africa,' he said, 'but it won't here, and it won't in PAI-Force, where you're going. Get back to the ship.'

Aboard the Devonshire again, I found that in my absence the British uniforms had arrived. Bound to the wheels of the military machine which, once set in motion could not be stopped, the Quartermaster's department had spewed forth a wild assortment of stores, including not only the so-long-desired uniforms, but all the complex and in this case useless impedimenta supplied to troops, including anti-gas equipment, entrenching tools, camouflage netting, long-johns, to say nothing of razors and shaving brushes, the uses of which were mysterious to these hairless men.

The prisoners swarmed like bees, buzzing with excitement over the piles of equipment dumped in their midst. Suddenly the fog of inertia and depression had been dispersed. Golik, in an evilly-fitting battle dress, but full of martial zest, had become the hero of the day. Moral was ebullient, and even the heat and stench of the holds seemed to have subsided. When the men could find space to walk among these crowded bodies, they did so more briskly, and had straightened themselves up. The mullah had retired to the latrines, 'to await a great vision,' and here he remained for the rest of the day.

Within a few hours the last of the Russians had been kitted out as British soldiers, and the tailors among them were given shears and set to work adapting garments made for the big-boned well-fed men of the West to the smaller bodies of Asiatics bred in the main from generations of mare-riding nomads. With their upgrading, the prisoners were to be given full army rations too, and although these men had eaten human flesh, they refused the liver – which was all the meat we ever received – on religious grounds.

Our fully-fledged Russian Allies, as they now were, seized with the greatest delight on the three-fourths of this gear, which one would have supposed to be quite useless, and began to convert these to their special purposes. Working with extreme ingenuity and skill, they dismantled such objects as zinc water-bottles, mess-cans, and above all tooth brushes, nail brushes and combs; and pierced, spliced and amalgamated them to produce a variety of miniature musical instruments: strange antique-looking fiddles, lutes, pipes and rebecks. Soon the bowels of the ship quivered with the wild skirl of oriental music.

We sailed from Port Said on 2nd November with hope fizzing like an electric current through the ship. Golik, transfigured with optimism, had one more request to make. Included in the kit issued to each Russian was a truly superb Canadian blanket of the finest and fleeciest grey wool, and Golik now asked if he could be permitted to have a pair of these transformed by the tailors into a Red Army-style officer's greatcoat, in which he would like to make his appearance at the celebrating concert to be given by the ex-prisoners next evening. This, he assured me, would set the final stamp upon his authority.

It was hard to refuse Golik anything, especially as in any case our interests interlocked. All that mattered was to come to the end of a trouble-free journey. The coat was made in a day: a garment fastening high in the neck, and falling to within six inches of the wearer's toes. It would have conferred dignity upon a trader in the old camel-market at Ismailia. He came on deck to show it off when it was ready, standing at the rail against the hot glitter of the sea and the incandescent Arabian coast-line, and a couple of off-duty members of the escort, sunbathing nearby, got up awkwardly as if undecided whether to stand to attention. When we went below most of the prisoners saluted him.

The concert given by the Asiatics was unlike anything I had ever seen before, or have seen since. It was an entertainment to fill the steppes' great emptiness, and hollow in time, transplanted perfectly here in the faceless surroundings in which we crouched. The art of the nomads had grown up without the aid of stage props, and depended on mime and masquerade, plus a dash of shamanistic witchery; it lifted the mind clear away from unacceptable reality to glowing new worlds of the imagination. Costumes were procured by magical adaptations of camouflage netting and gas capes. Supreme theatrical art had transformed a man who had tasted human flesh into a tender princess, stripping the petals from a lily while a suitor quavered a love song; we heard the neighing of the horses and the thundering hooves of a Mongol horde on their way to sack the town. Whatever these men had suffered in the camps, nothing had been able to take their art away. It was to be understood that this spectacle devised for the entertainment of the princes of Central Asia would have little appeal for the soldiers of the British escort, for not a man attended. What was less easy to understand was the boredom of a European Russian like Golik, who, sweltering in his coat, fell almost instantly asleep, snoring heartily to the accompaniment of arcadian pipes.

Next day the process of rehabilitation went ahead according to Golik's plans. The Russians were allowed up on deck in batches, and a little space was set aside for Golik to conduct token inspections, check hair-cuts, and lecture his N.C.O.s on military tactics. The O.C. Troops making his rounds of the Russians' quarters in the holds, noted that at last these had been scrubbed out to his complete satisfaction, and Golik was complimented, and some further relaxations decreed. The mullah had been forcibly put into a British battledress, and for the moment little more was heard of him. We all began to breathe more easily. This interlude of calm was disrupted by a most singular happening.

The three interpreters were profoundly oriental in their backgrounds, an influence which especially showed in their attitude to gold. This they appeared to regard as a magical substance, quite apart from any value it possessed for its purchasing power. Sergeant Manahen wore a signet ring made from gold wrenched from the jaw of a dead Italian on the battlefields. This had become like an African ju-ju for him – something invested with its own spirit. He did not like the ring to be touched, and complained of feeling a slight headache whenever he removed it from his finger to wash his hands. Shor, from Aleppo had been give his first bath as a baby in a bath into which one hundred gold coins had been showered; and his parents, holding his arms and legs, had made him go through the motions of swimming 'so that he should swim in gold for the rest of his life.' Benjamin had spent his boyhood in a religious community in which only the Rabbi handled money, and it was an unfortunate chance for all of us that this young man, for whom gold until now had been a legend, should have been the one to have smelt out its presence on the ship.

Benjamin was cheerful in appearance and sympathetic in manner, and the prisoners confided in him more freely than they did with us. It was this special intimacy that had sprung up that clearly induced one of them to show him a gold coin he possessed, and Benjamin borrowed it from the man and brought it to me, agog with excitement, for a ruling as to whether it was genuine. Of this there was no doubt. The coin was an Edward VII sovereign, but the mystery was where it had come from, and I asked Benjamin to do his best to find out. Questions were met with a smokescreen of conflicting stories, designed it was to be supposed, to cover up guilty facts. Piecing the evidence together, we concluded that the sovereigns had been taken from a British agent parachuted into Northern Italy, who thereafter, in all probability, soon vanished forever. We knew that agents sent behind the lines were normally supplied with gold, either in the form of sovereigns, or five-dollar pieces which had an accepted value wherever they might be offered.

What proved to be of fundamental importance in these events was that Benjamin, by his probings, discovered the existence, and eventually the whereabouts, of many more coins – about 50 in all, and immediately set about devising a method of persuading the prisoners to part with their treasure.

The ship possessed its own NAAFI, open for an hour daily, and selling a limited supply of such things as chocolates, sweets, cigarettes, stationery and depressing souvenirs stocked up in its call at Port Said. Despite their new status the prisoners were not allowed to visit this, perhaps because it was assumed that they had no money to spend.

Benjamin got his hands on a NAAFI price list, bought a sample of each article in stock and went in search of those with hidden gold. When he found one he pushed a square of chocolate into his mouth, and let him hold a toy camel, or work a lighter shaped like a sphinx. His offer was to supply one pound's worth of NAAFI goods for every gold sovereign. This was sharp practice, for everyone but the intended victims of the swindle knew that sovereigns changed hands in the bazaar of any Middle-Eastern town at five pounds, five shillings apiece. Many of the prisoners were reluctant to pay up, and when one hung back, Benjamin brought into play a particularly disastrous form of salesmanship. His argument – as we learned too late – went, 'You'll be off this ship in a few days. After that what good will money be to you? Surely you know what's going to happen?' Sometimes at this moment, he went so far as to point a forefinger to his temple in a significant way.

In the end Benjamin succeeded in convincing most of the prisoners to discard hope in exchange for the pleasure of the moment, and they handed over the gold and went off chewing a Cadbury's bar, and often clutching a ridiculous toy. In this way the seeds of despondency were effectively sown, and soon the men began to go down with it, one after one, like victims of an epidemic disease.

The storm broke with the Straits of Hormus sinking below the lip of the sea behind us, and Khorramshahr waiting, like a frown on the face of destiny, only two days away. The prisoners had been allowed on deck and a slow swing of the pendulum of authority back to Golik had left the mullah isolated, as one by one his adherents again placed their neck under the yoke of military discipline. The Pilgrim of Truth had got rid of his uniform once more, and now wore a kaftan with voluminous sleeves and a large turban, both made from British army underwear. He still received the unctious attention of a hard-core of followers, most of them, it was said, having some special reason to fear Soviet retribution.

The mullah had professed all along not to understand Russian, so, when the final confrontation took place, and Golik ordered him to go below and put on his uniform, the Battalion Commander took care to be seconded by Junior Lieutenant Ghenghis Khan, still sullen, but finally subdued, who repeated the order in the Uzbek language.

Golik had prepared himself for what followed. The mullah, an agile man, jumped to his feet, shrieking to his supporters to follow him, slipped through the ring of Golik's guards, and jumped into the sea. Golik, close at his heels, went in after him. A number of men intent on suicide had been inspired to climb the rails, but their resolution was demolished by the general outcry of *akoola*! (shark). In fact, the twisting grey shapes of large fish were to be seen everywhere, swimming close beneath the surface. The mullah's kaftan billowed in the water, he spread his arms feebly as if trying to fly; his eyes were closed and the sea washed the memory of fury from his face. Golik had reached him in a vigorous dog-paddle and kept him afloat, while the ship hove-to, and a boat was lowered.

For the mullah, when he was lifted aboard, this was the end of the road. The Uzbeks had gone dashing along the rail for a last gaze into eyes full of the rapture of paradise, but all they saw was a man fighting to fill his lungs with air and wincing and puking like a drowning kitten. He had not been permitted to die, and his survival was a matter for humiliation and sorrow. They watched the artificial respiration being given on the deck, saw the mullah's limbs move and his eyes open; then they turned their backs, and went away.

The last day on board was spent in preparation for the hand-over, which was to be elevated to a military occasion; the men of the escort fussed endlessly with their equipment and practised the arid drill movements with which they hoped to dazzle their Soviet opposite numbers.

I saw Golik as he readied himself for the fateful confrontation.

'What do you feel about things now?' I asked.

'Optimism. As long as you people stand by us. At worst I'll do ten years in a camp. I'm twenty-five now. I've still plenty of life left.'

We squeezed through the narrow waterway of Shatt El Arab, and tied up under a cold drizzle in Khorramshahr. In this threadbare city the Russians and the West were in daily mistrustful contact. It was the military show-window of nominal allies who hid their aversion between unbending correctness and skin-deep affability.

We looked down over a glum prospect of marshalling yards

under the soft rain. All was greyness, befitting the occasion. In the middle-distance the strangest of trains came into sight, an endless succession of pigmy trucks, like those used in the West to transport cattle, but a quarter their size. It was drawn by three engines, the leader of which gave a sad and derisive whistle as it drew level with us. It stopped, and this was the signal for a grey cohort of Soviet infantry to come on stage and change formation before deploying to form a line between us and the train.

The escort party and the returning prisoners now disembarked, and there was more ceremonial shuffling of men, slapping of rifle stocks and stamping of boots. The O.C. Troops and the Soviet Commander then strutted towards each other, saluted, shook hands, exchanged documents formalising the completion of the hand-over, and the thing was at an end.

With the three interpreters, I had been quite left out of this. Our presence had always been an anomaly, a suffix to the O.C. Troops' authority for which the Army had provided no rules. Excluded from the ceremony, and ignored by both sides, we went our own way. Sergeant Manahem had actually passed through the line of Soviet machine-gunners, cast like identical tin soldiers, to inspect the trucks they were guarding, in which our Russians were to be transported back to their Fatherland. He came back to say that they had been used to transport pigs, and from the smell of them, he believed that they had recently served this purpose.

The British had about-turned and marched away back to their ship, but no objection was raised when we stayed on to watch the Soviet Commander and a following of goose-stepping subordinates inspect the front rank of the Russians, who were now prisoners once again. They came to Golik, standing, immensely stylish in ultimate defeat, at the head of his battalion. The Soviet commander circled him slowly in absolute silence. Both men were of the same height and build, and their great-coats were identical in cut and length, but Golik's was the better of the two. The Commander then turned in my direction and signalled to me, and I went over to him. He spoke good English, and his manner was pleasant. 'Comrade liaison officer,' he said. 'Please do me a favour. I prefer to avoid speaking to these pigs. I ask you to give them the order to board the train.'

I refused to do this, but told him that one of the interpreters might oblige him, and in the end, Benjamin did.

There was a bar in the port just out of sight of what was happening, and I sat there and listened to the sound of the train shunting, the clash of bumpers, the pig-trucks rattling over the points, and the train's whistle as it pulled out.

The three interpreters came in out of the rain.

'Any trouble?' I asked.

'Not a peep out of anybody, not even the mullah,' Benjamin said. 'They're going to be shot. Most of them anyway.'

'How do you know that?'

'I had a chat with the Major. He turned out to be quite a character. Full of jokes. Took a great fancy to Golik's coat. 'Whatever happens,' he said. 'I'll see to it they don't spoil *that*.' Russians have a funny sense of humour. It may have been one of his jokes, but I don't think it was.'

18

A Mission to Havana

I met Ian Fleming in 1957 at a party given by our mutual publisher, Jonathan Cape, which Fleming had attended with ill-grace. A shortage of space at the Cape headquarters in Bedford Square made it necessary to spread the occasion over successive days. We found ourselves immersed in this rump of the party, reserved Ian suspected – though certainly without justification in his case – for Cape's less prestigious authors, and he retired, disgruntled, to a corner, where I shortly joined him. He asked if I wrote poetry, and when I said I did not, he seemed disappointed.

Although already famous as the creator of James Bond, Fleming seemed to extract less pleasure than one would have expected from the writing of successful thrillers. He craved the society of what he thought of as 'serious' writers, above all poets, like William Plomer, who had introduced him to the firm of Jonathan Cape, and through whom all his business with Cape was done. Jonathan Cape himself much disliked Ian Fleming's writing, and refused to meet him, and could only be persuaded to publish his books by a united front established in Fleming's favour by the firm's other directors, and by William Plomer, their reader. Michael Howard, the junior director, told me that the decision to publish *Casino Royale* gave him sleepless nights, and a bad conscience.

The acquaintance made at the party developed into friendship, and Fleming and I saw something of each other over several years. I found him genial and expansive, although many people did not. His habitual expression was one of contained fury, relieved occasionally by a stark smile. He seemed to wish to inspire fear in others, and on several occasions said of some person under discussion, 'he is afraid of me,' a conclusion seeming to give him satisfaction. Another habit, which did not endear him to women, was frequently to explain in their presence that he had only taken up writing 'to make me forget the horrors of marriage.'

For some reason I could not at first understand, Fleming showed much interest in the fact that I had travelled in Central America, more particularly in Cuba, which I had visited a number of times. At that time he was Foreign Manager of the *Sunday Times*, and one day he asked me to come to his office to discuss a potential article for the paper.

He wanted me to visit Cuba for him, to see as many people as I could, including some to be named by him, and investigate the possibility of the success of the Fidel Castro revolt, of which little at that time had been heard in this country. It seemed that Fleming's desire for information was not only on behalf of the *Sunday Times*. It was generally known that he had been assistant to the Director of Naval Intelligence during the war, so I assumed that he was still involved in one or other of the intelligence organisations, probably in a department concerned with Latin American affairs. He said that he was unhappy with information about the progress of the revolt received through the Foreign Office, and also with the reports from his personal contact, Edward Scott, who lived in Havana. He showed me Scott's most recent letter. The revolt, said Scott, was contained in a small mountainous area, the Sierra Maistra, near the far-Eastern tip of the island, and should give no cause for concern. He predicted that with the United States solidly behind the dictator Fulgencio Batista, the revolutionaries would shortly be rounded up, and massacred to a man in local style, while the world turned its back. Fleming said, 'I simply don't believe it.'

For some reason he was convinced that Ernest Hemingway, who had been living outside Havana for several years, was in close touch with the rebels, and he was most anxious to have Hemingway's views on the prospects of their success. He made it clear that Hemingway was one of his heroes. Not only did he regard him as among the great writers of all times, but he had come to the conclusion through analysis of his writings, in particular his novel dealing with the Spanish Civil War, *For Whom the Bell Tolls*, that Hemingway had been in his day an extremely subtle and successful under-cover agent, and probably still was one. He had written to Hemingway, but had received no reply, but, uncharacteristically, Fleming had forgiven him, and still hoped that contact could be made.

Hemingway's oldest friend in England was Jonathan Cape himself, who had been successfully publishing his books for thirty years, and Fleming, unable to make a direct approach to Jonathan, suggested that I should do so and persuade him to write to Cuba and ask Hemingway to see me. Jonathan agreed, and a favourable reply was received. There was a personal interest for Jonathan in this introduction, because Cape and the literary world in general had been waiting some years for any signs of a new book from the Maestro, after the long pause in production following what had been hailed as his masterpiece, *The Old Man and the Sea*.

At the beginning of December, Fleming and I had a farewell lunch at the White Tower, after which we retired to his office for the briefing. Fleming said that it would be convenient for me to travel as a journalist, and the necessary accreditation was arranged with his paper. I was to take all the time I needed, and above all get out of Havana, and go into the country and see what was happening. He wanted to hear the viewpoints of Cubans of all kinds, from generals to waiters, and he still hoped that I might find some way of wheedling the fullest possible report out of the great Hemingway.

A few days later I flew to Havana, and, as suggested, took a room in the Seville Biltmore Hotel, in which Fleming's contact Edward Scott occupied a penthouse flat. We met within minutes of my arrival in the dark and icy solitude of the hotel's American bar. Scott was short, pink and rotund with a certain babyish innocence of expression that was wholly misleading. His manner, at first wary in the extreme, became congenial after he had read Fleming's letter.

Scott was the editor of the English language newspaper, the *Havana Post*, but appeared to have other, somewhat mysterious irons in the fire. He was a man Fleming much admired. Ian liked to have his friends ask him if his character James Bond was based upon any living person, and although he almost certainly believed Bond largely reflected his own personality, the standard reply was that he was a composite of a number of men of action he had known. When I asked the question that was expected of me, he agreed that Scott had contributed his share of the inspiration for his hero, while admitting that physical similarities were excluded in Scott's case.

I mentioned to Scott that Fleming had asked me to see

Hemingway and he seemed flabbergasted. The reason for his amazement was that of all persons, as he told me, he had just challenged Hemingway to a duel, following a fracas at a party given by the British Ambassador. Scott said that Hemingway had arrived in the company of the film actress Ava Gardner, who in a moment of high spirits had taken off her pants and waved them at the assembly. Scott, an ultra-patriotic New Zealander, had objected to what he saw as an insult to the Crown, and, following a bellicose scene with Hemingway, the challenge had gone forth.

Leaving the situation aside, Scott's view was that Hemingway had withdrawn from the political scene, and no longer bothered himself with such uncomfortable things as wars and the rumours of wars and that, this being so, his views on the Castro revolt would have little value. Nevertheless, the briefing being what it was, I telephoned Hemingway's home to be told that both Hemingway and his wife were ill with influenza, and were expected to be out of action for some days. I left my address and telephone number.

There seemed to be some uncertainty as to whether or not Hemingway would take up the challenge when he was on his feet again, and Scott, with whom I spent the first evenings in Havana, seeming to assume that any duel would be fought with pistols, always set aside a few minutes for target practice in a room fitted up like a range over his office. He used a pistol employing CO_2 gas as the propellent for lead slugs. This fascinating and presumably lethal weapon was quite silent. We took turns to shoot at various small targets, but rarely hit anything.

Havana, most beautiful city of the Americas, had quite suddenly become a dangerous place. Until the middle fifties, life there – at least as a tourist saw it – had seemed like a permanent carnival, but, by the time of my visit in 1957, the spectacle of violence was commonplace. There was a good view from the hotel window of the Presidential palace, and the garden-filled square in which it stood. The roads round the palace had been closed since March that year when twenty-one students had died in an attempt to shoot their way up to President Batista's office on the second floor. Now there were armed men everywhere.

I was standing at the window on the second evening of my

visit, studying this scene, when machine-guns in the square and on the palace roof opened fire, aiming it seemed in no particular direction, for a man standing on the balcony of a building across the street was hit, and fell, this being the first and last time in my life I had actually seen anyone struck by a bullet. Such nightly alarms had become part of the existence of Havana. That same evening I had just returned from a visit to the city morgue arranged by a reporter on the *Diario de la Marina*, where we saw the bodies of five murdered students recovered from the streets during the previous night. It was an only slightly grimmer harvest than average, the victims being members of one or other of the left-wing groups opposed to the dictatorship. Several had been savagely handled either before or after death, in one case the victim's eyes having been gouged out. Batista's police were held responsible for these outrages. Outside Havana, the situation was worse, and in the province of Oriente, a private army, led by Rolando Masferrer, was busily torturing and extirpating 'Reds' – in other words any members of the peasantry objecting to the feudal conditions in which they lived.

The Batista regime was in its death throes. This ex-army sergeant who had taken over power twenty-three years before, had shown himself the most capable, and in his social measures the most progressive president the country had ever known. The labour legislation he had enacted had established Cuba as one of the most advanced nations in Latin America. He had fought big business over his social security laws, and still had the support of the trade unions and the organised urban workers, whose wages were at this time the highest in Cuban history.

But now, old and tired, he governed by force rather than flair, and he was losing control. He had forfeited the affection of Cubans as a whole by his destruction of civil liberties, by press censorship, by the massive corruption he closed his eyes to, and the ferocious repression of dissenters.

I was in Cuba to gather information, a task providing simple rules to be followed to obtain the best results. In all countries there are sections of the population who know more than most about what is going on, and are usually happy, and often eager to discuss their experiences and opinions with anyone showing interest in them. These include most of those in positions of responsibility and power, and on a lower level, members of the legal and medical professions, journalists, and above all priests – who know of everything that happens in their parish.

In Havana I had excellent contacts including Ruby Hart Phillips of the *New York Times* who had arranged Herbert Matthews' visit to Castro in the Sierra, and who shared an office, with Scott. Through Ruby, Scott, and others, I met bishops, disaffected senior officers, disgruntled politicians, student revolutionaries, a Batista torturer, the two legendary generals, Loynaz and Garcia Velez, both in their nineties who had led the last cavalry charges in the war against Spain, but above all those great capitalists, including Julio Lobo, Chief of the sugar barons, without whose favour Batista's cause was lost.

From these encounters one certain fact emerged – that Castro's revolt, so far from being a proletarian revolution knew nothing of Marxism and took little interest in the industrial workers. This was the middle class in action, and the hundred or so sons of good families who had taken to the mountains were not only not Communists, but they were at daggers drawn with them. How was it possible to believe, as our American friends had succeeded in believing, that Castro, who was receiving financial support from half the sugar magnates of Cuba, could have been the advocate of world-revolution and the dictatorship of the proletariat?

It was a moment when the United States was about to repeat its classic error in Latin America by renewing its assumption that any movement opposing a right-wing dictatorship must take its orders from Moscow. But in the case of Cuba this was not so. How was one to explain why the Cuban Communist Party should have sabotaged Castro's 26th July Movement in every possible way?

The antipathy shown at this time by Communists for the Castro movement sometimes took extreme forms, and was returned in full measure. The chief concern of a Castro agent from the Sierra Maestra I met in Havana was that any of his former comrades who had become Party members might spot him and denounce him to the police. It was an attitude that provoked talk of reprisals among Castro's men, including serious discussions as to whether or not the Communists should be granted legal existence after the Castro victory.

I found that three-fourths of the Cuban people were either

openly or passively behind Castro, and it would have been logical for the United States to have thrown its weight behind him, too, in those days when every declaration from the Sierra was underlined by assurances of the wholly democratic intentions of the rebels, their respect for private property and for foreign investments, and of their determination to hold elections within weeks of taking over power. As it was, other decisions were taken, and the tottering figure of the dictator was supported by the Americans until the last. What little the majority of Castro's followers knew of Communism in December 1957, they distrusted or disliked. Three years later, largely through the success of the economic boycott organised by the United States, they had been herded into the Communist fold.

Fleming had said, 'go into the country,' and I did so, travelling by bus from one end of the land to the other. The first discovery was that the mental attitudes of the countryman were radically different from those of Cubans who worked for their living in the towns. The industrial worker had been converted to a kind of conservatism through his expectation of fairly steady employment the year round. The countryman enjoyed no such security. One fourth of Cuba grew nothing but sugar; and the single fact overshadowing the life of the Cuban peasant was that the sugar harvest occupied five months, to be followed by seven months of unemployment. He was ready therefore for a revolution of any kind that would help to fill his stomach in the seven lean months, and relieve him from such feudal bullies at Masferrer and his thugs.

Santiago, capital of the sugar country, was of necessity, where the action was, and I went there to talk to cane-cutters and sugar magnates, and also on a strong recommendation from Havana to make contact with a famous clairvoyant, Tia Margarita, said to be consulted on occasion by Batista himself, and to know as much about what was going on as anyone in eastern Cuba. The astonishing statistic had been offered that one person in three in Cuba, regardless of colour, was a secret adherent of one of the cults introduced by the Negro slaves; and Tia Margarita happened to be high-priestess of Chango, Yoruba god of war, most powerful of the deities of the African jungles.

She proved to be a comfortable-looking middle-aged black lady of compelling humour and charm, living in a small sub-

245

urban house with a garden full of sweetpeas, attached to the usual straw-thatched voodoo temple. Women of her kind were to be found in every town in Cuba, combining in their operations all the exciting mumbo-jumbo of horoscopy and divination with the real social service performed in solving personal problems of all kinds, and in treating the sick from their wide repertoire of herbal remedies.

Tia Margarita ushered me into a chamber cluttered with the accessories of her profession, the skulls of small animals, the withered bats and the dusty salamanders, gently kicking aside the live piglets and cockerels that would provide the material for future sacrifices. A faint culinary odour suggested the preparation of her celebrated remedy for nervous tension – a thick soup made from the bones of dogs. I added my contribution – a pair of dark spectacles – to the homely offerings, including roller skates, tubes of toothpaste, and a jar of Pond's Cold Cream, stacked under the war-god's altar. I noted the framed autographs, offered in gratitude by famous personalities: senators, baseball-players and motor-racers who had come here with their troubles.

The mild maternal eyes scanned the print in the open book of my face, and her expression was one of slightly puzzled amusement. She expected to be called upon to demonstrate her speciality by forecasting the exact date of my death; instead of which I asked her what the people of Santiago thought about the war, and its likely outcome. If that was where my interest lay, she said, who better to discuss the matter with than Chango himself – surely the final authority on all such matters – who spoke through her mouth at seances held at the temple every Saturday night? Unfortunately this was a Monday, and when I asked Tia Margarita for an opinion off the cuff as to the way things up in the Sierra were likely to go, she was oracular and obscure. 'Chango says victory will be to whom victory is due,' she said. Still, something came out of the interview, because Tia Margarita went into a kind of mini-trance, lasting perhaps ten seconds, then said that the war would be over in a year – which, give a few days, it was.

In the few days I had been in Santiago, warlike activity had recommenced. From the roof of the hotel in Cespedes Square, the night sparkled distantly where Castro partisans had gone into the cane-fields, to plant candles with their bases wrapped in paraffin-soaked rags. There was gun-play every night, usually when revolutionaries took on the police, but on one occasion when Castro's 26th July Movement and the Communists decided on a shoot-out. By custom, the first shots were fired precisely at 10 p.m., giving the citizens the chance of a quiet stroll in the cool of the evening before the bullets began to fly. With a half hour to go, and all the street lights ablaze, the promenaders began to stream out of the square and make for their homes, where they clustered at their doors like gophers ready to bolt for the shelter of their burrows when the shadow of an eagle fell upon them. Then, as the cathedral clock struck ten all the lights went out, and the streets were cleared for battle.

Back in Havana a call came through from Ian Fleming in London. We had made a loose arrangement for a meeting in Jamaica, but there was a change in dates. He asked how things were going, and I told him fairly well, adding that there was not a lot more to be done.

'Have you talked to the Big Man?' he wanted to know.

By this I understood that he meant not the President, but Hemingway. I told him that Hemingway had been ill, adding that Scott did not seem to feel that a meeting would be specially rewarding.

'Never mind Scott,' Fleming said. 'Do your best to see him.'

I assured him that I would, and Fleming said that he had just read *The Old Man and the Sea*, again, and had found it even better on second reading. He had the book open by the phone, and proceeded to read out a fairly long passage that he had found of special appeal.

A letter arrived from Hemingway next morning. It was neatly hand-written and formal in tone. He said he would be happy to see me at his farm, La Vigia, on the outskirts of the city, and would send his car to pick me up, suggesting the next afternoon for the visit.

Hemingway's concern for his privacy was in strong evidence at his farm, the roof of the building being screened by a high fence, with a gate secured by a chain and an enormous padlock. The driver got out to unlock the padlock, drove the car through the gate, then stopped to go back and chain and lock the gate again. I was ushered into a large room, furnished in

247

the main with bookshelves, where I found Hemingway, in his pyjamas, seated on his bed. He pulled himself to his feet to mumble a lack-lustre welcome.

I was stunned by his appearance. At sixty years of age he looked like a man well into his seventies, and he was in wretched physical shape. He moved slowly under the great weight of his body to find the drinks, pouring himself, to my astonishment, a tumblerful of Dubonnet, half of which he immediately gulped down. Above all, it was his expression that shocked, for there was exhaustion and emptiness in his face. This was an encounter that might have been dangerous and undermining to any young man in the full enjoyment of ambition and hope, because it presented a parable on the subject of futility. Hemingway's mournful eyes urged you to accept your lot as it was, and be thankful for it.

Some people, and Fleming and I were among them, regarded this man as one of the great writers of the twentieth century, and at this time, three years after he had been awarded the Nobel Prize, he had only just overtopped the pinnacle of his fame. He was a man who had gained all that life had to offer. He had crammed himself with every satisfaction, driven his body to the utmost, loved so many women, dominated so many men, hunted so many splendid animals. It was hard to believe that anything Hemingway had set out to do he had left unachieved. Yet after all his conquests he seemed ready to weep with Alexander, and, looking into his face, it was hard to believe that he would ever smile again.

We talked in a desultory and spiritless fashion, and it was Hemingway who brought up the subject of his publishers, showing little affection for them, but ready with criticism. He found them parsimonious, nervous of spending money on publicity, and this, he said, had had an adverse affect on the sales of his books in Great Britain, which were disappointing compared with those in the United States. He disliked the dust-jacket of the English edition of *The Old Man and the Sea*. A leading artist had been commissioned at great expense to produce the American version, which he showed me, and it had to be admitted that it was attractive enough to increase sales.

The release of this unexpected grain of information about his literary affairs led to my undoing. It seemed, mistakenly, to open a suitable opportunity – although Jonathan Cape had warned me that this was a topic to be approached with extreme caution – to mention that his publishers were eager to know whether anything new from him could be expected in the near future. The reaction was instant and hostile. A wasted and watery eye swivelled to watch me with anger and suspicion. What had I come for? What was it I wanted of him. In the coldest manner he asked, 'Is this an interview?' and I hastened to reassure him that it was not.

There was something in this scene with the faint remembered flavour of an episode in *For Whom the Bell Tolls*, featuring Massart 'one of France's great modern revolutionary figures,' now Chief Commissar of the International Brigade, a 'symbol man' who cannot be touched, and has come with time to believe only in the reality of betrayals. With infallible discernment Hemingway had described this great old man's descent into pettiness; and now I was amazed that a writer who had understood how greatness could be pulled down by the wolves of weakness and old age, should – as it appeared to me – have been unable to prevent himself from falling into this trap.

Suddenly the talk was of Scott, and there was a note of harsh interrogation. Did I know him well, and had I heard about the challenge? I admitted that I had. I added quite sincerely that I regarded it as childish and absurd.

He seemed appeased, almost amicable. 'Take a look at this,' he said. He put in front of me a copy of a letter he had sent to the *Havana Post*. In this, couched in the most conciliatory language, he had taken note of the challenge to a duel made by its Editor, Edward Scott. This he had decided not to take up, in the belief that he owed it to his readers not to jeopardise his life in this way.

I nodded approval. It was the best thing in the circumstances that he could have done. For all that I was surprised, and in some way disappointed at the wording of the letter, as I felt that his readers might have been left out of it.

The problem now was how Fleming's demands – seeming more eccentric with every minute that passed – were to be satisfied. And yet Hemingway's opinions on Cuba *ought* to have been worth listening to. He had gone there in search of 'paydirt' for his post-war fiction many years before, and remembering his passionate involvement in the Spanish Civil War and in the politics of those days, it was hard to believe that suddenly he had torn himself free from all involvement with his times and that Cuba for him was nothing but a tropical setting for the pursuit of visiting film actresses and gigantic fish. He downed another half-pint of Dubonnet, yawned, and I got up to go. He followed me to the waiting car. All his anger had passed and I imagine that he felt little but boredom. 'A final word of advice,' he said. 'As soon as you get back to the hotel, I'd change that shirt.'

The shirt was a khaki affair, with convenient buttoning pockets of the kind it was hard to find in London at that time, and I had picked it up in an army-surplus shop in Oxford Street. 'By their standards that's a uniform,' he said. 'You could find yourself in a whole heap of trouble.'

I pointed out that I was wearing seersucker trousers with the shirt. 'It doesn't matter,' he said. 'It's still a uniform the way they see it, and they make the laws. A lot of cops on this island with itchy trigger-fingers. They have a rebellion on their hands.'

There was nothing to be lost. I took the plunge. 'How do you see all this ending?' I said. Comrade Massart's cautious, watery, doubting eyes were on me again. 'My answer to that is I live here,' Hemingway said. In my letter to Fleming I wrote. 'Finally I saw the Great Man, as instructed. He told me nothing, but taught me a lot.'

19

The Bandits of Orgosolo

Towards the end of October 1962, Edmund and Vera Townley, a middle-aged British couple on holiday from Kenya, who
were making their way back to England by easy stages, arrived
in Sardinia. Edmund Townley was employed by an import-
export firm in Nakuru as well as possessing a half interest in an
apiary which was doing well. He was also a notable jack-of-all-
trades, who had been farmer, miner, and road-engineer in
turn, as well as a bit of an amateur detective. The Townleys
were regarded as a quiet couple, who didn't go out much,
happy in their home life. They were a good-looking pair, and
Vera had once been almost beautiful with strong, classic
features. Edmund has been described by those close to him as
being capable sometimes of aggressiveness and he was
outstandingly devoid of physical fear.

While the life of the Kenya highlands suited them very well
on the whole, they were both uneasy about the prospects for
European settlers in independent Kenya. In Edmund Townley's case, there was some special additional motive for ner-
vousness. He had been actively involved in the Mau Mau
emergency, both officially as a screening officer, and as a private individual organising his own information network which
had been responsible for the capture and death of several ter-
rorists. Now he had learned that his name was on the ultra-
nationalists' black-list. This holiday, therefore, was to serve a
double purpose. On the way home, the Townleys decided to
visit the Mediterranean, and in particular Italy, with the idea
perhaps eventually of buying land there for their retirement.
Like so many Britons in their situation who have passed the
active years of their lives under the African sun, they found
it hard to believe that they could reconcile themselves to the
climate of their native land.

The Townleys had always enjoyed pioneering, and now

they were on the look-out for a place where they could start from scratch once again, clear a piece of land and start a bee-keeping project. They had nearly settled for the Canary Islands, but as Mrs Townley spoke fluent Italian, it seemed more sensible to settle in a place where this could be put to use. Sardinia seemed the next best choice, and here, at least, there would be no language problem while, from their first enquiries, all the other natural advantages they hoped to find in their new homeland seemed to be present.

Sardinia, indeed, had a great deal to offer. In spite of the Aga Khan's luxurious settlement near Olbia in the north, the country was largely undiscovered by tourists, and land prices had not begun to soar as they had elsewhere in the Mediterranean. Nor so far had the coastline been disfigured by chaotic development projects, as for example had the Costa del Sol in Spain. The cost of living was substantially less than on the Italian mainland, the beaches were the finest in the Mediterranean, domestic help was cheap and plentiful, the people charming and hospitable, and the towns clean – some of them built round a core of noble architecture. This was a land, in fact, possessing all the warmth and geniality of Italy, minus slums, smells and noise. If anything more was asked of it, it was an archaeologist's paradise, littered with dolmens, prehistoric 'giants tombs', *nuraghi* (only one out of 7,000 scientifically excavated), Punic cemeteries, shrines to the gods of Carthage and Rome, and rocks bearing mysterious inscriptions.

The Townleys planned to spend two weeks touring Sardinia, and, having flown from Rome to Sassari, they hired a Fiat car and set out for the interior. Ten days later, they arrived in Nuoro which is roughly in the centre of the island. Here they were in the foothills of the Barbagia – some of the wildest and least-known mountains in Europe. Sardinia is an island, but it is also a country in its own right, and it is big enough – 170 miles in length from north to south – to possess real rivers and impressive mountain scenery. The sense of confinement, and in the end the claustrophobia of the small island, does not exist in Sardinia. Looking southwards from the window of their hotel room the Townleys might have imagined themselves confronted once again by a vast African horizon, although not so much the Africa of their own green highlands of Kenya as the Africa to the far north of their home on the barren frontiers of Ethiopia.

Nuoro has many attractions for the discerning tourist. It has stood apart from this century, a leisurely introspective town built in a graceful but haphazard fashion on the lower slopes of the sugar-loaf mountain of Ortobene. It is supremely Sardinian, and women in from the country still walk its streets in the bold flamboyant folk-costumes inherited from the Middle Ages. Official brochures claim the view from the top of Ortobene to be the most striking in Europe. In fact, one looks out across a wide valley at an awe-inspiring recession of granite plateaux and peaks: a glittering hallucinatory whiteness where the sun striking the hard rock-surfaces counterfeits glaciers and snowfields. These are the mountains of the Barbagia – the word is from the same root as 'barbarian'. They are only 5,000 feet high, but almost as remote to humanity as the Himalayan peaks, and they are the last refuge of some of Europe's rarest animals, including a species of pigmy wild-boar, as well as the indigenous home of the moufflon, elsewhere extinct. *Insani Montes* – the dangerous mountains – Diodorus of Sicily called them in the atlas he made of Sardinia in the first century B.C. There has been no time in recorded history when outlaws have not roamed the Barbagia, and they are still as inaccessible to the prudent as they were when the Carthaginian, the Roman, and the Aragonese generals set up their out-posts on the further side of this valley of Nuoro, and went no further.

The Townleys stayed the night at the Jolly Hotel, one of an Italian chain set up throughout the country to relieve the asperities of tourism in such provincial towns. In the morning, they told the receptionist that they would be keeping their room again that night, but as it was a fine warm day, had decided to go for a drive in the country. They asked for and were given packed lunches.

Leaving Nuoro, they followed the main highway for five miles in the direction of Orosei, and then turned off into the narrow, winding and deserted road that leads to Orgosolo. Whether they knew it or not, the British tourists were now entering a most remarkable area. After two or three miles, the road passes through Oliena. Next comes Orgosolo where, barred by the mountain of Supramonte, the road loops away to the right to join the main Nuoro-Cagliari road five miles further on. The population of these small sad towns and of the mountains behind them are the descendants of Nomadic hunters that peopled Sardinia in pre-history. Of Orgosolo, Franco Cagnetta, the Italian social historian, had written, 'Here life is essentially unchanged after thousands of years; one is at the centre – all the more astonishing because the centre itself does not realise it – of a civilisation that is infinitely retarded; that has inexplicably survived. This is the most archaic community of the whole of Italy – perhaps of the Mediterranean basin.'

As the people, so the landscape that has in part formed them. The mountain of Supramonte, which blocks the horizon south of Orgosolo like some flat-topped iceberg, is the bed of the sea thrown up by a cataclysm of 100 million years ago; its surface strewn with rocks gouged by the wind into fantastic shapes. The mountain has been hollowed out by vanished rivers, there are fissures a half-mile deep, vast unexplored caves, primeval forests of chestnut and oak, and the ruins of nuragic villages visited only by armed shepherds. The visitor to these parts from the outside world is warned not to leave the road, for this is the traditional stronghold of the bandit and of the vendetta.

Orgosolo, too, with its aroma of immeasurable antiquity has something to detain the traveller. In the greyness and the ugliness of its streets, one still sees figures from pre-history: old men in the stocking caps of the bronzes of the Nuragic period of 1,000 B.C.; an occasional shepherd carrying the triple reed-pipes depicted in the same bronzes. Sixty years ago, the whole town was built of *fughiles*, the most ancient of stone habitations consisting of a single circular windowless room (in which it was impossible to stand upright) and a hole in the roof to let out the smoke of the fire burning in the centre of the floor. A few *fughiles* still exist even if they are disguised these days behind the facades of normal houses. Students of folklore find Orgosolo of extreme interest, and the high spot of any celebration is the apparition of the *mamutones*, the ancestral spirits, in sheepskins and tragic masks carved in wood, transporting the onlooker into an eerie animistic world that lurks here in the shadows behind a perfunctory stage-setting of Christianity.

The invisible life of the community is as singular. Nothing but lip-service has ever been offered to the state, and the only laws respected are the ancient customs codified in the *Carta de Logu* of 1388, on the eve of the extinction of a thousand years of

Sardinian independence. Never since the overthrow of the rule of the Sardinian Judges by the Kingdom of Aragon has the presence of authority possessed legal validity in the eyes of Orgosolo, which initiated nearly 600 years ago perhaps the longest resistance-movement in human history. Within the provisions of the famous *Carta* are laid down in minute detail the rules for the conduct of the vendetta. Orgosolo's only building of significance is the Church of San Leonardo with the famous churchyard and its row after row of small wooden crosses marking the graves of men who have met tragic deaths. It has been stated in the Italian press that of a population of 4,500, over 500 men have died through the vendetta since the war alone. By local standards, none of these killings have been crimes: at the most, they are the malefic links in a chain of cause and effect, the payment of debts of blood, the almost mechanical retributions decreed by a revengeful Stone Age Jehovah.

The spot chosen by the Townleys for their picnic-lunch was a tiny triangular field half-a-mile from the outskirts of the town. Looking down from Orgosolo, it is the only green and pleasant place to be seen in any direction among the browns of the lean, sun-scorched earth. The owner of this small oasis of wild flowers and grass died mysteriously leaving no heirs to cultivate it. By chance, it offered an unusual amenity in the form of a small, oblong, flat-topped rock. It was the obvious – the only place for a picnic along the whole of the road they had come, and the Townleys, having pulled their small car into the roadside, climbed the low bank into the field, unpacked their luncheon boxes, and set out the contents on top of the rock. This would have been about mid-day, and the Townleys had their lunch and were perhaps given a little time, too, to relax in the pleasant sunshine before they were interrupted by the appearance of a stranger.

Two days later, on October 30th, the London *Times* published a short description of the discovery of their bodies by shepherds. They had been riddled by bullets but, said the *Times*, 'the motive for the killing is not clear. Wrist watches and other objects of value were left untouched. The theory is that they may have come across a band of outlaws, who impulsively shot them and fled.'

Other reports were more erratic and fanciful and, in the case of *The Daily Telegraph*, even self-contradictory. '... they were preparing for a picnic ... the couple must have stumbled on a bandit hideout, and the bandits in the dusk mistook them for approaching police and opened fire.' And a few lines further on: 'According to a reconstruction of the crime, the attack took place (by the roadside) shortly after the passing of the regular bus in the early afternoon.' *The Daily Telegraph* has the couple killed by a large calibre shotgun which it erroneously describes as 'the customary weapon of Sardinia', but next day it found that Mr Townley's own pistol had been used. This report ends by sketching in the Orgosolo background, where some years before more than twelve people were killed 'one by one after announcing the next victim's name in crude paint on the white walls of the churchyard.'

But even the *Times* theory was not a tenable one. The Sardinian outlaw is rarely a pathological criminal, but almost inevitably a man who considers himself an unfortunate victim of circumstances with as clearly defined a moral code as the man who has not been obliged to take to the mountains. Under pressure of hunger, he will commit acts of banditry, but the Robin Hood image is always there at the back of his mind. He robs with a certain flair, never molests a woman, never takes from the poor. If obliged to kill, such a man does not act impulsively but after extreme premeditation. Never in these mountains had a bandit been known to kill a foreigner. Seventy-five years previously, in fact, when two Frenchmen had been abducted by bandits who had believed them to be Italians, they were released as soon as the mistake was realised and sent back to Nuoro laden with propitiatory gifts. All Sardinia was aghast at this meaningless tragedy and, in due course, other and even less profitable theories were produced in an attempt to explain the inexplicable.

One of these was an attempted sexual assault on Mrs Townley, but it had to be dismissed as more than unlikely, for not only was the lady fifty years of age, but there were no signs whatever of any interference or struggle. A local newspaper improbably suggested that the Townleys' death might have been the result of a suicide pact and printed an interview with a fellow guest at their hotel who, although he understood no English, claimed to have overheard them quarrelling. But if this was so, how was the fact to be explained that the Townleys had been killed with an Italian weapon which was never found?

By the middle of November, more sinister allegations were appearing in the Italian press. The suggestion now was that the apparently motiveless killing of the Townleys had been an act of terrorism designed to disrupt the nascent Sardinian tourist industry, and to discourage such projects as the Aga Khan's development on the Costa Smeralda. On 15th November, Le Ore said: 'Sardinian banditry is perhaps divided into two camps; one committed to impeding the country's tourist development in which numerous financial interests are involved, and in particular those of the Aga Khan Karim; the other to protecting the operation. Naturally, the bandits of the first group are in the pay of obscure personalities and the most reactionary cliques, who are interested in keeping the island in backwardness and misery. In this light, the murder of the English couple would appear not as a stupid and meaningless crime, but an act of purposeful intimidation intended to terrify the future clients of Sardinian Tourism.'

A far-fetched solution, perhaps, but not without its germ of possibility. In our own days, vestigial feudalisms, which have survived centuries of opposition by political reformers and well-meaning governments, have collapsed and died when exposed to a tourist boom lasting hardly more than a decade. In 1950, in the South of Spain, where the conditions in those days were roughly comparable to the most distressed areas in Sardinia at the present time, the Andalusian field worker was paid 15 pesetas a day, and when laid off between sowing and harvest, sometimes lived on such things as roots, frogs and snails. The same man, transformed into an unskilled labourer on a holiday building site on the Costa del Sol or in Majorca, is now paid 300 pesetas a day. His daughter, rescued from the expiring feudalism of the South to become a chambermaid, earns almost exactly the same in one week as in a year in service in one of the great houses of Andalusia. Despite all the increases in the cost of living, the advance in the standard of living of the labouring class is huge.

The object lesson is not lost on the landowners of such countries as Sardinia where tourism remains an infant in swaddling clothes. Labourers employed on the Aga Khan's project near Olbia receive at least ten times the pay of a peasant on an estate, and work an eight-hour day as opposed to anything up to fifteen hours demanded from his workers by one of the landowners of the old school. A shepherd, who has been tempted from his skilled and ancient trade to become a waiter in one of the Costa Smeralda's luxurious and expensive hotels, may occasionally expect to receive in a single tip as much as he could have earned in a week trudging over the desolate mountains after his sheep. Insidiously and indirectly, everywhere, a tourist boom destroys privilege and imposes its own democracy whatever the form of the regime. It begins by mopping up the pool of unemployed upon which feudalism depends, and in the end entices away the workers that remain, thus depriving the feudalist of the labour he needs to carry on. He cannot possibly feel anything but hatred for the interlopers of the tourist trade, and if he is strong, unscrupulous and bred in a tradition of rapid authoritarian action, he may be ready to fight back – and with whatever weapon he can.

But the theory of the Black Hand of the diehard feudalist and devilish manipulations behind the scenes – however tempting to the Latin sense of the dramatic – had to be abandoned as a succession of macabre happenings, following immediately on the heels of the Townley killings, were considered and eventually related to the murder of the two British visitors. Now, too, the suicide-pact rumour, so eagerly seized upon by the Sardinians following the story that the Townleys had been shot by Edmund Townley's own gun, had to be relinquished.

On November 2nd, *The Daily Telegraph* said: 'The bullet-riddled bodies of two notorious bandits were found today under a bush less than two miles from the spot where a British couple, Mr and Mrs Townley, were killed last Sunday.

'One of them, Salvatore Mattu, 23, was said to have killed a policeman when he was only 19. There was a price of £600 on his head. The other, Giovanni Mesina, 40, was released from gaol a short time ago.

'Police investigating the deaths of Mr and Mrs Townley are inclined to admit that some connection exists between the two bandits' execution and the motiveless murder of the British couple. The most likely theory is that bandits executed the two for having killed foreigners.

'In addition, the bandits hoped that by "having done justice" for the murder of the British couple the duel between bandits and the police will again return to its previous comparatively leisurely course.'

The use here of the word 'executed' is significant, and it is correct enough in the case of Mattu, although a much less appropriate definition of the manner in which Mesina met his death. What this report does not make clear is that the discovery of Mesina's body followed that of Mattu. The story of Mattu's supposed murder of a policeman at the age of 19 cannot be confirmed. At the time of the Townley incident, Màttu was a fugitive from justice suspected of the kidnapping and murder of a rich landowner two years previously. Mesina, having come out of prison, had married and settled down in the town. Like forty per cent of the employable men of Orgosolo, he was without a job.

Four days after the Townleys met their deaths, Mattu's body was found – in accordance with local tradition, 'by a young and innocent child.' He had been shot to death and the corpse was displayed in what might be described as ceremonial fashion. Like a princeling of Ancient Egypt prepared for his journey to the underworld, his weapons and portable possessions had been placed at his side. This signified to a student of the mores of Orgosolo that he had indeed been executed following sentence by a secret court of the heads of the clan-families of the town. Someone let drop the fact that among the objects found with the body had been a pair of binoculars belonging to Edmund Townley. The natural assumption was that the crime for which Mattu had been judged, sentenced and executed in such short order was the Townleys' murder. But before the amateur investigators had had time to prise more information out of their contacts in Orgosolo, the situation was complicated by the discovery of Mesina's corpse. There was nothing this time to suggest a formal execution. Mesina had simply been murdered by a burst of fire from a sub-machine gun, and his body flung contemptuously face downwards on the ground. But the fact that both Mattu and Mesina had been found in the same place in some way linked their deaths together. It was known that Mattu and Mesina were sworn enemies.

In the meanwhile, police investigations had dragged to a standstill routed, as usual, by Sardinian *Omertà* – 'manliness' – the silence, the wilful ignorance, the honourable non-cooperation with the law, which is the normal citizen's defence against what is seen as the inhumanity and the essential 'foreignness' of Italian justice. Several hundred Carabinieri and members of the Public Security force abetted by a helicopter wandered aimlessly and forlornly about the rocky trackless wilderness of the mountain of Supramonte, lost themselves, broke their limbs when they fell into crevices, chased after shepherds who behaved like deaf mutes whenever they were cornered, and shone their torches into the blackness of caverns as big as cathedrals in which a thousand bandits could have hidden themselves and never been found. In Sicily, a politician was quoted as saying, 'a pity we can't lend them our Mafia.'

The middle-class Sicilian and Sardinian attitude towards both the Italian police forces are practically identical, one of amused contempt; and this quip was in recognition of the well-known fact that, after the Italian police (aided by an army division) had battled ineffectively against the thirty bands of outlaws infesting Sicily after the end of the last war, these bandits were liquidated in a matter of months, when the job was unofficially confided to the Mafia. But then there has never been a Mafia in Sardinia, where this famous and ferocious secret society is temperamentally as alien as it would be, say, in Holland or the West-Riding of Yorkshire. At the time of the Townley tragedy, there were ten outlaws on the mountain of Supramonte alone, despite the fact that a recent intensive police drive had resulted in forty of the citizens of Orgosolo being in prison serving life sentences.

As all these men would be normally covered by the blanket description of bandits, it is necessary to consider and attempt a definition of the word. Few of the forty lifers from Orgosolo dispersed about the island's maximum-security prisons would, in fact, have committed any crime by local standards. They would have been no more than the executors of long-standing feuds, quarrels passed down from generation to generation, faded and hardly identifiable hatreds taken over as a matter of social obligation by sons, grandsons and great-grandsons of the original disputants. Dimly reflected are the customs and the *lex talonis* of the nomadic hunters and migrant pastoral peoples of immense antiquity, of Homeric Greece and the Near East of the Old Testament, people without settled property forced to push on endlessly in the search for sparse pastures, or follow the movement of hunted animals into territories claimed by other tribes. These conditions still persist in the Barbagia in Sardinia, and they have been fostered by poverty, isolation, the remoteness of the central government, and by tradition. In such fossilised societies, the power normally confided to the State in a more advanced civilisation is stubbornly retained by the family – the Mediterranean 'compound family' of the anthropologist, which may number anything up to 100 members – a tribe in miniature composed of the 'senior father', then sons and grandsons, and all the wives (the women leave their parents to live in the patriarchal home). The family inhabits a single house, or a number of adjacent houses, is ruled by a Council presided over by the 'senior father', and holds all family property in the way of buildings and livestock in common. The compound family's strength lies in its utter self-sufficiency and its single will, and its weakness is its terrible memory. It is found in remote corners of Sicily and Corsica, as well as in Sardinia. Even in the tiny Spanish island of Ibiza – hardly visible on a small-scale Mediterranean map – a few such archaic family amalgams still exist, living in fortified towers, *atalayas*, which are architecturally related to the *nuraghi* of Sardinia, dominated by formidable patriarchs who a generation or two ago would have seen to it that their commands were enforced, if necessary by knife or gun.

A life-sentence for carrying out the obligations of the vendetta carries no social stigma in Orgosolo – in fact, quite the reverse: it is seen more as a kind of sombre accolade, the admission to the exclusive club of men who have not hesitated to sacrifice themselves on the altar of honour. In gaol, the *ergastolano* with an honour killing or two to his credit is usually a model prisoner, entitled to an Olympian aloofness, treated with respect by prisoners and warders alike, often addressed by prison officers using the polite form *lei* where a swindling millionaire must content himself with the familiar and contemptuous *tu*. From *Enquiry on Orgosolo* by Franeo Cagnetta: 'An ex-prisoner who comes back from serving a life-sentence finds a wife who has awaited him in perfect fidelity, and who has brought up and educated his children. Thereafter he occupies in the community a position of special respect.'

Cagnetta was referring here to the vendetta killer, but another and far more numerous class of outlaw must be included in the general category of bandits. This is a purely Sardinian speciality, the *dogau*, or semi-bandit, who is the creation of a catastrophic error on the part of the police. The police's mistake was the employment of secret informers, and action was taken without any check being made on the veracity of their reports. This created an immediate vested interest in banditry. The informer – paid a small lump sum for every arrest – denounced all and sundry, and a single anonymous accusation was enough to secure a man's arrest and imprisonment perhaps for years while awaiting trial. Worse still, acts of banditry were encouraged and organised by informers, who took a share of the loot before selling the participants to the police. The logical outcome was that when a man – however impeccable his previous record – had reason to believe that someone had denounced him to the police, he took to the mountains. After that, it was usually only a matter of time before hunger drove him to become a bandit in reality.

These borderline outlaws – suspects who cannot be charged with any specific crime – still exist off and on by the hundreds in the mountains of central Sardinia, and they form a pool of tough and embittered humanity – Samurai of our times, who are available for employment in any kind of dangerous or illegal activity. Last year, when possibly a record number of animals were stolen in Sardinia – no official figure is available because less than half the losses are reported – a rich man, the descendant of one of the original Italian 'Colonists', for whom the Sardinian underdog cherishes an inherited detestation, complained to a magistrate that the police couldn't protect his property. 'Why come to me?' was the magistrate's astonishing reply. 'Surely there are plenty of *dogaus* about on the look out for a job? Take on a few like everybody else does. You'll find you'll have no more trouble.' Cagnetta believes that practically every male citizen of Orgosolo has been a *dogau* at least once in his life.

The ill-fated Mattu and Mesina, the one presumed to have been sentenced and executed by a secret court, the other whose death still remained a mystery – although almost certainly linked with the execution of Mattu – had both started their careers as *dogaus*. After that, they kept the wolf from the door by staging a few unimportant hold-ups. These happen by the hundred in the remoter parts of Sardinia, are often carried out in an apologetic fashion with the nearest approach to courtesy possible when one man is holding a tommy-gun pointed at the chest of another, no-one is hurt, and the bandit gets away with the equivalent of a few dollars. From modest hold-ups of this kind, however – almost enforced charities – Mattu and Mesina graduated to kidnapping, in this way passing the point of no return. Public opinion in Orgosolo would still have remained sympathetic to them as the victims of circumstances, and when either man came into town to visit a parent or relation, he would have been given food and shelter, protected from the eye of the informer, and smuggled back after the visit to the safety of the labyrinths of Mount Supramonte. Even if Mattu or Mesina had found themselves compelled to kill a policeman while avoiding capture, it is unlikely that Orogosolo would have held it against them. But the purposeless murder of a foreigner would be regarded with horror, as a stain on the honour of the community and, therefore, to be dealt with implacably.

Orgosolo was once more in the limelight. Newspapers delved into history for accounts of the exploits of the innumerable bandit chieftains it had produced. The masterpieces of the illustrations of the old Tribuna Illustrata were rediscovered and reproduced, and they offered a highly-seasoned choice of scenes full of heroic action, savagery and anguish. A favourite was the attack on the Cagliari–Ussassai train carried out in 1922 by a force of about a hundred bandits. Another was the last stand of Salvatore Pau. It shows the bandit perched on one leg – the other having been broken by a bullet – waving his pistol defiantly while smoke spurts simultaneously from the muzzles of the rifles of the dozen soldiers who have him cornered. A third records the return of troops from a successful anti-bandit operation – the bandits roped to the backs of horses and the commanding officer receiving the congratulations of a government official, who receives him with raised bowler hat. There was also a highly imaginative reconstruction of the marriage in 1929 of the bandit chief, Onorato

Succu, celebrated in the Church of San Leonardo in Orgosolo after the regular publication of the bans, and followed by a banquet at which members of the local police force and government functionaries were entertained.

This was all very well, but most Italians took the view that such things belonged to the romantic past, and they were startled to learn that despite half-a-dozen full scale military expeditions since the turn of the century, the bandits were still there. A few serious commentators stopped to enquire into the anomaly that at a time when the nation's industrial growth-rate as a whole was the highest in Europe, areas existed in Sardinia where a tourist's life was not safe and where the social pattern typified by the tradition of the vendetta hardly differed from the description of such authors as Diodorus and Strabo.

Isolation, poverty and neglect no doubt explained the situation in part, but there were other areas – in Calabria and in much of Sicily – even more poverty-stricken, if slightly less isolated. This being so, the determining factor must be sought in history.

The Mediterranean islands, Sardinia included, became the colonies of the ancient world as soon as the continental nations developed into sea powers. Their colonisation was brutal, wasteful and forthright; analogous to the destruction by the Spanish conquistadors of the Caribbean Indians, and their replacement with plantation slave-labour brought from overseas. In the late Bronze Age, the indigenous civilisation of Sardinia had reached a degree of prosperity evidenced by its trade in luxury articles with Egypt, Phoenecia and Eruria, and it was protected by 6,500 fortresses – the *nuraghi*, some of them most ingenious and complex in construction, and large enough to shelter a whole village in times of danger. By the end of the sixth century, the Carthaginians had occupied all but the mountainous areas of the island, dismantled the *nuraghi* and massacred all the natives within reach. These they replaced by Libyan slaves, who laboured and died to produce wheat to feed the Carthaginian armies. Diodorus noted that a few Sardinians managed to survive by building underground shelters, and these could only be caught by waiting until they were forced to come out to visit their religious shrines – a problem the Romans surmounted by importing police dogs to chase the refugees from their hideouts.

New conquests brought new masters. After the Romans, came the Byzantines, then, following a thousand years of independence, the Aragonese – bringing with them their own brand of torpid feudalism – the Piedmontese and the Italians. Only the mountains of central and eastern Sardinia were never occupied and settled – visited at the most by punitive expeditions – and here in the Barbagia with its spiritual capital, Orgosolo, a little of the old independent Sardinia, however degenerate, survived intact.

All the men, who farmed in the plains, made roads, and built towns, were strangers and enemies to the untouched mountain peoples, and the Italians, who took over Sardinia in 1848, were as foreign as their predecessors. With the Italian arrival, the Sardinians got their first taste of capitalism and found it even more bitter to their taste than the anachronistic feudalism they were accustomed to. First of all, the common grazing lands were expropriated, sold by auction, and acquired at knock-down prices by the church. After that, a law was passed permitting any Italian colonist to claim as much land as he could afford to build a wall round. Italian timber companies then came on the scene and cut down the forests – a project which was completed in ten years. As a result, the climate changed and a number of small rivers dried up. The equivalent of the Elizabethan 'Statute of Sturdy Beggars' was enacted to deal with the vagrant dispossessed, who soon filled the prisons. 'The time has come to ask ourselves if, in the past, we have not wasted scruple', Cavour said. '... Treat them as the English treat the Irish.' The Italian police and troops, who poured into the island, did their best to comply with true Britannic ferocity.

Until 1848, the people of Orgosolo had lived as semi-nomadic shepherds, pasturing their animals on the mountains in the summer and moving down to the valleys in winter. Now they found access to the old grazing grounds denied to them, and much of the hill pastures had withered away. Some starved, but many turned to banditry. The acts of legalised robbery, by which they were deprived of much of their livelihood, have never been forgotten and are the unfailing justification for the criminality of these days. When a bandit kidnaps a rich man and holds him to ransom, he says, 'They robbed us, didn't they? I'm only getting back a bit of what belongs to me.'

The loss of the traditional grazing lands meant that the law of the survival of the fittest was applied with mathematical exactitude in central Sardinia. In good years, the herdsmen of Orgosolo contrived to pull in their belts and carry on somehow, living on their sheepsmilk curds and the occasional animal rustled from the flocks of the rich Italian settlers. But after a bad winter, the choice was rebellion or death from hunger. The best pastures were claimed by other villages further down the valleys, and over and over again they were forcibly taken over after terrific pitched battles. These were the notorious *bardanas*, raids organised for the extermination of competitors for meagre food supplies, and every man of Orgosolo expected to be conscripted by the shadow council of village elders for such an expedition at least once during his lifetime. All the nearby villages, Oliena, Marmojada, Formi, Desulo, Arzano, and Locoe, were the targets of these assaults. Locoe had to be abandoned for a number of years, and in an attack on Tortoli in 1894, every male inhabitant was either killed or wounded. More than once armed bands from Orgosolo fought their way right across Sardinia to Oristano on the coast to capture the salt needed for their cheese-making.

The men of Orgosolo went to the *bardana* to clear the way for their flocks, on foot, on horseback, even on bicycles; a small, compact and infallibly victorious horde reflecting in microcosm the sorties of famished Asiatic nomads into the plains of Eastern Europe of the Middle Ages. Orgosolo, the tiny microcosm of a State and conscientiously ignoring the State that contained it, saw these local conflicts as necessary, justifiable and as patriotic as the wars waged by the nation in pursuit of its larger interests. Reprisals by police or army were never more than temporarily effective. One might as well have tried to debar the bedouins of Arabia from their oases.

Parallel with these wars in miniature went the endless internal struggle of the poor against the rich – against the descendants of the Italian colonists, who had established themselves in the fertile valleys, and the rich native families, who had slowly accumulated grazing land which they now let to the disinherited at extortionate rentals. The shepherd steals with perfect conscience from the rich proprietor and, year by year, the number of cattle thefts increases. There is little trace of the Christian ethic in these mountains where Christianity

266

gropingly established itself only by the early seventeenth century. The impoverished, self-sufficient, semi-nomadic shepherd simply cannot understand the philosophy of non-resistance, of turning the other cheek, of laying up for oneself treasures in heaven. The very word 'good' has its own special meaning in Orgosolo. A good man in the Orgosolo version is one who never puts up with an injustice, and his opposite ranks with a cuckold in the scale of public contempt. Meekness and submission belong to the code of the man who has allowed himself to be disarmed.

A final factor – one that is not completely detached from the subconscious – completes the picture of the shepherd-warrior mentality. Wealth, possessions and the *strength* they imply are magical substances, wholly good. The unconcealed ambition of every shepherd is to possess flocks and land, and to lead the life of a rich man. To be rich is to be virtuous and if in seizing the possessions of others more virtue is acquired, then the act is sanctified by the end.

Both Giovanni Mesina and Salvatore Mattu were the sons of families that had never quite got on their feet, that had always lacked the mystic attribute of possessions, and could do no more than reproduce generations of landless, hired shepherds, who still in the year 1966 must be on watch all day or all night over their master's sheep for a payment in kind of 20 sheep per year.

Both men had been *dogaus* many times. In a criminal or semi-criminal capacity, Mesina – who was by this time on the threshold of middle-age – had made something of a reputation for himself. He was bold and intelligent, the stuff of which the founders of the powerful families of Orgosolo are made, and he could stand alone. In Sicily, he would probably have been a fairly influential member of the Mafia.

Mattu, in his early twenties and having still to win his spurs, had become a junior member of a band by October 1962. In 1960, both men had been denounced to the police as implicated in the murder of Pierino Cresta, who had been kidnapped and then killed as a matter of principle when the ransom was not forthcoming. Giovanni Mesina had been arrested, but Mattu had managed to escape and had been in hiding ever since on Supramonte. After two years, Mesina was released but found himself under a cloud back in his home town, where it was rumoured that he had secured his release by putting the blame for the Cresta killing on the missing Mattu.

By a strange, almost exhibitionist quirk in the occult mind of Orgosolo, newspapermen are warmly received and spoken to with surprising frankness, and the friendships they form in this most reticent of towns show them glimpses of a secret life, which is completely denied to the police in their isolation from the community. Thus it was that although the Townleys' killing remained officially a mystery, by the end of the month Italian newspapers were publishing an account, pieced together from inside information, of what had happened at Orgosolo shortly after noon on October 28th, and the succession of bloody events of the week that followed.

Mattu, it is accepted, had challenged Mesina to a duel to be fought in traditional style, 'at high noon', and the place chosen for this encounter was none other than the green field where the Townleys had stopped for their picnic.

It was Mattu who arrived first, and found the English couple resting after their picnic. He kept out of sight and waited for some time, and then, as there were no signs of Mesina, decided to return to his mountain hideout. At that moment, he noticed a pair of binoculars left by Edmund Townley on the ground beside the rock that had been used as a table, and although Mattu is supposed to have protested, when hauled before the secret tribunal that sentenced him, that he had no intention of robbing the Englishman, he said that he felt justified in his present emergency in helping himself to the binoculars.

A fearsome figure he must have appeared to the Townleys as he came into the open, unkempt from his two years in the mountains, and armed with pistol, sub-machine gun, handgrenades, and a dagger. What precisely happened next? In the light of what we know of Townley's character, his aggressiveness, was he imprudent – even contemptuous – in his handling of this desperate man? The facts as accepted are that Townley, realising that Mattu was a bandit, put his hand in his pocket, perhaps to offer him money, and Mattu, mistaking the movement for an attempt to draw a gun, drew his own pistol and shot him dead. He then destroyed Mrs Townley – out of pure compassion, as he claimed 'so as not to leave a widow.' The cynics of Orgosolo say that he simply decided to eliminate an eye-witness.

At this moment, Mesina, attracted by the sound of shooting, came on the scene and immediately realised what had happened. He hid until Mattu had gone off, taking Townleys' binoculars with him, then scrambled down the hillside for a closer inspection of the bodies. He is alleged to have said that he realised that there could be no question of a duel now because he would have considered himself dishonoured to fight with a common murderer. Instead, he went back to Orgosolo and told all he had seen – not, of course, to the police but to the shadow authorities of the village. Mattu was promptly caught, interrogated, sentenced and executed. But in the light of what followed, one has the feeling that Mesina had few sympathisers in Orgosolo – a man the whole town believed had allowed himself to be broken by the police.

It appears too that Mattu had left powerful friends, who were not disposed to allow the matter to rest as it was. He had been an associate of the then celebrated Muscau band, and a mutual allegiance may even have been established by an archaic blood-mingling ceremony. However much the Townley murders undoubtedly scandalised the bandits on Supramonte, there were loyalties that could not be dissolved, and consequently only one course to be followed. Within hours of the traditional exhibition of Mattu's body, Mesina had been spirited away from the house where he lived with the wife he had married only twenty days before, and was never seen again alive.

The stern obligations of the vendetta now fell upon the Mesina family, and ritual vengeance was entrusted to twenty-year old Graziano, a young man of saturnine good looks and acute intelligence, as he frequently demonstrated in his subsequent trial. At the time of his brother's death, he was being held by the police in gaol under investigation over a charge of sheep-stealing, and on being told what had happened, he carried out the first of his many gaol-breaks.

The Mesinas had once before been involved in a vendetta. This was the celebrated Great Quarrel – a small war à outrance, lasting from 1903 until 1917, conducted between a number of allied families over a disputed inheritance. In the course of this, although the Mesinas survived, some families lost all their males – including any children over the age of thirteen. One faction was headed by the town's priest, the 'senior father' of a group of a half-dozen families, a sinister cleric whose popularity in Orgosolo was such that he was accustomed to celebrate Mass with an armed policeman standing on each side. Father Diego Cossu, a rich man, and an efficient deployer of the power inherent in his position, hit on the ingenious idea of buying the complicity of the police to have his opponents – the Mesinas included – declared bandits. This was effective in terms of short-term policy – perfectly honest

citizens, who happened to be the father's opponents and who decamped in terror, being promptly shot down by the police. In the long run, the plan failed simply because the many fugitives the police failed to imprison, or kill, were transformed into real desperadoes. The Great Quarrel produced several novel situations in the history of outlawry and the vendetta. There were occasions when the police masqueraded as bandits and murdered along with the bandits, and others when bandits dressed up in borrowed uniforms and passed themselves off as police. Some rich sports even formed a band as a diversion from the boredom of hunting and cards – Robin Hoods in reverse, who armed and disguised themselves to rob the poor.

This was the golden age of Orgosolo's special contribution to the arts, the funeral lament; and Bannedda Corraine, most famous of Orgosolo's professional mourners, found her vocation when at the beginning of the vendetta her brother died in ambush. She was eighteen years of age and the most beautiful girl in Orgosolo. She sang,

Oh, my brother Carmine, flesh of platinum and porcelain
Where is Carmine, tinkle of precious metals, glimmer of gold?

Her laments have the passion and the imagery of the poetry of Garcia Lorca, perhaps occasionally even of the *Song of Songs*, and are still sung at Orgosolo funeral wakes. Some of the figures Bannedda clothed in death in her hyperbole seem unsuitably described. Onorato Succu – 'the golden-eyed flower' he was to become in death – was a bald, middle-aged man of repellent ugliness, who had committed twenty cold-blooded murders, and had made no attempt to stop a lieutenant from strangling two thirteen-year-old children of the enemy clan – 'to save an effusion of innocent blood' the man said, when asked why he had not shot them.

There has always been a class of professional peacemakers in Orgosolo, whose office it is to compose the differences of warring families when things appear to be getting out of hand. This they usually do by arranging a marriage between suitable members of the opposing parties. Such a traditional marriage convenience was once attempted in the Great Quarrel, but was quashed by the macabre Father Cossu who objected that as all the families were related, the laws of consanguinity would be endangered by the proposed solution. However, with the near-extermination of family after family, peace had to come in the end and when it did, it was the relief of all Italy. The petty slaughter in Sardinia had been an unpleasant distraction to a nation in arms, absorbed with the patriotic holocausts of the First World War. Seven bandits, who had been in prison six years awaiting trial, were pronounced innocent and released as a gesture of good will on the authorities side. A celebratory banquet at Orgosolo followed at which the survivors were reconciled. It was graced by the presence of the Prefect of Sassari, the Bishop of Nuoro, a member of parliament, numerous police officers and the richest of the local landed gentry. Civic dignitaries and men, who had committed multiple homicide with huge prices still on their heads, embraced and got drunk together. Mesina's grandfather knelt with the rest to receive the Bishop's blessing, but nothing is recorded of his action in the vendetta. He was one of the small-fry who had served without distinction or notice in the band led by the golden-eyed flower.

On November 3rd, 1962, the day after Giovanni Mesina's death, the body was taken to the Mesina house for the lying-in-state. Here, with all the members of the family present, the professional mourners entered the room and began their dirge. Only in the last verse, after a recital of the virtues of the dead bandit, of his strength, his charity, his courage, and his manly beauty, came the moment so long awaited: the shrieking denunciation by the leading wailing-woman of the name of the man held responsible for his death. However much this may have been common knowledge beforehand, the mourners would have kept up a ritual pretence of their ignorance of the killer's identity until this moment. But now, against the sobbing of the women of the household and the shrieks of the corps of wailers, the calls for vengeance were heard. This is the moment when the death sentence of the family council is entrusted to the member or members of the family most fitted to carry it out.

In a large clan well-supplied with vigorous males, the execution will take the classic form – a purely Sardinian variation on the theme of the vendetta in which the honour and responsibility is shared by several volunteers. These, because justice should be seen to be done, choose a public place to approach their victim, draw him aside, whisper his sentence to him, and shoot him down. Instantly, the streets empty, passers-by slip into obscure alleyways and disappear. Doors and windows close. Nobody has seen or heard anything. The town averts its head and acquiesces in its muteness in what has happened. But a small family like the Mesinas must cut its coat according to its cloth. The only suitable male – if one exists at all – may have emigrated, or he may even be in gaol. When the news of his brother's death reached Graziano Mesina, he was in prison, held as a suspect. By feigning madness, he had himself transferred to the prison infirmary, and from this he easily escaped and made for the region of Orgosolo.

For ten days he scoured the bandit hideouts, the caves and grottoes on Supramonte searching for the men who had killed his brother. Failing to find them, he decided to enter the town itself and arrived there on November 13th just after dark. He was incited by others, the prosecution said at his trial, to do what he did.

He was seen by a number of people that evening as he walked up the narrow, badly-lit main street. His appearance must have been dramatic indeed, for despite the presence of a strong body of police in the town, he was armed to the teeth including the inevitable hand-grenades and sub-machine gun, and it was evident to the bystanders from his 'iron face', as they described it, that he was about to accomplish a 'mission of honour'.

Mesina went into the town's principal bar almost opposite the town hall, which is hardly larger than a cell and furnished with a few shelves carrying bottles of wine and cognac, an enormous refrigerator and three low tables with even lower bench-seats about nine inches high. Antonio, the bar's proprietor, was refilling a row of the tiny wine glasses used in Orgosolo. 'As he came in our eyes met, and I knew what he had come for,' he says. Mesina said nothing. He simply gestured with his machine-gun, and the patrons quietly left their tables and lined up against the wall. Among them was Giovanni Muscau, 22 year-old brother of Giuseppe Muscau. Mesina believed Giuseppe to have been Mattu's friend and protector and to have ordered the killing of his brother, and so – as Giuseppe could not be reached – he had decided to make do with Giovanni. Graziano beckoned to Giovanni Muscau to leave the men standing against the wall, shoved him against the bar with the barrel of his gun, and then fired two bursts into his chest. Muscau slid to the ground and Mesina gave him a final burst as he lay there.

Now Mesina turned to leave and the incredible happened. The custom of Orgosolo absolutely forbids interference in a vendetta by outsiders, and even recommends an onlooker, who believes a vendetta killing to be about to take place, to throw himself face downwards on the ground, to avoid seeing, and therefore being capable of identifying the assailant. The deed is done; the women draw their black veils over their faces, the men slip away into the shadows, the executioners pocket their weapons and disappear.

In this case, to the astonishment of all Sardinia, what happened was that as Mesina turned to leave the bar, someone picked up a bottle and struck him on the head from behind. He fell to the ground, stunned, and was then overpowered and handed over to the carabinieri. This was a break with the past indeed, and the notables of the town are said to have shaken their heads in consternation at what was regarded as evidence of the moral corruption of their young men. Terrible reprisals were predicted but, so far, the Mesina faction seems to have been content to bide its time. Memories are long in vendetta country and it is nothing for a man to nurse his private vengeance for ten years or more – even to appear to have become reconciled to his enemy – while he awaits the right time and place for the settlement of the score.

A few days after my arrival in Sardinia, Graziano Mesina stood up in the iron cage, in which he had been kept like an animal in the courthouse of Cagliari, to hear sentence passed upon him. This conclusion of the sanguinary episode in the bar at Orgosolo had been long deferred because, in the meantime, Mesina had broken Italian records by escaping from five different gaols and one prison hospital. He had never used the slightest violence in these evasions, nor had he attempted to avoid re-arrest. Throughout the trial, he had shown no more than the mildest curiosity in what was going on, 'the master' – as one report put it – 'of a sphinx-like imperturbability.' When asked why he had killed the innocent young Muscau, Mesina considered the question for a moment and said, 'It was his brother Giuseppe I was after. I thought that by killing Giovanni I might tempt him down from the mountains to settle accounts with me.'

Present to hear this admission along with a great contingent from Orgosolo, the women with their black veils drawn half across their faces, the men in stiff dark suits kept for trials and funerals, was none other than the famous Giuseppe himself. Giuseppe Muscau had been captured and put on trial for banditry a year or so before, and as happens in about two such cases out of three, he had been acquitted for lack of sufficient proof. He is now unofficially the town's leading citizen, described as the possessor of great dignity and charm as well as something of a poet, and the highest honour Orgosolo can confer upon a visitor is to arrange for a presentation to the great man.

Giuseppe's demeanour on this occasion remained stolidly unrevealing, matching in every way in correctness by the standards of Orgosolo that of the protagonist in the dock. Both men were in the eye of a critical public. One supposed that one day if things hadn't changed by then, it would be Giuseppe's sacred duty, or that of his son, to kill Mesina – but it would be many, many years before that day could arrive. Only once Mesina was stirred from his apparent indifference. This happened when the Public Prosecutor suggested in his final speech that Mesina had killed a helpless and unarmed lad because he had been afraid to confront this smallish, mild-looking, middle-aged man sitting there with bowed head and clasped hands in the body of the court. Mesina smiled.

The defence's only hope was to extricate him from the ultimate calamity of a life sentence, and the strategy employed was an uphill struggle to create sympathy for a man who clearly hadn't had much of a chance in Orgosolo's battle for survival. 'The negative circumstances of his childhood', as the defence counsel called them were enumerated. Graziano Mesina had been orphaned at the age of twelve, and then a few years later, the family suffered 'moral and economic disintegration as a result of the arrest of the three adult brothers who were kept two years in prison on suspicion of murder before it was decided to release them as innocent. Graziano had had to support his mother and sisters through the long months of misery and near starvation. Then came the Townley affair, and the eldest brother's death. 'Don't think of Graziano Mesina as a cold-blooded murderer,' his counsel pleaded. 'He's just an impulsive headstrong boy, incapable of premeditation.' He gave a few instances of Mesina's typically impulsive actions such as tearing down the sheepfold of a man who had killed his dog, and then, perhaps to demonstrate that his client was essentially reasonable, recalled Mesina's protest earlier in the trial: 'After all, the younger brother was in the bar as well, and I might have finished him off too while I was about it. But there was no question of that. One was enough.'

A psychologist's report was read out in court, which described Mesina as legally sane and above average intelligence, although egocentric and remarkable for his 'moral coldness'. Sentence of twenty-six years was then passed, and the judge added that only a consideration for the special social climate, of which the prisoner was a product, had prevented him from sending him to gaol for life. Emotional scenes are not unusual in Italian courts at moments like this, but here Orgosolo dominated in its taciturn acceptance of victory or defeat. The sombre men and women in the public gallery got up and filed away in silence. No-one looked again in the direction of the prisoner still standing motionless and expressionless, hands clasped behind his back in the cage, waiting for the chains to be fastened on him.

On the cross-country journey to Orgosolo, one need only leave the main coastal road at Cuglieri to experience an immediate transition from a familiar to an alien civilisation. In a matter of minutes, the Bruegel-like world of the laborious peasant bent over his crops, is left behind, and one finds oneself enclosed without warning in noble and arid landscape, devoid of humanity. In this hard air, details of rock, tree and ruin are painted with gothic exactitude; rusted ferrous earth is relieved with the greyish green of oaks; sun-flayed mountains lie all along the horizon; there are no isolated houses, no small villages; an occasional town like Santa Lussurgiu is the site of an ancient nomad encampment built where precious water gushes miraculously from a rock. Besides the flinty chatter of wheatears and the occasional screaming of an eagle, there is an omnipresent sound that is at once gay and sinister. This is the lively discord of bells – all of different tones – as a flock of goats goes by. They come through the dark bloodily-red trunks of the cork-oaks at a quick, stealthy trot moving as fast as a man can walk. One knows that the shepherd is there too slipping from tree to tree, or out of sight over the lip of a ravine, or behind the rocks; never coming into view. The sensation is an uncomfortable one remembering that there is nothing of the meekness of the shepherd of Christian parable in this man, that he is a cruel, hungry dreamer with a gun, and that in this austere, archaic world where human life counts for so little, the shepherd is often separated by a hair's-breadth from the bandit.

Santa Lussurgui is a cheerful-looking village unusual for the fact that most of the houses have flower-gardens, and, here on a hillside in the pinewoods, the government has built a tourist hotel with a swimming pool and children's playground, and picnicking areas with fountains and waterfalls among the trees. Nightingales were singing in all the bushes when I was there. I was the only guest staying at this hotel, which has some fifty rooms, and the barman was also waiter, chambermaid and receptionist.

'Thing's aren't so bad as they were,' he said. 'Two years ago, we had hold-ups almost every day, but last year it calmed down a bit. We're keeping our fingers crossed ... Dangerous to go out alone? Not really, but it's a smart idea not to carry too much money on you if you go out for a stroll.'

The day's newspaper from Nuoro was open in front of me and there was Santa Lussurgui itself in a headline: 'Like the Wild West,' judge says. I read on. 'In this part of the world, life seems more and more to imitate the standard Western movie, a continual real-life battle between outlaws and the sheriff and his men – and all we ordinary citizens can do is to look on.'

In the year 1966, in fact, there are estimated to be a hundred bandits at large in Sardinia, about ten of them regarded as particularly dangerous. The majority are centred in the province of Nuoro where the Questore (the chief of the Public Security Police) recently said: 'At nine o'clock, people shut themselves in their houses. Outside you'll find only police and soldiers. All traffic stops at night. If there's a car on the road, you can safely say it's a bandit's.'

Through the window, I could see the barman's children picking wild narcissi at the edge of the wood. Santa Lussurgui looked as peaceful at that moment as a garden-suburb of London.

'The other day they put the pressure on a neighbour of ours, Francesco Atseni,' the barman said, 'You can see his house from here. Told him to hand over 5 million lire – or else. He went straight to the police, and while he was about it, bought himself a new rifle. What good did it do him? They got him all the same, and not only him but his shepherd Salvatore. Waited outside the house one night and machine-gunned the pair of them. We've learned our lesson now ... I expect you've heard of the famous Antonio Michele Flores of Orgosolo. He used to operate round here until the police killed him last year. He was only twenty-five when he died and he'd been a bandit since he was fifteen. I saw him once or twice. Good-looking kid, but his eyes scared me stiff.'

I brought up the fact that Orgosolo was thirty-five miles from Santa Lussurgui, but the barman said that that was nothing to the special kind of bandit Orgosolo produced. They'd been known to cross the country and carry out a raid as far afield as Oristano, fifty miles from their base. When I told him I was going to Orgosolo next day, he was astonished. Not one Sardinian in a thousand has ever visited Sardinia's most famous town.

Sedilo was two villages, one *nuraghe*, and a cavalcade of gypsy horsemen further on. It looked deserted, and in fact half its population happened to be in Cagliari at that moment for the trial of Pepino Pes (sometimes known as the bandit of the decade) who had been born there. Pes, a lover in the grand manner, as well as a mere killer, with some facial resemblance

277

to young Ramon Navarro, was alleged at the trial to have paid 40,000 lire (55 dollars) for a killing, when too busy to attend to the job himself. He had many friends in Sedilo still, and one of them had written that day to each of the judges of the Supreme Court threatening them with death. 'Not perhaps the best possible part of the world to be in for the next week or two', the senior British resident in Cagliari had said of this region. 'Always a fair amount of highway robbery when a big bandit trial's going on. These people's families need money for their defence counsels. They're very punctilious about paying for their legal advice.' To avoid discouraging me, the lady then added, 'Mind you, the chances of being held up aren't terribly high. Say, one in ten at the most.'

The last stop before Orgosolo was Oliena. This town has stood a dozen times in the path of the erupting Orgosolo horde, and as a result has a makeshift and haphazard frontier character. Carlo, the guide I had picked up in Nuoro, was a native of Oliena, and he pointed out a local Alamo where, in the days of his grandfather, a last-ditch battle had taken place between townsmen and invaders. Now cautious and exploratory friendships were beginning to link the two communities. The two wars had exercised a liberalising influence, and the fierce endogamic rule of Orgosolo had been relaxed to permit one or two outside marriages. Carlo was very proud to have friends in Orgosolo.

Oliena seemed to believe that tourism would eventually appear like some fairy prince to rescue it with a kiss from the servitude and drudgery of the present, and as an act of faith, and quite astonishingly, a roadhouse had been built on the outskirts of the town, overlooking a natural curiosity, a deep, onyx river gurgling out of an unexplored cavern in the mountainside. Thirty or forty tables were laid in the dining room, in a vaguely Hawaian ambience, neat little waitresses with pretty identical Sardinian faces stood by, and the menu offered *porchetto* (roast sucking pig), but no guests arrived. The only customers at the bar were police, and armed shepherds in velveteen who stacked their repeater rifles in the corner before ordering their drinks. A rich farmer of the neighbourhood, Antonio Listia, had been carried off from his home by four armed men on the previous day, and as the mechanism for paying the ransom had broken down, his life was feared for.

The shepherds were members of a search-party.

Hereafter, followed a Sardinian no-man's-land, a deserted landscape composed of the cautious greens of spring, but dramatised with a bold infusion of red – the red-washed walls of a refuge for road-menders; the sanguinary red of newly-flayed oak trunks; the bluish bruised-red of the Sardinian prickly pear, which grows here everywhere and is quite unlike the prickly pear in other Mediterranean countries. Supramonte rose up over the horizon, silhouetting the green hills against the skull-whiteness of its rock.

A last curve in the road revealed Orgosolo clinging to a hillside, drab as the outskirts of some mean industrial town. Greystone unfinished houses stood among old middens of building materials. In a moment, a dejected street began, hardly wide enough for two cars to pass. Then an arched doorway under the sign *Municipio*, through which a man could be seen hunched over a desk in a dim bare room, announced that we were in the administrative heart of the town. Black hairy pigs cantered up and down the street, and a sharp penetrating odour of animals hung on the air.

A few yards up the street from the decrepit Town Hall was Tara's barber's shop re-opened some years back under new ownership. Tara himself was under one of the wooden crosses in the churchyard. He had been suspected of informing to the police, and after his assassination, his body had been exposed with the corners of the mouth carved to the ears (the punishment prescribed for the false witness in the ancient *Carta de Logu*).

The atmosphere of this town was furtive. Although architecturally it was at first sight quite formless – a jumble of mean, dissonant buildings – one soon divined premeditation in this anarchy. Houses were built at more than one level on steeply-sloping, zig-zagging alleyways having in many cases, I learned, multiple exits, escape routes to inter-connecting cellars, concealed passages and rooftops. It was a town designed to shelter the fugitive; a labyrinth behind blind walls and barred windows, where a sick or wounded outlaw unable to face the life on Supramonte could take refuge for weeks and months at a time. Paska Devaddis, Orgosolo's only female bandit, who died of tuberculosis in 1914 after a short life full of trouble, never once left the town.

But one extraordinary circumstance separated Orgosolo from any other town I have ever been in with the exception of a Welsh mining village: the people sang. Groups of sombre Goya-esque figures gathered outside the small taverns waiting for room at the tables inside, and the sound of music and of splendid male-voice choirs poured out into the street. By now, Carlo had found his friends, and after a whispered discussion as to the suitability of such a visit, I was conducted to the bar where Graziano Mesina had killed the young Muscau and shown the bullet holes left by the fusillade.

In this bar, too, they were singing *sos tenores*, seated at dwarfs' tables, one man leading with the first verse, and then three more joining in with the chorus, their hands cupped over their mouths to form a kind of resonant chamber; and in this way imparting to the voice a harsh, nasal quality recalling the sound of bagpipes. Musicologists say that *sos tenores* are African or Asian, rather than European, in their musical affinities, but beyond this they appear to know little about them. They are very beautiful, strange and exceedingly melancholic. All the songs I heard that afternoon were on the themes of parting, sorrow and death, and a typical one began: 'Let me live on in hope. Don't tell me my days are numbered.'

The women of Orgosolo were hardly to be seen – black-shrouded creatures that flitted from doorway to doorway with no more than a brief Islamic revelation of the eyes. Their men-folk both in appearance and manner demolished another pre-conception. One would have expected the reputation of Orgosolo to have been reflected in at least some hint of fierce-ness or facial brutality. But nothing could have been less true. On all sides, one saw faces of great sensitivity and refinement – often not the faces of our time, but rather of the heroes of Attic and Etruscan pottery: long straight noses with the slightly recurved nostrils of the bedouins, bold Iranian eyes, and mouths often of feminine softness.

And the last thing they wanted to talk about was bloodshed and banditry. One of them, Orgosolo's most celebrated singer, a 24-year-old unemployed shepherd, said, 'What's so import-ant is to understand the social background of these things.' Guiseppe Muscau was a heroic figure as a man of action, that was agreed (I was invited to meet him when he got back to

Orgosolo), but higher still in the social scale were the troubadors – *sos poetas*. The high spot of their year was the August *festa* when the professional singers and poets came down from the mountains to take part in the contests in improvised verse – marathon calypsos lasting as much as twelve or fifteen hours on a subject announced by the judges without previous warning. Last year's subject, to which several thousand verses had been dedicated, was 'space travel'.

Late that evening, the time came for the pilgrimage to the small green field by the roadside below the town. Three shepherds went with us, including the singer, Salvatore, and we climbed the bank and stood among the grass and the flowers, and the men took off their caps. An old man leading a goat down the road stopped to cross himself.

Salvatore said, 'The people put up two crosses, and the children used to bring flowers every day. In the end, the authorities had the crosses taken away. I suppose they wanted to do their best to forget the thing.'

He added, 'All Sardinia turned its back on us. In Nuoro, they sell the cheeses we make in Orgosolo, and the shops sent them back. You might say that we ourselves were stunned. People kept asking each other how such a thing could have happened? Understand me, a man gets killed for some reason, and then his relations get together to even the score. That's the custom. But this thing didn't have any meaning. We felt as if there was a debt to be paid, and it was hanging over us. It threw everything out of balance. We are not criminals. We are an oppressed people.'

The time had come to return. The men covered themselves. Orgosolo was ahead, a dark jagged silhouette against the fateful shape of Supramonte, glowing benignly in the evening light.

A shepherd said, 'Something has changed since then. People showed a little of what they felt when they caught Mesina and handed him over to the police. We were sick of the whole thing. The papers said that the fellows, who turned Mesina in, weren't long for this world, but you can see for yourself, nothing has happened to them at all. There's been a change of heart. Even the police feel differently about us these days. They leave us in peace.'

281

Salvatore said, 'One of the *poetas* composed a beautiful lament for the two strangers. You must come back in August if you can, and you'll hear him sing it.'

20

High Adventure with the Chocos of Panama (six hours required)

Panama City on election eve was like a medieval town placed under an interdict. My plane touched down at about eleven-thirty, and at twelve, midday, all the bars and cafes closed down as this torrid land went dry for thirty-six hours. A sullen, fevered preoccupation with politics had entered the Panamanian blood. People sat at home listening to interminable radio speeches and prepared themselves to go to the polls on the morrow – which in Panama can be an exciting and dangerous experience. Having decided that these two days might be well spent in seeing something of the country's interior, I was dismayed to learn that travel was restricted during this period. As a precaution against citizens attempting to register their vote in more than one district – a fairly common practice in the past – all movement between voting districts was under a ban. The prospect of seeing anything of Panama in the short time I had to spare seemed a gloomy one. The discomforts of the moment were increased by the fact that the rainy season had just started and it could be expected to rain punctually every afternoon. In fact on that first afternoon in Panama I sat on the hotel's verandah watching a deluge unequalled in a single day, so the papers said, since 1905. That evening in desperation, and for the first time in my life, I visited a tourist agent in the hope he might be able to suggest some way of escape from this burden of other people's politics, and rain.

The travel agent, a genial New Zealander named Kemp, who seemed amazed that anybody should actually require his services, at first half-heartedly recommended a visit to the ruins of old Panama. 'That's if you like ruins,' he added. 'Some people seem to get a kick out of them. Why I can't imagine. The trouble is you've got a whole morning to use up, and the ruins only take a couple of hours at the most – and that's too

283

long.' He thought again. 'You could go to Colon. There's no restriction of movement in the Zone itself. Can't say I particularly recommend it though. It laid down and died when they closed the naval base. It's not a place that had much appeal for me at any time, but the way it is now, it's like a wet Sunday afternoon in Hull. Say now, how about a trip to see the Indians? You can at least use up six hours that way, and be back before the rain starts.'

He handed me a sheet of paper headed: 'Tour number six. See the Choco Indians (six hours required).' I read on: 'This exciting excursion takes you right into the heart of primitive, untouched Panama. Here you will see primeval man, strange birds, extraordinary beasts, and rare animals, all in a breathtakingly exotic jungle setting. Transported by commodious motor launch, you will be the privileged spectator of the mysterious way of life of the Choco Indian – intrepid hunter, and most remarkable of all Panama's indigenous peoples. With your experienced native guide (English speaking) you will penetrate to the hidden places of the jungle rarely seen by the white visitor. The keynote of this tour is high adventure. Especially recommended to those prepared to tolerate some discomfort in exchange for a unique travel experience. Bush clothing, and rope-soled shoes for walking over shingles are suggested.'

'The bit about discomfort is to warn off elderly ladies,' Kemp explained. 'This is supposed to be a real expedition in miniature. I mean you could get your feet wet or have a wasp sting you. I can't take any chances about someone starting a court action over a case of sunburn.'

'Have you ever done this trip yourself?' I asked him.

'No,' he said. 'When you're in the business you don't. You can't be bothered. Haven't got the inclination. In any case I can't say I'm wild about Indians. If you go for that kind of thing you'll enjoy seeing the Chocos, though. There's nothing like them. You'll see them going around by the hundred without a stitch on. Paint their bodies all the colours of the rainbow. Mind you, they can be dangerous if you go too far into the jungle. Liable to shoot a poisoned arrow into you. You'll be all right with our guide though. Whatever you do, don't forget to take plenty of colour film, or you'll never forgive yourself.'

284

Next morning at six, the experienced native guide called for me in a station wagon. I was surprised by the cut and quality of his clothes, his signet ring, his brown suède pointed shoes with white inserts, his bow tie, his fairly competent English and his well-bred reserve. I was unable to associate this man with jungles. To me he offered in his way an example of adjustment to an environment as delicate as that of the armadillo. But his environment was the city. I soon discovered my suspicions to be exact. Dominguín was an expert on what the New Zealander called his 'Slumming Tour' which took in Panama's night spots (3 hours required). He frankly admitted that he'd only seen a jungle from the outside. It turned out that the jungle tour expert was working that day as an officer at one of the polling stations. However, this presented no problem, because all Dominguín had to do, he said, was to drive us to a point where the road touched the shore of Lake Madden, where an Indian would be waiting with the commodious launch. Thereafter the Indian would take over.

'These Indians,' he explained, 'live on the water. They know their way round the jungle like we know our way round the town. If you and I went into one of those jungles by ourselves we'd never come out again. These Indians know every creek, every tree. It's their life.'

This seemed reasonable enough to me. Our road now, in fact entered the jungle, and for the first time I saw the rain forest typical of South America, the authentic Green Hell, which begins here on the east bank of the Panama Canal, and extends as a trackless sub-continent of vegetation for 1,200 miles to the edges of the Pampas of the Argentine. Suddenly the grass on the road's verge had become monstrous – a hedge of green bayonets. Beyond, the jungle pressed forward under its armour of varnished and sculpted leaves, held back at the very edge of the tennis courts and playing fields of the Canal Zone. I stopped the car, got out and enjoyed this confrontation. Twenty paces and I had passed through the green wall into the gothic solemnity of the forest's interior, into the borderland of millions of acres of twilight and vegetable decomposition. The odours of sap and mould, of roots and rain and leafy decay hung as thick as a London fog. Nothing stirred, but the distances were full of the chuckling and jibing of hidden birds. I came out and struck my foot against a flower, a confection of white waxen tiers jutting leafless from the wet earth. It shattered like glass. Huge morpho butterflies, blue and iridescent, were using the road like traffic, flying along it, up and down, very deliberately, in straight lines, and so slowly that I was able to reach up and snatch one out of the air as it was passing by.

A few miles further along, a side road took us down to the shore of Lake Madden. Here a small handsome indifferent Indian waited with a dug-out canoe, of the type known as a cayuco. The cayuco was fitted with a neglected-looking outboard engine, and it held an inch of brown water, and two or three small dead and malodorous fish in its bottom.

The Indian, splendidly bronzed and muscular, a miniature Apollo in faded bathing trunks, appeared not to notice our arrival. He was standing on one leg with the other flexed, and the sole of his foot pressed against the knee in a posture commonly adopted by the nilotic tribesmen of the Upper Sudan. Dominguín went up to him and started a conversation in Spanish. 'Are you Juan?' Dominguín asked him.

The Indian brought his leg down. 'No,' he said.

'I was told to look for Juan. Where's Juan, then?'

'Juan's away voting so they sent me.'

'They sent you. All right, well look here. This man wants to see Indians.'

'Why?' the Indian asked.

'Don't ask me. He just wants to see Indians. He's on a tour.'

'There aren't any Indians around here.'

'What are you talking about? The jungle's full of Indians. They're all over the place.'

'There aren't any Indians here. They don't come down here. There's nothing for them. There's only one boat comes down here. They sell cabbages. There's no business to be done round the lake.'

'We can go up the side creeks and look for them, can't we?' Dominguín said. 'This man is paying to see Indians.'

'You can't get this cayuco up the creeks,' the Indian said. 'There isn't enough water in them. It hasn't rained enough yet. Why don't we go fishing. There are plenty of fish in the lake.'

'What kind of fish?' Dominguín asked. 'Catfish – tarpon?'

'Mojarras,' the Indian said. He pointed to the small, shrivelled, sardine-like objects in the bottom of the boat.

Dominguín now supplied an English version of what had passed between them. 'He says there aren't any Indians around just now. He says you come back next month when it's rained some more and he'll show you all the Indians you want.'

At this point I decided to take a short cut in the conversation and tackled the Indian in Spanish.

'Where do you live?' I asked. I assumed that he lived in a village that might be worth a visit.

'I live on Mr Coronado's farm. I'm the one that does the odd jobs.'

'Coronado's the guy who hires the boats to my boss,' Dominguín explained.

'Yes,' I said. 'But where is your home? Where do you come from?'

'I'm a Cuna. I come from San Blas,' the Indian said.

'Then you don't know these parts very well?'

'I've been here a month. I've been up the river once, that's all.'

'That's the River Chagres,' Dominguín said. 'It's full of Indians. I know people who've been up that river. The Chagres is where you see the Indians. They have a big village up there.'

'Did you see any villages up the Chagres?' I asked the Indian.

He thought about this. 'Yes,' he said. 'I saw villages. There were many villages.'

I detected a trace of eagerness in his tone. Indians everywhere are over-anxious to be the bearers of pleasing information.

'What were the houses like?'

'They were houses.'

'Yes, but with walls, or with open platforms, and just a roof.'

'I cannot remember. Perhaps they were open.'

'And the Indians – did they wear clothing?'

'Some wore clothing. Others did not.'

'This man doesn't know anything,' Dominguín said. 'What's to stop us going and taking a look ourselves? I tell you, if you want to see Indians, the Chagres river is the place where

287

you're going to see them.'

'Can you find the Chagres river?' he asked the Indian.

'I think so,' the Indian said.

'He thinks so!' Dominguín said. 'Can you imagine that? A guide who thinks he can find a river half a mile wide. Well, anyway, let's go.'

We lowered ourselves cautiously into the cayuco which responded to the slightest imbalance with a violent rocking. Dominguín manoeuvred a handkerchief into position between his posterior and the seat. He took off his shoes and placed them in his lap, put on a pair of darker glasses than the ones he had been wearing hitherto, and then grasped the gunwale with both hands. Perhaps fifteen minutes passed while the Indian tinkered with the engine, and then we were off.

The lake was majestic and unruffled, darkly mirroring the firm clouds of summer. We roared over its surface alternately spray-soaked and sun-scorched towards a curving horizon of forest, rising out of the water. Shortly, the rampart of trees ahead of us divided, and we entered the mouth of the Chagres river. Half an hour passed comfortably, a pleasantly monotonous passage through an ever-narrowing channel. Small trusses of lavender flowers relieved the unchanging green façades on either side. A few herons broke into flight ahead of us at each bend in the river. And then, with an unpleasant jolting, the propeller shaft struck the shingle of the river bed. We were in shallow water. The Indian stopped the engine, fixed it into the tilted position with the propeller clear of the water, and got out a single paddle with a wide, spear-shaped blade.

Paddling against stream our speed was reduced to less than walking pace. In the next half hour, we covered only two or three hundred yards. Then the bottom of the cayuco began to drag on the shingle. First the Indian got out and began to wade, pulling the cayuco along. Then Dominguín and I found ourselves in the water too. I now remembered Kemp's warning suggestion about taking rope-soled shoes on this trip. It was agony to walk barefoot over the sharp pebbles, especially when hauling at and half lifting the cayuco. At practically the same moment Dominguín and I decided to sacrifice our shoes. Relieved of the pain of bruised cut feet we staggered on, sometimes plunging waist-deep into a pool, sometimes being forced almost to carry the cayuco through shallows where the water was only a few inches deep. Finally we came to a stop, exhausted, and Dominguín called to a mulatto, the first human being we had seen since the start of the boat trip; he was sitting in a hammock just above the water's edge.

The mulatto pulled himself to his feet, straightened his body joint by joint, and came wading out to meet us. He was shaking his head and clicking his tongue, roused into a kind of easy shallow anger at the spectacle of our foolish ineptitude. This man was a member of the half of humanity that lives for ever on the slippery edge of bare subsistence. A short life – perhaps thirty-five years – of utter want had left him toothless, lacklustre of eye, with sagging body; and his mahogany skin was blotched with an ugly yellow as if he had been splashed with acid. Despair hung about him like a ragged shapeless garment. A grey crone of a wife and a brood of sickly children crept out of a shack in the background to watch us.

'Greetings Uncle,' Dominguín said. 'How far do we have to go to get into deep water again?'

'Deep water?' the mulatto said. 'There isn't any. From this point on upstream it's nothing but pools and rapids. It beats me what makes people like you try to get up this river when there's no water in it, in whaling ships the size of that. I'm always being dragged away from whatever I'm doing to give someone a hand. Where are you going anyway? There's nothing but a few million trees up there.'

'This man's looking for an Indian village,' Dominguín said.

'There's an Indian village, all right,' the mulatto said, 'but you'll never get to it in that boat. You'd better leave that deep sea vessel with me and wade upstream if you want to go. You'll probably find the Indians fishing on the other side of the rapids. Maybe they'll take you up in their canoes.'

This seemed the only solution to our problem. We dragged the cayuco across to the bank under the mulatto's shack and tied it up.

'Who are you voting for?' Dominguín asked the mulatto.

The mulatto's angry laugh turned into a cough. 'Who'm I voting for? Why, I'm voting for the only chap who's ever done anything for me. Myself.'

'You should vote,' Dominguín said coldly. 'This is your chance to show your sense of civic responsibility.'

'Listen to me,' the mulatto said. 'I don't throw my vote

away. If they want to do the right thing by me, all well and good. Last time I only got a half a sack of rice out of it. They'll have to do better than that. They offered to send a boat to pick me up. But I told them, I said it's got to be something substantial this time. We never know where our next mouthful is coming from.'

We left enough of our food with this man to hold back the frontiers of hunger for another few hours. He was a colonist of a forgotten world; limited by his depleted store of energy to burning off a few square yards of jungle a year, thereafter depending on the meagre return of seeds sown in uncultivated soil, left to themselves. He and his like – and there were millions of them – were condemned by malaria, semi-starvation, and by civilisation's total neglect, to an endless servitude of years spent lying in a hammock by the waters of such rivers. His cash income, on average, would hardly be more than fifty dollars a year.

We began to splash on upstream again. 'They haven't much civic feeling,' Dominguín said. 'The Chocos are like that, too. You can't get hold of them to make them vote. The Cunas vote because it's easy to round them up on the islands, and set up polling stations.' He began to reminisce happily. 'Last election, I was working as an agent for Don Fulano' (he mentioned the name of a presidential candidate). 'He was interested in buying the votes of the Cuna Indians in bulk, so we went down there to fix up a deal with their cacique. Well, we figured it was no use telling these people about the improved drains we were going to put in in Panama City, so we told the cacique we were fixing up a rain-making ceremony and we would like to have his people's help. The cacique was pretty flattered to have us come to him with a proposition like that. They're nice people, the Cunas. They like to help. We gave the cacique an outboard engine and he saw to it that we got every Cuna Indian vote.' Dominguín made a face. 'The way things went, it didn't do Don Fulano any good. The opposition got to hear about it. They hi-jacked the boat taking the ballot papers back to Colon, and threw them into the sea.'

Fortified by the opium of his memories, Dominguín struggled on philosophically. By now we would certainly be unrecognisable as the men who had left the urbane precincts of the Panama Hilton hotel only four hours earlier. Our clothes

290

were wet, shapeless and bedraggled, and smeared in places with the blood from minor abrasions suffered when we had slipped and fallen among half-submerged boulders. All the exposed parts of my skin were brilliant with sunburn. At this stage of our journey, we experienced a single dramatic moment when we saw a long thin pink snake swimming vigorously towards us. Our Indian, alerted by Dominguín's yelp of horror, reached under the surface, found a large stone and with what seemed to me incredible marksmanship hit the small agitated target represented by the snake's head fairly and squarely at a distance of perhaps twenty-five feet. The snake, seemingly stunned, lay still on the surface for a few seconds, and then began to wriggle towards us again, whereupon the Indian coolly repeated his feat. This time the snake gave up and turned back. Dominguín said that he recognised it as the most deadly of all snakes, an aggressive monster known in Spanish as *quatro narices* whose bite produces infallible and agonising death in ten minutes. The Indian, on the other hand, said that it was quite harmless.

This whiff of Kemp's high adventure reminded me of the other extraordinary animal life his leaflet had promised.

'Do you have any jaguars in these parts?' I asked the Indian.

'No. We have small cats. No jaguars.'

'Tapirs, then?'

'What are tapirs?'

I described one, modelling the form of its pigmy trunk with my hands.

'There is no such animal. They do not exist.'

I didn't want to argue about it. 'Deer?' I asked.

'There are no deer.'

'There must be some animals,' I said. 'What animals are there?'

He thought for a few seconds. 'Rats,' he said. 'There are many rats. And iguanas. We eat the iguanas.'

'I know,' I said. 'They taste like chicken.'

'No, no,' he said. 'Much better than chicken.'

This conversation was going on sporadically while we were by-passing the rapids, forcing our way through the vegetation along the river bank. Many thorny bushes and saw-edged reeds blocked our advance. These left the Indian unscathed but Dominguín's hands and my own were soon bleeding freely, and rents began to appear in our clothing.

Fortunately, as the mulatto had promised, two Indians were fishing just above the rapids. Our Cuna spoke to the two Chocos in some Indian lingua-franca, and they agreed to lend us their canoes. The Cuna was to take me in one canoe, and Dominguín was to go with one of the Chocos in the other. This Choco was taller and slimmer than our Cuna. He had the face of an Eskimo, a polished helmet of black hair, and wore cotton shorts. I found a pair of ordinary skin-diver's goggles in his canoe along with his spear, and his morning's catch of two tiny fish. Dominguín asked him why he did not paint his body, and the Choco said that he did not have the time.

Our progress, although faster now, was still laborious. The river had become a series of pebbly shallows, separated by fairly deep pools. We paddled through the shallows where the water was just deep enough to float the empty canoes, and when we came to a pool the Indians ferried us across. It must have been midday before we reached a steep path leading up to what was described as the Choco village. When we got there we found a single house surrounded by the usual meagre, weed-infested fields, and half-charred tree trunks. The house was in reality an open-walled platform, made of branches roped together and thatched with reeds. As we came up the steep path, the Choco Indian shouted, and the house was suddenly full of running people who were either completely or nearly naked. I soon realised that they were rushing for their clothes. Skirts were hastily going on and blouses being pulled over heads. Only a row of children with enormously distended stomachs, who stood peering down at us, were not involved in this excitement.

Presently a young woman carrying a baby came down the ladder. She was dressed shapelessly in a kind of shift made from a sack that had contained fertiliser, and she wore gypsy earrings of city manufacture and several necklaces of bright, crude beads. Her face was completely devoid of expression. The Choco who had brought us conferred at length with her, and then turned to me and announced in pidgin Spanish that she and the other members of the household agreed to be photographed with their clothes off for four dollars.

Dominguín was able to throw some light on this proposition. He discovered that several months previously a camera-armed party of tourists had been here, and through these the Chocos had learned that their normal state of nudity had become a marketable asset.

And were their bodies in fact painted in the geometrical designs one had heard about? I asked.

No, they were not it seemed. These were civilized Chocos who had learned to despise barbarism of that kind. They lived by growing a little grain and fruit – principally bananas, for the market, and while they waited for the maize to come up and the bananas to ripen they had nothing much to do but keep alive. Recreation? The Choco's face was incapable of amazement, but he clearly didn't know what I was talking about. Music? – Surely the young men still piped tunes on their primitive flutes? He shook his head. They'd had an old gramophone once, but it was broken now. Dominguín became impatient of my naivety. 'What do they do? Why, they sleep, of course.'

A powerful, heavy-faced matriarch now appeared. She was the cacique's wife. The cacique was away voting. With some pride she admitted that his vote had cost a pair of trousers and a vest.

'But the village?' I asked. 'Where are the other houses?'

'They've fallen down,' the woman said. 'There used to be many houses but the people all died or went away. Now what's left of us live in the one house. The cacique forbids the young men to go and work in the town, but they go all the same, and leave the women and children to look after themselves.' This year alone a woman had died in childbirth and the fever had carried off two children. Doctors? Unemotionally, the cacique's wife continued her saga of neglect. 'Two years ago a doctor came here and stuck a needle into everybody's arm. Why, I couldn't tell you. We haven't seen one since. The uncivilized jungle people have a medicine for fever, but it takes two days to get there, and the Shaman expects something like a pig in return. They're supposed to be Indians like us, but they're just as bad as the townspeople the way they take advantage of us.'

My eyes went back to the primitive shelter, only one degree removed as human habitation from the cave. Around us for a distance of twenty or thirty yards, the earth was scattered with stinking debris. Pigmy diseased-looking pigs squealed and rooted among the rubbish. 'Why do you live here?' I asked.

'This is our home,' the woman said. 'We're civilized people. Planters. We believe in God. We grow bananas, and sell them in the town. The only trouble is they see you coming when you're an Indian. If it's a load of bananas you've got to sell, they'll tell you they're the wrong kind, or they're past the season. Supposing you offer them a monkey you've caught in a trap, they'll tell you it's going to die. It's a question of half price, take it or leave it. We're Indians. We have to take whatever they like to offer us. They know we can't argue with them.'

A shadow fell across us. I looked up. The sun had just fallen out of a last enclave of blue sky into curdling clouds. Thunder came galloping to meet us over the tree tops, and raindrops began to spatter all round. We said goodbye to the Chocos, scampered back down the path to the canoes, and began the journey back. Now I knew what the real high adventure of Kemp's tour was to be. It was to be an adventure of rain.

When the rain started in real earnest, it seemed to close in on us until we were in a prison-cell of water. At first the trees were still visible, lightly sketched in by a Chinese artist behind the curtains of rain. Then the rain washed out all the landscape. Dominguín's canoe, only a few yards ahead, had vanished. We slid forward over a vapour of pulverised water. Lightning glared all round us in prismatic colours, but a soundproof wall of rain held back the roar of thunder. Huge severed leaves came flapping down and fell in my face and on my lap. I found it helped to hold a hand over my nostrils to avoid breathing water. Presently I felt the canoe's bottom scrape on the shingle. We got out and began to grope our way ahead, repeating the laborious procedure of the upstream journey, alternately hauling the canoes along and then dragging ourselves into it to ride a few yards as soon as the water deepened.

Suddenly the sky had emptied itself. The clouds overhead were torn apart, and sunshine poured through. Dominguín and the Choco took shape in a brilliant mist, standing knee-deep beside their canoe. There was a faerie-like quality in this scene that transformed them into the creatures of some watery Celtic legend. It seemed that we had reached the head of the rapids, and the Choco had a suggestion to put. It would save time, he said, as well as being a perfectly safe and reasonable thing to do if we shot the rapids. The Chocos themselves, he said, did it as a matter of course, and without a second thought, every time they went down the river. He would go first to show us the channel to take, and all we had to do was to follow him.

We set off and headed for the waters prancing and leaping between the high banks ahead. Somehow the rapids had taken on a fiercer vitality than they had possessed when we had passed them going up stream. Our plan of action instantly collapsed when the Cuna, instead of remaining behind the Choco, shot into the lead. I was startled at the speed we were travelling at, and tried hard to comfort myself with the thought that the Cunas were an island people, miraculous watermen, who passed nine-tenths of their lives in boats. The canoe sat so low in the water under our weight that it only had about three inches of freeboard, and among the rocks, the races and the whirlpools of the rapids, small agitated wavelets broke continually over the side. With growing disillusionment and concern, I watched the water in the canoe's bottom deepen. It would have been impossible to bale because the slightest movement on my part would have upset us. Black rocks crested with flying water hurtled past on each side. The six inches of water in the bottom implacably deepened to a foot. The Cuna, who had been inclined to show signs of amusement since the beginning of this difficult passage, was now laughing outright. This chilling sight prepared me for the inevitable. Indian impassivity is rarely disturbed by anything short of catastrophe. I remembered agonisingly the last Indians that I had seen laughing in this way had been the survivors of a bus crash in Guatemala.

Water poured over the gunwale now. Our weight slowed us and I saw the Choco with Dominguín bearing down. The Choco, too, was convulsed with laughter. He waved his paddle in what was perhaps a farewell gesture as our canoe sunk under me, and I found myself being carried away at such a speed that it was impossible even to influence my direction by trying to swim. A moment later I was bumping on shingle. For another twenty yards I scrambled, slipped and struggled in the water trying to find my feet before I landed on a sandbank. The current tugged like wrestlers' hands at my ankles. Only when the water was less than knee-deep could I stand upright.

Dominguín and the Choco had passed but were clearly *in extremis*. As I watched, Dominguín still seated bolt upright, and strangely spruce and dignified in this moment of truth, appeared to be lowered gently below the surface. An instant later water, too, cancelled out the Choco's happy grin. Fortunately for Dominguín, who couldn't swim, he was carried straight on to a small island, where he squatted rather miserably, until he could be rescued. Both Indians were washed up a hundred yards or so away, and came clambering back over the rocks to recover their canoes. They were in high spirits.

Perhaps an hour later we reached the mulatto's shack. By this time our clothing had dried on us. We found the mulatto waiting for us. 'I've been thinking about doing something about voting after all,' he told Dominguín. 'Any chance of your finding anyone who can do better than a half sack of rice, if I come along with you?'

Dominguín with his connections in the city thought he might be able to do something.

We took our seats in Kemp's commodious launch and the mulatto excused himself. He came back carrying something like one of those straw capes which Japanese peasants are depicted as wearing in the old colour prints. This he fastened round his shoulders.

'Going to rain in a minute again,' he said. 'And it won't be a shower this time either, like the last one.'

I looked up. The sky was turning into porridge.

'Another couple of hours,' Dominguín said, 'and we'll be home.'

MEMOIRS OF A
BENGAL CIVILIAN

JOHN BEAMES
The lively narrative of a Victorian district-officer

With an introduction by Philip Mason

They are as entertaining as Hickey . . . accounts like
these illuminate the dark corners of history.
Times Literary Supplement

John Beames writes a splendidly virile English and
he is incapable of being dull; also he never hesitates
to speak his mind. It is extraordinary that these
memoirs should have remained so long unpublished
. . . the discovery is a real find.
John Morris, The Listener

A gem of the first water. Beames, in addition to being
a first-class descriptive writer in the plain Defoesque
manner, was that thing most necessary of all in an
autobiographer – an original. His book is of the
highest value.
The Times

If you wish to receive details of forthcoming publications,
please send your address to
Eland Books, 53 Eland Road, London SW11 5JX

A VISIT TO DON OTAVIO

SYBILLE BEDFORD
A Mexican Journey

I am convinced that, once this wonderful book
becomes better known, it will seem incredible that it
could ever have gone out of print.
Bruce Chatwin, Vogue

This book can be recommended as vastly enjoyable.
Here is a book radiant with comedy and colour.
Raymond Mortimer, Sunday Times

Perceptive, lively, aware of the significance of trifles,
and a fine writer. Applied to a beautiful, various, and
still inscrutable country, these talents yield a
singularly delightful result.
The Times

This book has that ageless quality which is what
most people mean when they describe a book as
classical. From the moment that the train leaves
New York. . .it is certain that this journey will be
rewarding. When one finally leaves Mrs Bedford on
the point of departure, it is with the double regret of
leaving Mexico and her company, and one cannot
say more than that.
Elizabeth Jane Howard

Malicious, friendly, entertaining and witty.
Evening Standard

*If you wish to receive details of forthcoming publications,
please send your address to
Eland Books, 53 Eland Road, London SW11 5JX*

VIVA MEXICO!

CHARLES MACOMB FLANDRAU
A traveller's account of life in Mexico

With a new preface by Nicholas Shakespeare

His lightness of touch is deceiving, for one reads *Viva Mexico!* under the impression that one is only being amused, but comes to realise in the end that Mr Flandrau has presented a truer, more graphic and comprehensive picture of the Mexican character than could be obtained from a shelful of more serious and scientific tomes.
New York Times

The best book I have come upon which attempts the alluring but difficult task of introducing the tricks and manners of one country to the people of another.
Alexander Woollcott

Probably the best travel book I have ever read.
Miles Kington, Times

His impressions are deep, sympathetic and judicious. In addition, he is a marvellous writer, with something of Mark Twain's high spirits and Henry James's suavity ... as witty as he is observant.
Geoffrey Smith, Country Life

If you wish to receive details of forthcoming publications,
please send your address to
Eland Books, 53 Eland Road, London SW11 5JX

Previously published by
ELAND BOOKS

TRAVELS WITH MYSELF AND ANOTHER

MARTHA GELLHORN

Must surely be ranked as one of the funniest travel books of our time — second only to *A Short Walk in the Hindu Kush* . . . It doesn't matter whether this author is experiencing marrow-freezing misadventures in war-ravaged China, or driving a Landrover through East African game-parks, or conversing with hippies in Israel, or spending a week in a Moscow Intourist Hotel. Martha Gellhorn's reactions are what count and one enjoys equally her blistering scorn of humbug, her hilarious eccentricities, her unsentimental compassion.
Dervla Murphy, Irish Times

Spun with a fine blend of irony and epigram. She is incapable of writing a dull sentence.
The Times

Miss Gellhorn has a novelist's eye, a flair for black comedy and a short fuse . . . there is not a boring word in her humane and often funny book.
The New York Times

Among the funniest and best written books I have ever read.
Byron Rogers, Evening Standard

*If you wish to receive details of forthcoming publications,
please send your address to
Eland Books, 53 Eland Road, London SW11 5JX*

THE
WEATHER
IN
AFRICA

MARTHA GELLHORN

This is a stunningly good book.
Victoria Glendinning, New York Times

She's a marvellous story-teller, and I think
anyone who picks up this book is certainly not
going to put it down again. One just wants to go
on reading.
Francis King, Kaleidoscope, BBC Radio 4

An authentic sense of the divorce between Africa
and what Europeans carry in their heads is
powerfully conveyed by a prose that selects its
details with care, yet remains cool in their
expression.
Robert Nye, The Guardian

This is a pungent and witty book.
Jeremy Brooks, Sunday Times

This edition is not for sale in the USA

*If you wish to receive details of forthcoming publications,
please send your address to
Eland Books, 53 Eland Road, London SW11 5JX*

A STATE OF FEAR

ANDREW GRAHAM-YOOLL
Memories of Argentina's nightmare

For ten hair-raising years Andrew Graham-Yooll
was the news editor for the Buenos Aires Herald.
All around him friends and acquaintances were
'disappearing'; and as an honest and brave
reporter he was under constant suspicion from all
sides in Argentina's war of fear.

Because of the author's obvious honesty and
level-headedness, we get an especially frightening
picture of life in a society where the slightest
deviation may cause you to disappear for ever.

'It is the story of trying to do two contradictory
things: write honestly and keep alive . . .
Gripping.'
Andrew Thompson, Guardian

'Will become a classic document about 20th
century Argentina . . . It is a small masterpiece.'
Hugh O'Shaugnessy, Financial Times

If you wish to receive details of forthcoming publications,
please send your address to
Eland Books, 53 Eland Road, London SW11 5JX

Previously published by
ELAND BOOKS

MOROCCO
THAT WAS

WALTER HARRIS

With a new preface by Patrick Thursfield

Both moving and hilariously satirical.
Gavin Maxwell, Lords of the Atlas

Many interesting sidelights on the customs and
characters of the Moors. . .intimate knowledge of
the courts, its language and customs. . .thorough
understanding of the Moorish character.
New York Times

No Englishman knows Morocco better than Mr W.
B. Harris and his new book. . .is most entertaining.
Spectator (1921)

The author's great love of Morocco and of the Moors
is only matched by his infectious zest for life. . .
thanks to his observant eye and a gift for felicitously
turned phrases, the books of Walter Harris can claim
to rank as literature.
Rom Landau, Moroccan Journal (1957)

His pages bring back the vanished days of the
unfettered Sultanate in all their dark splendour; a
mingling of magnificence with squalor, culture with
barbarism, refined cruelty with naive humour that
reads like a dream of the Arabian Nights.
The Times

*If you wish to receive details of forthcoming publications,
please send your address to
Eland Books, 53 Eland Road, London SW11 5JX*

FAR AWAY
AND LONG AGO

W. H. HUDSON
A Childhood in Argentina

With a new preface by Nicholas Shakespeare

One cannot tell how this fellow gets his effects; he
writes as the grass grows.
It is as if some very fine and gentle spirit were
whispering to him the sentences he puts down on the
paper. A privileged being
Joseph Conrad

Hudson's work is a vision of natural beauty and of
human life as it might be, quickened and sweetened
by the sun and the wind and the rain, and by
fellowship with all other forms of life. . .a very great
writer. . .the most valuable our age has possessed.
John Galsworthy

And there was no one – no writer – who did not
acknowledge without question that this composed
giant was the greatest living writer of English.
Far Away and Long Ago is the most self-revelatory of
all his books.
Ford Madox Ford

Completely riveting and should be read by everyone.
Auberon Waugh

If you wish to receive details of forthcoming publications,
please send your address to
Eland Books, 53 Eland Road, London SW11 5JX

A DRAGON APPARENT

NORMAN LEWIS
Travels in Cambodia, Laos and Vietnam

A book which should take its place in the permanent literature of the Far East.
Economist

One of the most absorbing travel books I have read for a very long time. . .the great charm of the work is its literary vividness. Nothing he describes is dull.
Peter Quennell, Daily Mail

One of the best post-war travel books and, in retrospect, the most heartrending.
The Observer

Apart from *The Quiet American*, which is of course a novel, the best book on Vietnam remains *A Dragon Apparent*.
Richard West, Spectator (1978)

One of the most elegant, witty, immensely readable, touching and tragic books I've ever read.
Edward Blishen, Radio 4

*If you wish to receive details of forthcoming publications,
please send your address to
Eland Books, 53 Eland Road, London SW11 5JX*

Previously published by
ELAND BOOKS

THE
HONOURED
SOCIETY

NORMAN LEWIS
The Sicilian Mafia Observed

New epilogue by Marcello Cimino

One of the great travel writers of our time.
Eric Newby, Observer

Mr Norman Lewis is one of the finest journalists
of his time. . .he excels both in finding material
and in evaluating it.
The Listener

It is deftly written, and every page is horribly
absorbing.
The Times

The Honoured Society is the most penetrating book
ever written on the Mafia.
Time Out

*If you wish to receive details of forthcoming publications,
please send your address to
Eland Books, 53 Eland Road, London SW11 5JX*

Previously published by

ELAND BOOKS

NAPLES '44

NORMAN LEWIS

As unique an experience for the reader as it must
have been a unique experience for the writer.
Graham Greene

Uncommonly well written, entertaining despite its
depressing content, and quite remarkably evocative.
Philip Toynbee, Observer

His ten novels and five non-fiction works place him
in the front rank of contemporary English writers . . .
here is a book of gripping fascination in its flow of
bizarre anecdote and character sketch; and it is
much more than that.
J. W. Lambert, Sunday Times

A wonderful book.
Richard West, Spectator

Sensitive, ironic and intelligent.
Paul Fussell, The New Republic

One goes on reading page after page as if eating
cherries.
Luigi Barzini, New York Review of Books

This edition is not for sale in the USA

*If you wish to receive details of forthcoming publications,
please send your address to
Eland Books, 53 Eland Road, London SW11 5JX*

Previously published by
ELAND BOOKS

A YEAR IN MARRAKESH

PETER MAYNE

A notable book, for the author is exceptional both in his literary talent and his outlook. His easy economical style seizes, with no sense of effort, the essence of people, situations and places ... Mr Mayne is that rare thing, a natural writer ... no less exceptional is his humour.
Few Westerners have written about Islam with so little nonsense and such understanding.
Times Literary Supplement.

He has contrived in a deceptively simple prose to disseminate in the air of an English November the spicy odours of North Africa; he has turned, for an hour, smog to shimmering sunlight. He has woven a texture of extraordinary charm.
Daily Telegraph

Mr Mayne's book gives us the 'strange elation' that good writing always creates. It is a good book, an interesting book, and one that I warmly recommend.
Harold Nicolson, Observer

*If you wish to receive details of forthcoming publications,
please send your address to*
Eland Books, 53 Eland Road, London SW11 5JX

Previously published by
ELAND BOOKS

KENYA DIARY (1902–1906)

RICHARD MEINERTZHAGEN

With a new preface by Elspeth Huxley

Those who have only read the tranquil descriptions
of Kenya between the two Wars may be surprised by
Meinertzhagen's often bloodthirsty diaries. They do
not always make pleasant reading, but they offer an
unrivalled and startlingly vivid account of life during
the early days of the colony.

One of the best and most colourful intelligence
officers the army ever had.
Times, Obituary

This book is of great interest and should not be
missed
New Statesman

One of the ablest and most successful brains I had
met in the army.
Lloyd George, Memoirs

Anybody at all interested in the evolution of Kenya
or the workings of 'colonialism' would do well to
read this diary.
William Plomer, Listener

*If you wish to receive details of forthcoming publications,
please send your address to
Eland Books, 53 Eland Road, London SW11 5JX*

Previously published by
ELAND BOOKS

JOURNEYS OF A
GERMAN IN ENGLAND

CARL PHILIP MORITZ
A walking-tour of England in 1782

With a new preface by Reginald Nettel

The extraordinary thing about the book is that the writing is so fresh that you are startled when a stage-coach appears. A young man is addressing himself to you across two centuries. And there is a lovely comedy underlying it.
Byron Rogers, Evening Standard

This account of his travels has a clarity and freshness quite unsurpassed by any contemporary descriptions.
Iain Hamilton, Illustrated London News

A most amusing book. . .a variety of small scenes which might come out of Hogarth. . .Moritz in London, dodging the rotten oranges flung about the pit of the Haymarket Theatre, Moritz in the pleasure gardens of Vauxhall and Ranelagh, Moritz in Parliament or roving the London streets is an excellent companion. We note, with sorrow, that nearly two centuries ago, British coffee was already appalling.
Alan Pryce-Jones, New York Herald Tribune

*If you wish to receive details of forthcoming publications,
please send your address to
Eland Books, 53 Eland Road, London SW11 5JX*

A CURE FOR SERPENTS

THE DUKE OF PIRAJNO
An Italian doctor in North Africa

The Duke of Pirajno arrived in North Africa in 1924. For the next eighteen years, his experiences as a doctor in Libya, Eritrea, Ethiopia, and Somaliland provided him with opportunities and insights rarely given to a European. He brings us stories of noble chieftains and celebrated prostitutes, of Berber princes and Tuareg entertainers, of giant elephants and a lioness who fell in love with the author.

He tells us story after story with all the charm and resource of Scheherazade herself.
Harold Nicolson, Observer

A delightful personality, warm, observant, cynical and astringent. . .Doctors who are good raconteurs make wonderful reading.
Cyril Connolly, Sunday Times

A very good book indeed. . .He writes a rapid darting natural prose, like the jaunty scutter of a lizard on a rock.
Maurice Richardson, New Statesman

Pirajno's book is a cure for a great deal more than serpents.
The Guardian

In the class of book one wants to keep on a special shelf.
Doris Lessing, Good Book Guide

If you wish to receive details of forthcoming publications,
please send your address to
Eland Books, 53 Eland Road, London SW11 5JX

Previously published by
ELAND BOOKS

NUNAGA

DUNCAN PRYDE

Ten years among the Eskimos

Duncan Pryde, an eighteen-year-old orphan, an ex-merchant-seaman, and disgruntled factory worker left Glasgow for Canada to try his hand at fur-trading.

He became so absorbed in this new life that his next ten years were spent living with the Eskimos. He became part of their life even in its most intimate manifestations: hunting, shamanism, wife-exchange and blood feuds.

This record of these years is not only an astonishing adventure, but an unrivalled record of a way of life which, along with the igloo, has vanished altogether.

He tells us stories, which he seems to have been born to do.
Time

One of the best books about Arctic life ever written . . . A marvellous story, well told.
Sunday Times

If you wish to receive details of forthcoming publications,
please send your address to
Eland Books, 53 Eland Road, London SW11 5JX

Previously published by
ELAND BOOKS

THE LAW

A novel by
ROGER VAILLAND

With a new preface by Jonathan Keates

The Law is a cruel game that was played in the taverns of Southern Italy. It reflects the game of life in which the whole population of Manacore is engaged. Everyone from the feudal landowner, Don Cesare, to the landless day-labourers are participants in the never-ending contest.

Every paragraph and every section of this novel has been carefully cast and seems to be locked into position, creating a structure which is solid and formal, yet always lively. . .while we are reading the novel its world has an absolute validity. . . *The Law* is an experience I will not easily forget.
V. S. Naipaul, New Statesman

The Law deserves every reading it will have. It is and does all that a novel should — amuses, absorbs, excites and illuminates not only its chosen patch of ground but much more of life and character as well.
New York Times

One feels one knows everyone in the district. . .every page has the texture of living flesh.
New York Herald Tribune

A full rich book teeming with ambition, effort and desire as well as with ideas.
Times Literary Supplement

*If you wish to receive details of forthcoming publications,
please send your address to
Eland Books, 53 Eland Road, London SW11 5JX*